THE HAMLYN BOOK OF
FOOTBALL
TECHNIQUES AND TACTICS

THE HAMLYN BOOK OF
FOOTBALL
TECHNIQUES AND TACTICS

RICHARD WIDDOWS
Illustrated by Paul Buckle

TREASURE PRESS

ACKNOWLEDGEMENTS
The author would like to thank the following
for their assistance during the preparation of
this book: Janette Place, for her skill and
patience in layout and design; Paul Buckle,
for his unrivalled illustrations; Martin Tyler,
for his valuable advice and for contributing
the text on the chapter 'The Nature of Team
Play'; Simon Moore, for his help with picture
research and the glossary, and for compiling
the index; Philippa Inskipp and the staff of
Zambril, Bury St Edmunds, for colour
separations and page make-up; Lyn Watson
and the staff of Rowland, Bury St Edmunds,
for typesetting; Peter Arnold, sports editor at
Hamlyn; plus Chris Jameson, Cherry Knock,
Jessica, Sam and anyone else who may have
suffered inconvenience or hardship.

First published in Great Britain in 1982 by
The Hamlyn Publishing Group Limited

This edition published in 1988 by
Treasure Press
Michelin House
81 Fulham Road
London SW3 6RB

Reprinted 1989

ISBN 1 85051 292 2

Produced by Mandarin Offset
Printed and bound in Hong Kong

PICTURE ACKNOWLEDGEMENTS
Associated Press: 39
Capital Press: 16
Central Press: 120
Colorsport: 11, 12, 17, 22, 30, 36, 40, 41, 48–49 (4), 50 (3), 66 (2), 94–95, 97 (2), 122, 136–137 (4), 146–147 (4), 150, 152 (4), 158, 160, 187
Michael Grimes: 36–37
Peter Robinson/Mick Alexander: 10, 34, 54, 60–61 (2), 82, 89, 91, 96, 105, 116, 117, 148 (bottom), 151, 163, 166, 180
Popperfoto: 103
Presse Foto-Baumann: 95
Sportapics: 84(4)
Sporting Pictures (UK) Ltd: 93
Sportsimage: 19, 43, 51, 57, 68, 72, 126, 130, 148 (top), 157
Syndication International: 70, 71, 81, 106, 174, 186 (3)
Bob Thomas Sports Photography: 13, 14, 15, 18, 25, 27, 28, 29, 38, 45, 46, 52, 58, 59, 62 (2), 65, 73, 75, 76 (3), 77, 79, 83 (2), 85, 86, 87, 90,
98, 100 (4), 102, 108, 109, 110, 114, 119, 124, 125, 127, 128, 129, 130 (3), 134, 135, 137, 139, 142, 143, 145 (4), 151, 154, 164, 178, 179, 183
D. G. Waters: 113

CONTENTS

INTRODUCTION

One of the great attractions of association football, and one of the reasons for its unrivalled position as the world's most popular sport, is that it does not at any time exclude certain members of a team from the action. To some extent, every person in the side is participating continuously throughout the match. All players are involved at all times. This book sets out to help you make the most of that involvement. It seeks to increase the extent and raise the standard of your participation by improving the two broad areas of your game: technical ability and tactical appreciation.

Those areas are not easy to separate and divide up for the purposes of presenting a publication—and nor should they be. To think of the game in terms of neat compartments would be to fail to understand its greatest asset, the flowing, unrestricted, unpredictable nature of its movements. Technique and teamwork fuse into one: solid technique is wasted without the knowledge of when, where and how to use it; tactical awareness is useless if you lack the tools with which to apply it.

No amount of planning and organisation can overcome poor control, inaccurate passing or shooting, weak heading or bad goalkeeping. The logical place to start is getting these elements right—but without losing sight of the context in which they are used. The 'action replays' thus show how these techniques were employed to the best effect by top players in important matches.

At the same time, you can expect your actual contact with the ball to be extremely limited during a game, somewhere between one and two minutes in all. For the remainder of the time the ball is in motion, around an hour of play, you are moving without the ball—marking and covering in defence, supporting and running off the ball in attack. The skill here relies on appreciation of time, space and movement, not how well you can dribble, pass or shoot. The tactical section tries to provide a framework in which you can perform these crucial 'hidden' roles far more effectively.

The book has been governed by two basic 'themes'. The first is simplicity. Football *is* a simple game, and the key to good team play is to do the simple thing quickly and do it well—again and again. It is the bad amateur who takes risks, the good professional who strives to erase the 'unforced errors' from his play, to be the master of his craft. Only then can an individual or a team afford to explore the limitless scope of creativity that the game offers—the second theme of the book.

No book, of course, can teach anyone to play football; you have to practise, regularly and hard. So do the best players in the world. But practice doesn't necessarily make perfect—it makes permanent. The wrong practice will cement bad habits, while the right practice will instil good habits. This book suggests the correct practice for each technique and shows how, with the right attitude, you can not only develop your skills but also learn how to apply them in the most productive way in match situations.

GOALKEEPING

Basic technique

▲ *A fine example of handling from Liverpool's Steve Ogrizovic as he takes a high ball at Highfield Road in August 1980. He has kept his attention focused entirely on that ball—despite the challenging presence of Coventry striker Tommy English—and is well balanced to make the catch. Note the perfect positioning of the hands, the fingers spread wide with the thumbs almost touching, to prevent the slightest chance of the ball slipping through. Hours of dedicated practice mean that good keepers can rely on such abilities time after time—though for Ray Clemence's deputy this goalless draw was to prove the only first-team outing in a frustrating season in the Anfield squad.*

The days are long gone when the goalkeeper was regarded as the footballer with a little too much courage and not quite enough sense, a player somehow divorced from the rest of the team. Ever since Gyula Grosics began acting virtually as a sweeper for the great Hungarians of the mid-1950s the keeper has gradually extended his sphere of influence to a point where he is expected to dominate in defence, a point where he is seen not only as an integral part of the side but often as its most important member.

Over the same period men like Lev Yashin, Gordon Banks, Sepp Maier, Dino Zoff, Pat Jennings, Peter Shilton, Ray Clemence, Ronnie Hellström, Ubaldo Fillol and Luis Arconada have elevated the actual techniques of goalkeeping to a craft—an achievement resting as much on doing the basics superbly well as on bringing off those heart-stopping saves that linger in the memory.

Goalkeepers need very special qualities. Some apply to any member of a football team, but he requires them all to be good at his unique job. First there are the physical prerequisites: excellent eyesight and judgement, shrewd positional sense and an awareness of angles, agility, speed, suppleness, anticipation, sharp reflexes and, of course, a 'good pair of hands'. It's often thought, too, that he must be tall; but while height is an obvious advantage, all-round strength and athleticism are far more important. At the start of the 1981–82 season, in fact, there were 14 keepers on the books of First Division clubs who were under six feet tall.

The mental factors are in some ways even more demanding. Most apparent, perhaps, is courage, since the keeper has to go in regularly where it can really hurt. He must be confident of his judgement and his ability—indecision is a basic cause of poor goalkeeping. He must be a strong personality to command his area and direct his defence—controlling, warning, cajoling. He must be cool under pressure, able to perform well in the knowledge that he is the last line of defence, to handle testing periods of sustained attack, to play well after he or a teammate has conceded a soft goal. He must be determined not to be beaten—become possessive about the area he guards. He must be alert, concentrating even when the play is not near him for long periods. And he must be dedicated: becoming and remaining a good keeper is hard work, with much of the tough training done away from the rest of the side.

With this daunting list it's hardly surprising that there are so few unquestionably fine keepers. While an outfield player can sometimes 'hide'—avoid the action for a spell or have his mistakes covered by a colleague—the goalie can afford no errors, no slips, no lapses in concentration. One piece of bad judgement or slow reaction can, in an instant, waste the patient work of ten other players.

It's a lonely occupation at times, carrying a huge responsibility. If his performance is poor he can lose the match on his own; if it's good he can not only prevent the opposition scoring but also spread confidence right through the side, inspiring teammates to play far better, while at the same time demoralising opponents. That trust in the keeper's abilities will come far more from getting the essential aspects of his trade right again and again than from the occasional breathtaking save—and those aspects are based on good handling and catching.

The principles of handling are, by definition, the fundamental rules of goalkeeping in general. And while no two keepers are or could be identical in style, ability and temperament, they should be borne in mind at all times.

First, and most essential, is to keep your eyes fixed firmly on the ball. This may sound almost ludicrously obvious, but the keeper operates in what can often be a crowded part of the field, and the slightest glance to check on the position of opponents can spell disaster, even when everything else is correct. Second, always use both hands whenever you can. Third, don't reach for the ball if you can secure it

more easily by moving your feet to get into position. Fourth, get your body behind the ball if at all possible, even for the simplest takes. Last, 'catch it if you can' rather than punch—but only if you're sure the ball will stick. We'll expand on these basic aspects later when covering shot-stopping; here we're concerned with the essential techniques of fielding and catching the ball.

There are roughly four heights at which the ball comes to you: at and around your feet, between your thighs and chest, at head height, and above head height. It's important to remember that while there are basic techniques to deal with each of these any number of factors can affect them—the ground conditions, the pace of the shot, the spin on the ball and so on—and the vital thing is to field the ball confidently and securely.

It is perhaps a reflection of the individualistic nature of goalkeeping that there are two quite different approaches to its simplest skill—fielding a ground shot when there's time to get into the correct position. Keepers can favour either the stooping or the kneeling technique, but others may use both, bending for a back pass and crouching for a firmer shot or in certain circumstances—for a spinning ball, on wet ground or with an opponent closing in quickly. Until they learn the trade and discover a preference, aspiring

▲ *Using the space available, Peter Shilton of Forest takes a short run and jumps to convert a ball just above head height into a safer catch to his chest. The head-high take can be a deceptively difficult one because of the temptation to move your head sideways away from the line of flight as the ball approaches and thus take your eyes off it at the vital moment; even an experienced England international is aware of such amateur errors. Shilton personifies the new breed of top-level keeper—strong, athletic, dedicated. Forest's management team of Brian Clough and Peter Taylor secured his services for £250,000 from Stoke in September 1977 and the man who began his career as an understudy to Gordon Banks at Leicester conceded just 18 goals in 37 League games as Forest cruised to their first ever Division 1 title. Taylor maintained that Shilton was worth ten points a season to the side—and its most important member.*

▼ There are two basic approaches to fielding a ground ball, and while the decision can depend on a number of factors—the pace of the shot and the weather conditions, for example—for most keepers it's often simply a question of personal preference. Some use the stooping technique for easy balls like soft shots and back passes and employ the kneeling method for stronger shots, on slightly bumpy pitches or in tricky conditions. The latter is certainly a safer approach, since it provides three layers of insurance rather than two: hands, leading knee and the foot which tucks in behind the knee, placed side on to increase the surface area facing the ball. The hands are held fingers down, the palms opening to scoop the ball in. This technique is the one for youngsters to adopt at all times; it may seem ostentatious for a simple back pass, but it leaves little room for error and obeys a basic maxim of goalkeeping . . . 'safety first'. The answer is to try out the other method in training—never experiment with such basic approaches in a match—and settle for the one which feels right and gives you most confidence.

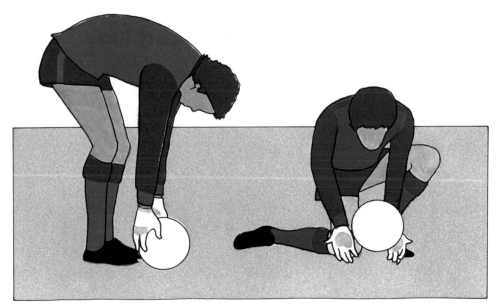

young keepers can do no worse than employ the kneeling method, with its three layers of cover, for all ground balls.

The bouncing ball can cause real problems, and for this the best position is often more of a compromise between the two fielding techniques, with the shielding knee kept off the ground as the ball is taken on a slight rise. It's as true of a simple ground shot as a fierce drive into the corner that the most awkward ball for a keeper is the one that bounces just in front of him.

The most basic 'save' is the shot taken at stomach or chest height. Here it's important to get your body behind the ball, cupping your hands round it to form a cradle. Your body should 'give' on impact to prevent the ball bouncing away: the harder the shot, the more your body gives with the impact of the ball.

For balls coming at head height and above, your hands point upwards. Positioning of the hands is crucial here, because there's no body or legs behind them as extra insurance now. The fingers should be spread wide but relaxed, the thumbs almost touching, with the hands forming a basket for the ball. Cushion the ball rather than hit it (bending the elbows a little will help here) and when it has stuck secure it to your body as quickly as possible as you come down.

With the high ball you should aim to make the most of your legal advantage by taking the ball at the highest possible point. A run to the ball obviously makes this easier, taking off on one leg and thrusting upwards with the free leg like a high jumper. This lifting of the non-jumping leg not only provides momentum: it also acts as useful protection

against the challenge of opponents. Avoid the temptation to raise both knees: this will increase the chances of your body spinning or turning and may make a safe 'landing' difficult.

If it's not possible to get a run to the ball, and your jump is all upwards, move around on your feet and bend your knees to overcome the inertia of your body-weight. The resulting jump will then be quicker and higher.

Any aspiring keeper should take every opportunity not just to improve his all-round agility but also to strengthen his arms and hands; they are the tools of his trade. There are the obvious exercises like chin-ups in the gym, while press-ups can be done anywhere, even at home. Two handy tips are to do press-ups on your finger-tips and to squeeze a tennis ball whenever you have a spare moment.

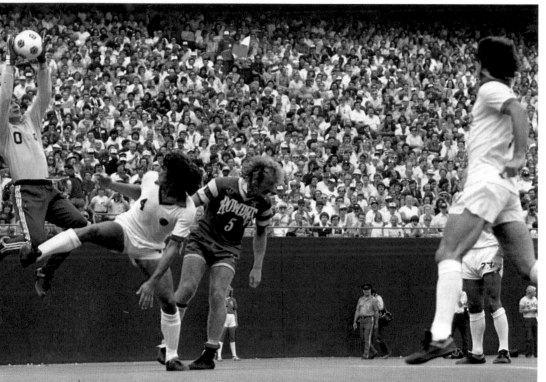

◄ *Cosmos keeper Jack Brand makes a convincing catch during the 3–1 Soccer Bowl win over Tampa Bay Rowdies in 1978. The basic technique is flawless: eyes fixed firmly on the ball, hands firmly behind it and the leading knee bent slightly for protection against the possible challenge of opponents and team-mates alike—in this case Rowdies' Davie Robb and Cosmos captain Werner Roth. Catching high balls is about doing the right thing well, making full use of your legal advantage to secure the ball no matter who else is around, whether friend or foe. Decisive action (and a clear call) lets your defenders know where they stand; they can then concentrate on the job of marking their men. And just as plucking high balls confidently out of the air will inspire your team so will it demoralise the opposition. Brand, a shoot-out specialist with a truly international background—born in Germany, Canadian citizen, playing in the USA—replaced the flamboyant Shep Messing for the 1978 season as Cosmos retained their NASL title, and American players in general seemed well able to cope with this aspect of the game since their ball traditions all require safe handling.*

► As with all practice routines for skills, start off with the simple approach in order to completely master the basics. For the high ball, begin with gentle throws to learn how to catch cleanly with your hands placed firmly behind the ball. Build up the distance and the height gradually to long throws from various angles before adding an 'opponent' to challenge for the ball. Finally move on to kicking the ball to the keeper—again adding a third person going for the header to make the practice more realistic—and then on to genuine crosses from the flanks. If the person playing the ball in is sufficiently accurate, you can of course start off with kicks, but throws also help if both players are aspiring keepers, since the second player is at the same time improving that department of his game.

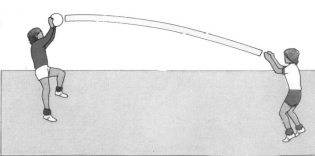

Dealing with crosses

One of the goalkeeper's basic attributes must be an ability to cope confidently and consistently with the high crosses that will inevitably invade his area, and to handle them when that part of the pitch is often crowded with players of both sides. Many crucial decisions are involved—the choice of starting position, whether to go for the ball and, if so, when to go and whether to catch or punch. Yet while it is a testing skill it is regarded as a fundamental aspect of the craft and one that must be mastered early.

Unlike a shot goalkeepers invariably know when a cross is on and usually have time to assess its flight; with today's more protective referees, it's most unlikely they will concede a valid goal after being fouled; and, most obviously, they have the massive advantage of over two feet in extra reach—and it's this more than anything which leads observers at all levels to demand reliability on the cross.

Taking up the right starting position will make the operation that much easier. If the player is well out on the flank you should be near the far post; this allows you to see a much greater part of the danger area more readily and it's a good deal easier and safer to go forward—and take the ball—than it is to go back. If the player in possession cuts in then you move towards the near post. Judging whether to start from the line or a little off it is something that comes with experience, but naturally if the player with the ball is near the goal-line you must be aware of the chance of a snap angled shot. As a general rule, the nearer the halfway line the cross is made from the further you can afford to be out of your goal.

The decision to stay or go will be made mainly on seeing the trajectory of the cross

and the pace of the ball—but not entirely. There may well be instances when you decide that a ball well within range is best left alone because the route to it is hopelessly cluttered. Only practice and, more pertinently, match experience (where players really are trying their hardest to make good contact) will guide you here. Anything inside the six-yard box, of course, should be yours by right. In his Liverpool days Ray Clemence operated on the principle that he would go for every cross played into his goal area; outside that, his defenders were expected to clear.

If you can reach the ball safely then you should attack it, but if there is any

doubt stay put and adopt an appropriate defensive position. If you decide to go, be positive. There's no place here for hesitation or a change of mind. Indecision is a bigger cause of mistakes on crosses than poor handling—and is often the reason for that embarrassing fumble in the first place. The keeper who hesitates not only risks failure himself; he also leaves his defenders wondering whether to cover him and mark opponents or go for the ball. A positive move by the keeper means nobody is in doubt, and an early clear call will let everyone know where they stand.

The technique of cutting out crosses, combining timing, agility and good handling, requires constant practice. Whenever possible catch the ball on the move in order to gain rhythm and momentum for the jump. From the moment you start to move watch only the ball: to know where

▶ *The arms of Ray Clemence protrude above a clutch of players as he tries to collect a difficult cross during the European Championship qualifier at Sofia in June 1979. Here his problem is not so much the Bulgarian forwards as midfielder Trevor Brooking, apparently doing sterling work in defence but in the end making the keeper's job more awkward for a ball which, on the edge of the six-yard box, should be automatically his. Clemence has not been able to get a clear run to the ball and take it at the highest possible point; it's now falling and despite bending his elbows his hands are still over rather than behind the ball. Though he in fact held on to it—and went on to record his 19th clean sheet in his 42nd full international—on the evidence of this picture a firm two-fisted punch would seem to have been the safer course of action, obeying the maxim of 'safety first'.*

You can't beat'em

Bristol Street Motors

◀ West Ham's Phil Parkes uses every inch of his 6' 3" frame and his legal advantage to pluck a high cross from above the head of Everton captain Mike Lyons during the teams' first FA Cup semi-final at Villa Park in April 1980. Note how he has turned to face the ball for better vision and protection, while getting both hands firmly behind it, with fingers spread wide and thumbs almost touching, to prevent any chance of a slip. Keepers at most levels can expect to be tested on their handling in the air early in a game—even when, as here, the opposition are well aware of Parkes' considerable experience and stature. This fine take, however, made just a few minutes after the kick-off, will serve only to boost Parkes' confidence and that of his teammates. They may properly expect a top keeper to do his duty, but it's still warming to see your man handling well. A few more like that and the opposition will have to think again about their tactical approach. If the keeper fumbles a few early on, of course, the reverse happens: he and his defenders get nervous, the opponents sense a killing. Other points are the covering of Billy Bonds and the possibility of a counter-attack: Parkes has a superb throw.

▼ There's no better practice than simply dealing with cross after cross, gradually getting to know every aspect from which foot you prefer to take off from to how to land properly. Throws will do in the early stages as long as they are accurate, but the important thing is to vary the crosses once the basics have been mastered. A third player will help with the whole question of concentrating and timing the run and jump. At the start he can be passive—a defender if you like—but later he should be competing for the ball, first as a defender and then as an attacker on a run. Ideally this type of practice should then involve at least two competing players, one in defence and one looking to head for goal.

the opposing forwards are—or to gauge where they could be after a run—glance up before the cross is made, but never once the ball is struck.

Take off on one foot (you'll soon discover which are your natural 'leading' and 'trailing' legs) and turn your body gradually to face the ball. This not only improves your vision and means your hands will be behind the line of flight; it also provides better protection against challenging opponents because you're meeting them side on. Try to time the run and leap to catch the ball at the highest possible point to make use of your handling advantage. Watch the ball all the way and not other players, securing it quickly to the safety of your body as you land. Distraction is a danger right to the last, so concentration is vital throughout. And the job isn't finished once you have the ball: the alert keeper will be looking to set up a quick attack with an intelligent throw.

The choice of catch or punch should be an early one, made as you decide to go for the ball. Late changes of mind, perhaps because an opponent has got into an awkward position or the ball has swerved unexpectedly in flight, are very risky, though of course they can't be ruled out. Your basic duty, after all, is to clear the danger. It's a problem that can bug the best, as Peter Shilton found out early on in his international career. Replacing the cup-tied Gordon Banks for his third cap against Switzerland at Wembley in November 1971, Shilton put England in trouble three times early on in the match when he produced poor punches on crosses that appeared to be comfortable catches

While many schoolboy goalies get little practice on crosses because few youngsters can centre a ball well, professional keepers often get bombarded early on in a game, particularly if they are thought to be suspect in the air. They must be ready for such searching examinations of their handling—and for the physical challenges than can accompany them. But a keeper who passes that test deflates his opponents, who then have to think again about their tactics, and boosts the morale of his own side. There was no better example of this than with England's seemingly disastrous World Cup defeat in Oslo in September 1981, when surprise choice Tor Antonsen plucked cross after cross out of the air (and conceded only a debatable goal on the ground) to help inspire his Norwegian teammates to play the game of their lives.

The best practice you can have is quite simply to deal with cross after cross, aimed at various areas of the goal and differing distances from it. If there's only one other person around or available that's as far as you can take it. But valuable though that is, handling crosses is about catching the ball under pressure, and if possible that must be simulated in practice. One other person will do, playing initially as a defender—first passive then active—before taking on the role of attacker, genuinely trying to head those crosses home.

With a total of five players it's easy to set up a continual, demanding routine. Three of them put crosses over from various angles, using two balls, while the fourth puts pressure on the keeper. As he collects

◄ Centres close to the crossbar present special problems for keepers, and catching the ball in such circumstances can be hazardous. Here St Etienne's Jean Castenada, under pressure from Paul Mariner of Ipswich during the UEFA Cup quarter-final at Portman Road in March 1981, has no choice but to palm the ball over for the relative safety of a corner. He does well to retain his poise, balance and concentration in a difficult situation, hitting the ball firmly with the whole of his hand before turning to 'follow' the ball. A casual flick may look cool, but it's important to get a good solid contact to get the ball away. This is an even bigger danger if you use the arm nearest the goal, which some keepers prefer because they can face the ball more easily. Which style is employed may be determined as much by the flight of the ball as by personal preference: Castenada, pinned right under the bar, has no option but to use the arm farthest from goal. This type of save is especially difficult—but particularly valuable—when a cross goes over your head towards the far post, when you're forced to retreat and as you back-pedal still achieve the height and accuracy to palm (or fist) the ball to safety. All such crosses should be dealt with for real in practice sessions, no matter how simple the routine or limited the number of players; the 'push-over' is far from that and can be a real life-saver for a keeper and his side. Palming the ball near the bar usually means jumping straight up, so move on your feet and bend your knees a little as the ball approaches to overcome the inertia of your bodyweight—your opponent may have had the benefit of a run, and even if he can't reach the ball he can still put you under severe pressure.

▼ While a keeper's main concern in cutting out crosses is to deal with the immediate danger and make a good catch, the matter doesn't end there; his run and jump can take him in to the perfect position to launch a quick counter-attack. Often this will be out of the question: he may have a difficult landing, he may be confronted by an opponent, or there may simply be no player available. But if he has made a good call and catch, defenders and midfielders can look for space, perhaps capitalising on the fact that opposing midfielders and defenders (particularly at set pieces) have gone for the ball and are temporarily out of position. An intelligent throw here can be devastating if the outfield players are aware of the possibilities. This should of course not distract a keeper from his main aim—he must never look for it as he goes for the ball—but he should practise the art of assessing the situation quickly once he has possession.

from the first 'winger' the keeper feeds the ball to the second one as the third outfield player sets up a cross with his ball. This is returned by the keeper to the first player and so on. This routine has the advantages of continuity and realism, the 'suppliers' being able to make various runs before crossing the ball.

This kind of practice, one essentially of familiarisation with the skill itself, assumes that the keeper can and will catch every ball. Learning to master the most crucial decision in dealing with crosses, however, can only be done with seven or eight players, since the basic reason for staying on the line (or electing to punch rather than catch) is the relative positions of attackers and defenders. Thus to be effective this type of practice requires at least two of each, plus wingers, to launch proper attacks. With a full team, of course, there can be a real split, with the keeper looking to set up 'attacks' to his spare defenders after taking the ball. As illustrated on the right, the high catch can also be the springboard for offense,

Punching

If there is one aspect of goalkeeping that divorces the British players from their continental counterparts it is the attitude towards punching. Many keepers in Europe (particularly in the 'Latin' countries) and South America seem to regard it as the first choice for high balls, and catch only if there is no other player within ten yards of them. Indeed one recent coaching book, written by a former French international, actually claims that every high cross should be met with a punch, irrespective of any further factors.

British coaches would have been converted long ago if these keepers had somehow proved it was steady and safe rather than spectacular and risky. The irony is that they don't appear to be very good at it; crowds at English and Scottish grounds are treated annually to appalling examples of mistimed punches by foreign club goalies, especially with one hand.

Home-grown keepers, however, still see the punch as the first reserve for dealing with high balls. They tend to follow two simple rules: 'catch it if you can', but 'if in doubt, punch'. Perhaps continentals adhere to these maxims, too: maybe they think they can catch the ball less often, maybe they have more doubts. The more likely explanation is that like so many aspects of goalkeeping the differences are based on tradition rather than just technical ability.

There are three basic instances in which a keeper elects to punch, or to be more precise is forced to punch. All of them are pressure situations in which the ball is 'in range', but in which the chances of a clean take and hold are considered too low. The first is when the ball is well within catchable height and distance but the area is just too crowded with players. The route is blocked or the actual point at which you could take the ball is above a cluster of bodies straining for the hopeful header. Even with a good catch, landing would be at best difficult. This, understandably, is most likely to occur at wide free-kicks and corners, where both sides have had time to pile players into the danger area for the expected cross.

The second instance is when you are moving or diving forward at speed for a slightly lower cross. Here, even when you're not under pressure from opponents, it can be awkward getting your hands behind the ball at full stretch and you don't have time to secure the ball to your body before landing. A punch in this position can be as good as a kicked clearance if the contact is good.

The third call for the punch is the lob, chip or very high cross that loops over your head, often towards the far post, when to make contact of any kind you have to back-pedal. Sometimes a catch is on, or if you're near the line you can palm the ball away for a corner; more often, however, this ball demands a one-handed punch to the safety of the opposite flank.

For the basic high cross the decisions you have to make are the same as if you were going to catch it—including the final one. But that decision should be made before you make the run or attempt the jump. A change of mind from a catch to a punch is extremely dangerous, although in certain circumstances—a sudden movement in the flight of the ball, a player getting into an awkward position, a poorer jump than expected, perhaps because of the muddy ground—it has to be done. But punching is all about being positive, about getting as powerful and solid a contact as possible, and that means really going for the ball all the way.

◀ *Spurs full-back Don McAllister covers as Barry Daines does everything right after electing to punch one-handed against Bolton's Alan Gowling in the First Division game at White Hart Lane in October 1978. He has assessed that the combination of the flight of the cross and the position of Gowling will give him no chance of a clean catch and that a good contact can't be guaranteed from a two-handed punch. So he aims for firm contact with one hand, punching through the ball rather than at or across it, going for height and distance and adding more safety by sending the ball back in the direction it came, to the wing. Solid contact was vital here to stop Gowling getting in a header at goal or a glance to Frank Worthington, on a run behind him.*

The fundamentals for catching the high ball and cutting out the cross apply again with punching, though the intention and end product are very different. Ideally you should use two fists whenever possible in order to put a bigger and flatter surface area in contact with the ball (and if a striker gets between you and the ball you're more likely to block the flick-on). But the very reasons for your punching at all also mean that frequently you can only make decent contact with one, when you have that extra little reach.

The key to punching is to go for height, distance and width . . . in that order. Like a defensive header, you're looking primarily for safety, getting the ball well away from the danger area. You should if possible hit the ball on the run, making contact at the highest available point of flight, and punch through the ball rather than at or across it, finishing the action with arm or arms fully extended for the maximum power.

This will bring you the height and distance. As for direction, aiming for the area of least danger, this simply means hitting it back the way it came for the near-post cross—and helping it on to the other flank for the far-post ball that has you stretching. The straight high ball presents problems for the puncher: you really need to get an angle, but until that comes in practice settle for the basic principle—go for the safety of distance.

However good a punched clearance is, there's always the chance of a quick cross as the other side regains possession. It could be a neat lob or chip if you've come well off your line—and especially after a weak punch. So it's important to cultivate the habit of recovering your position—and your poise—ready for the next move.

Practice for punching should really start with the actual contact on the ball—using the flat area of the fist between the knuckles and the lower joints of the fingers. You can try this at first on your own with a suspended ball, learning to master the take-off and timing aspects as well as the punching techniques, before moving on to the kind of routines with several players described in the section on handling crosses. After you have grasped the basics, try to ensure there is pressure on you in practice to avoid cultivating 'bad habits'. If there is no challenge and you have plenty of time and space, catch the ball as you would in a game.

Punching is not a first choice of action for a keeper: with its inherent uncertainty it's a last resort to be used only under pressure. Whereas a consistent 'catcher' can reassure his team and deflate opponents, a regular and risky 'puncher' will worry his colleagues—and allow the other side the luxury of hoping he will eventually be found out.

▲ *More decisive punching, this time with two fists, from Argentina's Ubaldo Fillol in the World Cup final with Holland. This is a sensible intervention by the River Plate star, even though it appears that his skipper Daniel Passarella would have beaten Arie Haan to the ball. But a keeper's duty in these situations is to be positive, to maximise safety and minimise risk in defence. When Fillol decided to go—and to punch—he did not know exactly how the players involved would perform as the cross came in, so despite the cluttered area he chose to make that ball his responsibility. The relative certainty of a good punch will always beat the possibility of a good defensive header, and no centre-back is going to complain about the ball being hit confidently to safety. And that's what the keeper accomplished as he sent the ball firmly towards the touchline. Unlike many South American goalkeepers he is not what Britons regard as an excessive puncher, and his balanced and consistent handling was a major feature of Argentina's success in 1978, when he conceded only four goals in their seven matches and saved a penalty against Poland.*

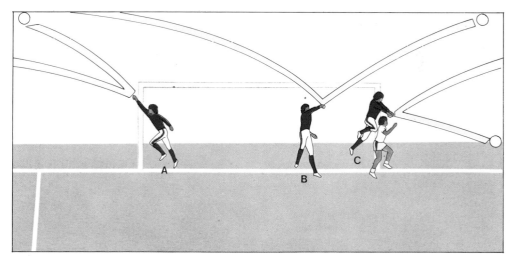

▲ **Each type of cross demands a different kind of punch.** For the high ball that comes in at the near post (**A**), it should be back in the direction it came from, really going for that height and distance as you aim for the area of least danger—the touchline. Some keepers like to use two fists whenever possible, but a minority feel happier with one; using the arm nearer the goal will give you slightly better vision in certain situations, but you'll soon discover in practice which one you feel most at home with. At times, of course, you can only rely on one hand, as in the example opposite. For the high far-post cross that has you going backwards and really stretching for the ball (**B**), aim for the opposite flank. Here the one-handed technique is almost obligatory as you're hitting across the line of flight. Again, hit through the ball (under the mid-line rather than over it) as you look for height and distance to take it towards the safety of the wing area. If this ball really has you struggling and you can't get that type of direction on it, punch firmly out for a corner, well away from the goal. The dipping or lower cross to the near post (**C**) will force you to break the rule about going for the big clearance, if an opponent is in the position shown here; he'll be looking for the header and you'll do well to get your hands slightly in front of him and bang the ball downwards, hopefully to a defender. Two hands are essential in this instance, and if he just beats you to the ball they'll also provide a block right after he has touched the ball. For any of these crosses, there should be no need to punch if you're not under pressure. **17**

Shot-stopping

A comparatively small percentage of a goalkeeper's touches during a game will be actual saves: usually crosses and even back passes will be more common. Indeed it's possible for keepers to go whole matches without making a save. Yet the diving stop and the reflex save remain the romantic heart of the craft. That is when the keeper has to earn his keep.

The shot doesn't permit the same luxuries as the high cross, rarely allowing cover or giving second chances. Often there is no warning. It comes at speed, against difficult backgrounds, possibly through a ruck of players. It can be cruelly deflected—by friend or foe—to leave the goalie helpless.

These are the times when the goalkeeper really is the last line of defence, when only his ability stands between a save and a goal. That is why the amount of practice required is out of all proportion to the number of times that skill is called upon during actual matches; that is why hours have to be spent in dedicated training mastering positional play, improving strength and agility, enhancing handling and sharpening reflexes for occasions that might amount to a few seconds a season.

At the same time, of course, the awesome responsibility and daunting tasks are matched by the rewards. If the goalkeeper can never quite attain the stature of the scorer his shot-stopping skills are nevertheless held in ever-increasing regard and his saves can provide heart-stopping moments for the spectator.

The range of shots a keeper has to cope with is almost endless. They can come from three yards or thirty; they can be on the ground or above his head; they can come full on or from an acute angle; they can be blasted or carefully placed; they can be dipping or rising, hard and straight or soft and swerving. He must learn to react to them all, but because of the immense variation it's not possible to master them by learning the art through logical steps, as it is with the cross. The answer is practice: practice until every conceivable eventuality has been encountered in training, and then more practice to ensure that both reflexes and agility are always at a peak. Even then all this must be constantly tested in match situations. This is one of the main reasons why goalkeeping is such a long apprenticeship, why so many internationals are in their thirties.

▶ *Corinthians keeper Jairo holds on to a high shot during the Brazilian National Championship game against Santos in 1979. Brazil have always tended to produce goalkeepers of the 'continental' style—agile and acrobatic but at times weak on basic technique and prone to lapses in judgement—and the national side won the World Cup three times with players who don't really stand comparison with the goalies of other victorious sides in the sport's premier competition. Gilmar (1958 and 1962) and Felix (1970) come nowhere near Banks (1966), Maier (1974) or Fillol (1978) in terms of reliability or, ironically, in terms of bringing off the spectacular save when required. Brazil triumphed with a policy of scoring more goals than they accepted they would concede; with a top keeper, as the Hungarians had before them, they would have been an even greater force.*

▼ *Positioning, reflexes, suppleness, agility and handling all combine to give Jean-Marie Pfaff a superb athletic catch for Belgium in their European Championship finals match with England at Turin in 1980. Many keepers would have been content to turn this shot over or round for a corner, but Pfaff's confidence, experience and ability enable him to make the ball stick. Note how he has maintained good vision despite the sideways dive and got his hands firmly behind the ball. The skill doesn't end here: he must ensure that he secures the ball to his body as quickly as possible to prevent the chance of losing it as he lands.*

There are nevertheless basic rules which should be followed, guidelines which govern the very essence of goalkeeping. First, remain alert to the possibility of a shot. Always be aware of the chance of a snapshot on the run, a quick turn and drive, a surprise effort from long range, an ambitious try from near the goal-line. Literally keep on your toes, legs slightly apart, ready to move in any direction at speed.

Second, always adopt a sensible starting position. In general terms this means being on an imaginary line drawn between the ball and the centre of your goal-line,

called the 'bisector', moving into line as play moves across your goal to give yourself the chance to make a save on either side with a minimum of movement.

Third, concentrate on the ball. Though there isn't the time—nor the temptation—to look around as on the cross, there are distractions in dealing with a shot, particularly in crowded areas or when an opponent is following up, hoping to cash in on a parry or fumble. This isn't to say you're not aware of the movements of players away from the ball—you should of course know what's going on in front of you and indeed instruct and warn your

defenders when necessary, especially when you can see things they can't because of your unique vantage point; but when the possibility of a shot exists, however slight, then your only concern is with the ball.

Fourth, whenever possible get as much of your body behind the ball, no matter what the type of save. While the ball can slip through your hands, it can't slip through your chest or stomach. Relax that part of your body in contact with the ball on impact and draw it away, 'giving' with the power of the shot to minimise the risk of the ball bouncing out of control.

◄ Shots close to the body can present bigger problems than those requiring apparently more difficult acrobatic saves. With the hard low shots between the body and the ground, the technique is to 'collapse' on the ball rather than dive for it, getting your legs out of the way quickly so that your hands, supported by your body, can be behind the ball. There's a temptation to 'overdive' with the higher shots near the body, but it's important to maintain balance and vision here, keeping your eye fixed on the ball and getting your hands firmly behind it. These saves are needed far more often than the athletic leaps, so they should be practised frequently and at length in training. All you need is someone firing in shots between three and ten yards away.

19

Fifth, avoid reaching for the ball with a dive if by first using your feet you can get into position with your body behind it, or at least make the actual take a lot easier. By seeing the ball early, by shrewd judgement and by quick but controlled footwork, really good keepers often make hard shots look easy.

Sixth, if you can't get your body behind the ball then apply the same essentials as for handling the high cross: hands behind the line of flight, fingers spread wide, thumbs almost touching, and secure the ball to your body as soon as possible.

Finally, whenever possible catch and hold rather than parry, punch, palm or 'tip' the ball. Many strong shots you'll be glad just to stop, and by any means available, including your legs, and as with high balls the basic maxim of safety first applies—a certain corner is preferable to an unsure save—but all too often keepers overreact, particularly on weak shots. Learning the delicate and difficult dividing line between 'catch it if you can' and 'if in doubt, don't' is a long and sometimes costly business—another reason for keepers reaching their playing peak when all around them are thinking of packing it in.

While it is the spectacular dives and acrobatic leaps that capture the popular imagination, goalkeepers often maintain that it's the apparently simpler shots that

can cause them most trouble—the ball that bounces a few feet in front of them, the seemingly straight drive that suddenly swerves at the last moment. And, ironically, one of the trickiest to deal with is near the body, the fast low ball around the legs that exploits the space between the body and the ground.

If you dive for shots close to you there's a chance that you'll dive over the ball. The problem here is literally how to get your legs out of the way, how to get down quickly so that your hands, supported by your body, can be behind the ball. The art of it is a 'dropping' technique, collapsing your legs so that your body is side-on to the line of flight. These shots are often hit with pace from close range—so the practice should emphasise that, with balls being struck from about four to ten yards. The first and third routines illustrated on page 24 are good examples.

The approach to handling much wider shots off the ground rests as much with the preparation for the save as the technique of actually executing it. It's all too easy to get pinned to the spot when better positioning, often using your feet, would make the save easier. Youngsters tend to lurch at everything, but with long shots in particular there can be more time than you think and an alert keeper, by picking up the flight of the ball early and taking a few

In any poll for 'the save of the century' the short-list would surely include a remarkable piece of action from Gordon Banks in England's game against Brazil at Guadalajara during the 1970 World Cup finals. The long-awaited tussle between the holders and the favourites was only 18 minutes old when the move which led to it began in the Brazilian half. 'Carlos Alberto hit an unbelievable ball with the outside of his right foot,' recalls Banks. 'It literally curled round Terry Cooper and dropped right into Jairzinho's path. He could motor too, but he took the ball towards the goal-line. There was no way he was going to shoot from there . . . but I had to take up my position at the near post because Tostão had made a run there. That's why I had so far to go across to make the save. As Jairzinho put the ball over I started back across the goal. I was sure it was too high for anyone to reach . . . but then I saw Pelé. The ball seemed to hang in the air and he seemed to climb higher and higher until he got the ball on his forehead, putting everything behind it . . .'

Pelé had drifted in behind Tommy Wright and caught the England defence ball-watching. Wright and Alan Mullery, Pelé's marker for most of the game, could only watch as the great man's powerful downward header sped towards the corner of the net with Banks still only halfway across his goal. Many of the fiercely pro-Brazilian crowd behind the goal were already rising to their feet to acclaim a score as Pelé landed. They, and the hundreds of millions watching on television, had reckoned without Banks. He launched himself off his right leg towards the ball . . . but it was already on the up after the bounce a few feet from the line. Forward force wasn't on—but a final stretch of the back meant he got his fingertips to it, flicking it upwards. Spinning furiously, the ball arced up in front of the crossbar and then over it in a gentle parabola for a corner. It's not easy to say who was most surprised. The crowd, almost all of them on their feet with their hands in the air; the England defence, rescued by a near miracle; Pelé, his arms raised, his second leap in jubilation suddenly stunted; or Banks himself. 'Never at any point did I think I couldn't make it . . . but I thought it had gone in. The crowd erupted, and I thought they'd scored.'

That staggering save, made in the blazing heat and high altitude of Mexico, made against the most talented team in the world's foremost tournament, and made in a stadium with 71,000 people baying for an England defeat, contains a host of goalkeeping lessons. Banks' original positioning to cover Tostão on the near post; his repositioning in following the cross; his footwork to get near the ball; his agility in getting to it. Less obvious factors played their part, too: Banks' confidence and determination in refusing to admit he was beaten; his bravery in throwing himself at a ball when a collision with the post was a probability ('. . . once I'd lifted my arm to cover the bounce of the ball I was looking where I was falling because I knew I was near the post'), and in fact he finished up curled round it; and not least a magic ingredient in goalkeeping—improvisation. Banks produced a save that isn't on the curriculum of any training course or in any coaching book. A combination of instinct and knowledge, of sheer physical ability and vast experience, produced the instant solution. 'At that moment I hated Gordon Banks more than any man in football,' says Pelé. 'I just couldn't believe it. But when I cooled down I had to applaud him with my heart. It was the greatest save I had ever seen.'

► Hard shots going for the corner are frequently impossible to hold, and the important thing here is to get to the ball at all. You'll need to see the ball early and often call on some nifty footwork as well as agility in the air to make contact. Don't try and parry the ball down for a recovery save: a certain corner is always safer than a risky rebound off your hand or arm. Make sure your fingers get a firm contact with the ball, even though the deflection needed is only a slight one. Throws can be more effective than shots for practising this type of save—particularly useful if you're training with another keeper, since he is then refining that aspect of his technique—but only deflect the 'shots' that merit it. If the ball comes in nearer to you, then make the appropriate save. The thrower should aim just inside the post, to either side, from a position around the penalty spot. A supply of balls will enable you to get an element of rhythm into the exercise.

◄ East Germany's Bodo Rudwaleit turns a fierce shot over the bar—and to the relative safety of a corner—during the 1980 Olympic final in Moscow against Czechoslovakia, watched by team-mate Rüdiger Schnuphase and Frantisek Stambachr (16). This type of deflection is a very different proposition from the one used for the high cross near the bar, which with its studied response and technique is almost in slow motion by comparison, though of course the intention and the end product are the same. Here it's all about speed and reflexes; sensible positioning is important, but it counts for little if you can't get the touch that matters. Often the finest of deflections is enough, even though the contact must be a sure one. Such reactions have to be developed and honed with patient and dedicated training, both with exercises and practice routines. Any exercise that improves agility is valid, but the practice is difficult to isolate. It's also a little dangerous: the essence of this area of goalkeeping is your response to the instant situation, and if you actually know that someone is about to try and throw or kick a certain type of ball then the whole thing is undermined.

► The tip-over save from the shot heading just under the bar often demands fast reactions as well as a high degree of suppleness and agility. Both the 'push' and 'swing' approach, as here, need patient practice; only a limited percentage of the balls coming at you will warrant the treatment (the rest should be saved by the correct means) and a fair number will no doubt sail over the top. Again, only a touch is required for the fierce shot, though the dipping shot or lob may need a more pronounced pushing action to get the change of direction. Strong hands are essential for goalkeepers, not least in the fingers for this kind of save and for the tip round shown at the top of the page. Finger-tip press-ups are an obvious and effective way of strengthening them, while a handy hint (and a method used by Pat Jennings) is to squeeze a tennis ball; this has the advantage that you can do it virtually anywhere at any time.

small steps before 'take off', can sometimes convert a difficult save into a relatively simple one. The movement is a sideways skipping motion on the balls of your feet—never cross your legs—maintaining poise, balance and concentration throughout. It's a shuffling action, not the big strides used in going for the cross.

The desire to be spectacular is a common fault in young goalkeepers. It is more important for your side to be safe, and this galls opponents: few things are as frustrating than to see a well-struck, well-placed shot plucked contemptuously out of the air. The keeper is saying that it will take something a bit special to test him, let alone beat him, and the top players tend to save their acrobatics for when they are really needed.

Though no two saves are identical, there is a specific technique to the diving save, whether you've used your feet to move across to it, whether it's at knee or head height. The bodyweight should be transferred onto the leg nearest the ball and you thrust off that leg to get the movement required. Dive sideways, not face down, getting your hands firmly behind the line of flight without 'twisting' your arms. Maintaining good vision is crucial here, and by practising you'll be able to decide precisely what adjustments are needed in the placement and angle of your arms in a given situation.

Your hands should 'give' a little on impact to take the pace off the shot, and the ball should be secured quickly by drawing it to your body as you bring your knees up on landing. A good catch means little if you then lose the ball as you reach the ground.

There are occasions, of course, when the rules go right out the window; when instinct, experience, sheer good fortune or a combination of all three seem to come to a keeper's aid. It usually happens once or perhaps twice a game—sticking a leg out at close range, making contact with a deflection after being wrong-footed, a ball somehow held when the technique was sadly lacking. But occasionally, as England found to their dismay in 1973, it can happen over a whole match; Jan Tomaszewski's performance at Wembley in the vital World Cup encounter was an amazing amalgam of skill, nerve, madness and luck, but it won Poland the point they needed to reach the finals.

Luck is a crucial factor in the keeper's most thankless task—facing penalties. Even Tomaszewski's ran out for Allan Clarke to equalise in 1973. The pressure, however, is all on your opponent: his side is expecting him to score, while no-one on yours is expecting you to save a well-struck spot-kick. If you do, you're a hero.

There are nevertheless some things you can do to add to the tension working in your favour. One, of course, is to try and discover which opposing player takes them for his side before a match. One of your teammates may have seen him take one before and can tell you which side he put it on that occasion.

You may be able to get another clue as your opponent places the ball, unable to resist the temptation to glance into one corner—though if it's pronounced he may be trying to fool you. The last chance you will get before contact will be the angle of his kicking foot as it comes to the ball; practising with your colleagues will help you recognise the way certain angles will affect the direction the ball travels.

A final tip is to dive slightly forward rather than across the goal-line. While this gives you fractionally less time to reach the ball, the shot is less likely to push your hands and fingers back. It's one of the most frustrating moments for a keeper to reach a firmly hit penalty but see it crash off his hands into the net.

Penalties are very much a personal area for keepers. Some favour the 'percentage' theory—by committing themselves in advance to going one way, their bodyweight already on that leg, they reckon they stand a better chance than by desperately trying to react in either direction; some prefer to stay put on the grounds that they can't make a well-placed shot but can save the one hit near the middle, no matter how hard and at what height; some really do try to respond to the actual kick; some, perhaps the majority, will vary the technique each time according to the player taking the kick, the ground conditions and so on. Whatever the method, the keeper deserves any luck that comes his way.

Goalkeepers must be alert to the possibility of having to make any type of save at any time the ball is near the danger area—as Leeds United's Scottish international David Harvey discovered during the First Division draw with Wolves at Molineux in November 1978. This tale of the unexpected came when a Steve Daley free-kick, from about 35 yards out, drifted fairly harmlessly into the space behind the Leeds defenders and towards Harvey. Suddenly midfield star Tony Currie—not apparently marking anyone but acting as an instant sweeper—took a couple of steps backwards and lurched at the ball to send it curling goalwards, wrong-footing the keeper. Harvey's superb reflexes, honed by endless hours of practice, served him well as he leapt to his left, palming the spinning ball with his left hand and then trying to gather it with his right as he came down. The ball 'got away', however, and he had to make a quick, brave recovery as Mel Eves closed in. The incident well shows the need for keepers to control their area and their defence, for the value of maintaining communication—a clear call may have been the simple answer—and for defenders to do the specialist defending.

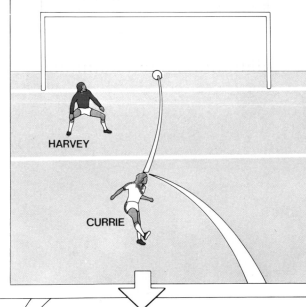

▼ Below are four practices, all used by professional clubs, for sharpening reflexes and improving shot-stopping technique. The first requires a stretch of grass (or sandy or earthy ground) next to a wall—one that can be used legitimately—with the keeper wearing appropriate protection, such as thick track-suit trousers, if the surface is at all difficult. This is a demanding routine in which you have to really push yourself and fling yourself around, but one which is enormously rewarding. Two players stand behind you and at an angle (you'll soon discover the right position, especially if you mark a small goal or target area on the wall) and throw or kick balls at the wall so that they rebound within handling distance to the man in the middle. If the two partners are also keepers, they'll probably prefer to throw the ball, and the target area on the wall can help them with that department of their game as they wait for their turn as the keeper proper. If they are outfielders they'll choose to kick.

They crash their ball in alternately, shouting 'Now!' as they release it, and the keeper has to save the rebound. It's a practice that can work at anything between three and ten yards. At the longer position you should expect to hold the ball; for the ones close in you're looking to parry or deflect it—at this distance the emphasis is on speeding up reactions rather than handling itself—but if you can make the ball stick then so much the better. The 'shots' should be as varied as possible, within reason, coming off the wall at different heights, angles and speeds. It has to be a fast, exhausting exercise to be effective, and though this can be achieved with three (if the keeper flicks the held balls back and the other two players retrieve the deflected balls quickly) it will be a far easier task with four players, two each side and armed with a generous supply of footballs. A simpler version for two players is for the keeper to face the same way as the kicker and turn to face the shot as he calls.

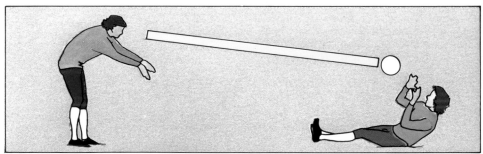

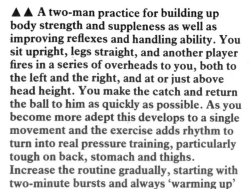

▲▲ A two-man practice for building up body strength and suppleness as well as improving reflexes and handling ability. You sit upright, legs straight, and another player fires in a series of overheads to you, both to the left and the right, and at or just above head height. You make the catch and return the ball to him as quickly as possible. As you become more adept this develops to a single movement and the exercise adds rhythm to turn into real pressure training, particularly tough on back, stomach and thighs. Increase the routine gradually, starting with two-minute bursts and always 'warming up' for it first with stretching exercises.

▲ This simple but exhausting 'piggy in the middle' exercise again uses speed and surprise to help improve reactions and handling. The two outfield players play in all kinds of shots to the area round the body, from chips to the stomach to firm shots to the side. The keeper makes his save, flicks or kicks the ball back to the first man then turns quickly to face the next shot as it comes in. The same idea can be done with just two of you: the 'keeper' faces the same way as the man with the ball, and the latter shouts 'Turn!' just before he shoots. A wall or net behind will save you retrieving the balls missed in this case.

▲ Most reflex saves are made in crowded areas with bodies often preventing a clear sight of the ball. This exercise tests the keeper's ability to hold a ball he sees late. A player stands right in front of the keeper and a third player, standing a few yards away, throws head- and shoulder-high balls straight for him. He ducks out of the way, down or to left or right, at the last possible moment. This idea can be expanded to shots and diving saves by having two keepers in a goal—one on the line and one just in front; any shot not saved by the first man (or 'dummied' by him) should be taken by the one behind.

Narrowing the angle

When a player is through on his own against a keeper he has an advantage and should in theory score, either by beating the keeper with a shot or by dribbling round him. That such a small proportion of such chances are converted is a testament to the skills, timing and above all the bravery of their adversaries.

Your first aim in these situations is to get your positioning right, shutting down the angle to reduce the size of the target area your opponent has to shoot at. It's worth noting here that the expression used for this, 'coming off your line', is rarely exactly that; keepers should and do patrol a few yards out, and will probably begin their advance of a player who is through from outside the six-yard box.

Closing down your man, let alone gaining possession, is not an easy tactic to master. If you go too soon, your opponent may pass; if you go too far, he may chip over you; if you go too fast, not really balanced and in control, he may find it a simple task to just dribble round you; if you don't go far enough, you can present him with a temptingly large target. Learning to get it right, when every new instance is different in some ways from those you've met before, takes a good deal of practice and a lot of experience culled from match situations.

Once basic rule will help: your advance should normally be as fast as possible while the ball is outside the playing distance of your opponent, but if he already has the ball, or when he runs on to a through ball, the approach should be more cautious and considered.

Your opponent is usually coming at you on some sort of angle, and your job is to force him wide. The ideal here is to actually rob him and gain possession; but if he does retain the ball you've drastically reduced the angle on the shot (and the options to shoot, since he'll now be virtually restricted to going for the near post) and gained time for a defender or two to get back behind you and cover for the shot or

the cross, whichever is now played in.

All this can be real cat-and-mouse stuff, in which both players try to conceal their intentions. The keeper can and should make use of any legal device to kid the opponent or put him off his stride as you force him to make the first positive move, in the direction you want. You can feint to rush in, then stay where you are; you can

make yourself as 'big' as possible and wave your arms about; you can lean well to one side to tempt him to go the other. If you know he has a weaker foot, incidentally, you may try to force him onto it, no matter what the position involved.

Forcing your opponent wide relies on a combination on good positioning and spreading yourself, that is further narrowing the angle by forming a lateral barrier—across the angle between the ball and the goal. This is where the keeper's courage is really put to the test because you have to go in 'head first' to stand a

▲ Stopping an opponent who breaks clear is about moving out and spreading yourself; narrowing the angle by coming off your line and then creating as wide a barrier as possible with your body. As well as making it more difficult to shoot by reducing the area he has to aim at, this side-on approach gives you a better chance of actually gathering the ball. The least you're looking for is to force the player wide to make his angle for the shot more acute and possibly gain time for your defenders to cover behind you. Though most goalkeepers are better on one side than the other here, you'll be a far more effective player if you can go down and make these saves on both sides when required.

▼ *The high point for Ray Clemence in an uncharacteristically jittery debut for Spurs in the Charity Shield—after signing from Liverpool in the summer of 1981—was a well-timed dive at the feet of Aston Villa's David Geddes. With the striker through on his own Clemence has carefully but purposefully come out of his six-yard area before choosing the right moment to go for the ball, when for a split-second it's outside the playing distance of his opponent. He then acts quickly, spreading himself wide to form a lateral barrier as he goes for the ball. While he is unable to get two hands behind the ball and secure it to his body, he uses one hand to rob Geddes, avert the immediate danger and eventually gain possession.*

chance of getting your hands to the ball. If you go in feet first you not only erase that chance but also leave a bigger angle for the shot or for him to go round you, since you are diving along the angle between the ball and the goal rather than across it. The lateral approach also means that if he cuts inside you've got another bite at the ball—with your legs. Many a match-winning stop has been made that way, with the keeper seemingly beaten and then just nicking the ball away at the last moment.

While your initial movement may be a little cagey, you should be quick and positive when you do go down for the ball; you'll only get one opportunity. Some keepers maintain you should watch for the split-second when he glances down at the ball—he has to look at it at some point—but others say that experience has taught them to 'read the feet'. Either way (and countless practice sessions will teach you which method is more effective) look for the moment when the ball is outside his playing distance, or at least as far from his controlling foot as it can be, and be decisive. Remember too that the pressure is more on him than you, and he may well be in two minds about his course of action.

You must really attack the ball, keeping your head steady as you go for it with both hands in a sideways dive as you protect your head with your trailing arm. Make sure your calf, thigh, hips and arm make a complete barrier on the ground. When you gain possession, fold your arms, head and knees to your body to smother the ball—and yourself—as you clutch the ball to your lower chest.

Sometimes this doesn't come off, but getting a touch with even one hand will often be enough, deflecting the ball so that your opponent has to check on a diverted run. If you don't manage a touch at all, at least you'll have forced him wider, and your priority now is a quick recovery to an appropriate position in goal.

Before going into a practice session make sure you are properly clothed, with adequate protection for both arms and legs. If you are a real learner start out on soft ground.

To begin with a friend should dribble the ball at a suitably gentle pace from about 30 yards out, and you come off your line to go down and rob him. He should gradually increase the speed of his run and vary the angle of approach until he is

genuinely trying to score: chipping you if you've come too far, dribbling round you if your approach wasn't correct, shooting 'through the hole' if your dive wasn't sideways down and so on. If you get a touch to deflect the ball, or if you miss the touch but divert his run, continue the 'move' by practising the art of recovering your position in goal as he tries a shot from a more acute angle.

Practising the timing of your run off the line to beat opponents to a through a ball requires two other players. From about 30 yards out one of them plays balls towards the inside of the area for his friend to run on to form a similar or slightly straighter position 25 or 30 yards from goal. You start just off your line and race to beat the second man to smother the ball as he closes in or at his feet. Again, play it for real: if he beats you to the ball he should try to shoot past you or take it round.

While goalkeepers need inherent bravery, these exercises will develop the timing and handling that lead to confidence in such situations. And a courageous, self-assured keeper will be a difficult proposition for a forward—even though he 'only has the keeper to beat'.

▲ The basic concern for keepers in one-against-one situations is to narrow the angle—coming off your line or out of your six-yard box to reduce the area of the goal your opponent has to aim at. But allied to this is the need to spread yourself wide to form a barrier across the angle between the ball and the goal, shrinking the target still further. The temptation to go down 'feet first' should be resisted; it means you'll be along the angle between the ball and the goal instead of across it, and it will reduce the chances of getting your hands to the ball. Opponents are more likely to shoot earlier on straighter runs than they are from wider positions, and you may be forced to make a save as you close your man down. Luck may play its part here, but good positioning, a sensible approach and fast reflexes will count for far more as you 'collapse' your legs and get your hands to the ball to prevent it slipping 'through the hole' between your body and the ground—a more common way of scoring against the advancing keeper than the dribble round him or the chip.

PONTE

McGOVERN

► *You may not have to be crazy to be a goalkeeper, as the saying would have us believe, but you certainly have to be brave. And nowhere is that quality more severely tested than with the save at the feet of an opponent bent on scoring, whether in a crowded goalmouth or in the wide open space of a player running on to a through ball. Here Nacional's Uruguayan international Rodolfo Rodriguez holds on after a courageous dive at the feet of Forest centre-half Larry Lloyd during the World Club Championship match at Tokyo in February 1981. He may be wearing tracksuit bottoms to protect his legs on the abrasive surface, but his hands and more particularly his head are cruelly exposed as he tenaciously guards his goal. While there are techniques for shielding yourself with most saves, circumstances sometimes dictate that you have to risk all to get that ball. This fearless pride remains an essential ingredient in the make-up of the good goalkeeper—at whatever level he plays.*

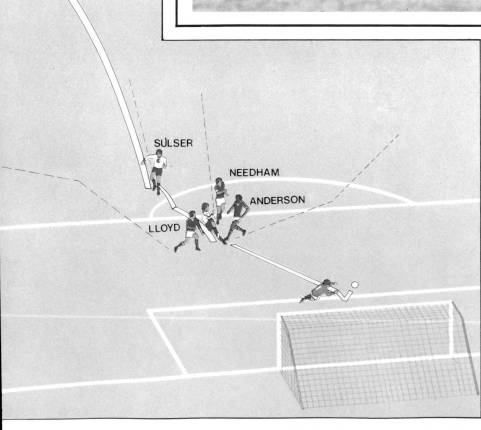

Nottingham Forest suffered some heart-stopping moments on their way to a debut European Cup success in 1979, not least in the first leg of the quarter-final against Swiss champions Grasshoppers at the City Ground. Forest were 2-1 up when Raimondo Ponte (who was to join the English club the following year) hit a long through ball from inside his own half for Claudio Sulser. The pass caught the Forest defence square and the speedy Sulser—who had already scored once to give the Zurich side the lead for his tenth goal of the competition—took the ball into the penalty area as Larry Lloyd and Viv Anderson tried to cover. But it was really one-against-one as Peter Shilton came off his line to narrow the angle and then 'show' Sulser, a very left-footed player, the area he would like to aim at, just inside the far post. The Swiss star obliged with a fierce low drive which Shilton, just five or six yards away, did well to reach at all, parrying it to his right. As the ball bounced away, Shilton was on his feet before anyone could cash in and made a neat recovery. A score then would have made it 2-2—a draw plus two valuable away goals—but Grasshoppers were foiled by a response honed in training.

Throwing

There is a world of difference between clearing the ball and passing it, between getting rid of the ball and using it constructively to maximise the chances of creating an attack. Today's keeper must think like an outfield player and be positive when he has possession.

It's not so long ago that he was expected to do nothing more than put in a big punt down the middle or, if he threw at all, it was automatically put out to the opposite flank from which it had been received.

The keeper's role now, however, is a far more thinking and involved one. In the modern game he must not only have an array of accurate throws and kicks at his disposal; he must also be as tactically astute and aware as any outfield player, giving his passes the same consideration as they do. He must think like a sweeper. The opposition are vulnerable after an attack breaks down, and a sharp throw to a man in space or an incisive kick upfield can pay rich dividends. He may be the last line of defence, but he can also be the first line of attack.

The goalkeeper has several advantages here over his teammates. He doesn't have to worry what's happening behind him; he is rarely challenged, let alone marked; and because he can use his hands he has available to him various throws and certain types of kick not possible for other players to use.

While the keeper can be a surprisingly effective instigator of attacking moves, taking out opponents with quick, well-placed kicks and throws, he will still find he is forced to hold the ball on the majority

► Ray Clemence lines up an overarm throw for Liverpool. Note how he uses his non-throwing arm for a sighting device as he looks over his left shoulder. With his hand firmly behind the ball and his throwing arm extended, he is perfectly balanced to transfer his weight onto his left leg and execute the throw. Experienced keepers use this 'javelin' technique as a genuine alternative to the kick—it can easily clear the heads of opponents quite a distance from goal—and it's an invaluable weapon for setting up the quick break in midfield, as the diagram above illustrates. Though this throw can produce a straight line of flight, keepers also produce and control a swerve on their overarm clearances with a slightly wider arm action: for the right-hander this will be a 'fade' from left to right. This can be used to take out opponents or keep the ball away from them, bending it 'behind' a forward into the path of a defender going up the right flank or away from one to find a team-mate going up the left. But get the straight throw right before trying those.

► The opposition can be vulnerable to the counter-attack after a keeper has taken a high ball—particularly if he has moved forward in taking a catch and after set pieces. In this instance, during the derby against Birmingham City at St Andrews in October 1979, Aston Villa took full advantage of both factors to set up a killing move. It began with keeper Jimmy Rimmer coming out to claim a City corner. Though he was forced to roll over as he landed, he was aware of the possibility of a quick break as he recovered. So was midfielder Dennis Mortimer, who was already moving into space as Rimmer caught the ball. The keeper put in a fine overarm throw into Mortimer's path. With a couple of defenders well out of position, still getting back from the corner, Mortimer hit a first-time ball to Andy Gray deep in the Birmingham half and he laid it off, again first time, to Brian Little. He ran on at an angle before sending a perfect pass for Andy Gray, stealing into space on the left of the area, to beat the advancing Jimmy Montgomery with a left-foot shot for the game's only goal.

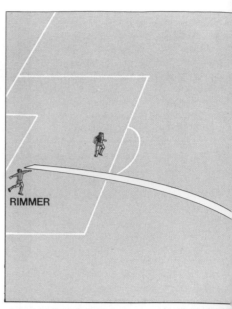

RIMMER

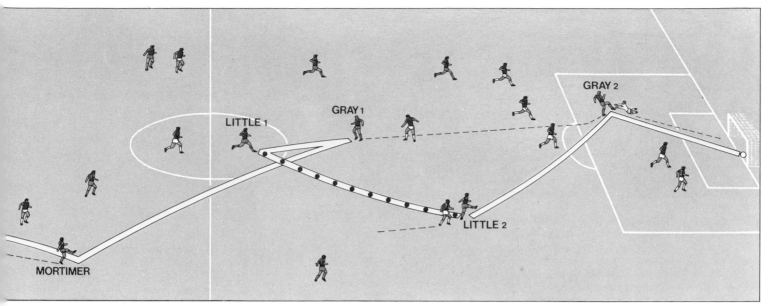

▶ Any aspiring goalkeeper can improve his throwing by practising on his own against a wall. Accuracy is the first concern, so with the overarm throw make a circle or a square on the wall a few feet off the ground and get your technique right before gradually building up the distance. Too many youngsters try to heave the ball 40 yards before they've got it right over 15 or 20, like a tennis learner trying to serve fast before he has the knack of getting the ball in the service court. Keep your throwing arm straight, your hand firmly behind the ball, and use your non-throwing arm as a sighter as you look over that shoulder. Transfer your weight to your leading leg and bring your throwing arm over full extension in an arc, avoiding the temptation to bend your arm. Follow through with your arm still extended in the same line. Later, after mastering the basic technique, you can move the mark down—the receiver will want the ball at his feet—and practice curving the ball to him. This 'fading' technique can be particularly effective in steering the ball away from opponents and drifting it into the path of a team-mate; but it takes time to learn how to control the degree of 'bend'.

▲ This simple three-man practice improves agility and handling as well as throwing technique. The aim is for the thrower to clear the player in the middle, who jumps from a specified position, and reach the third player. After a set time or number of throws one of the two throwers goes in the centre. The advantage with throwing practices is that, unlike most other routines for keepers, they don't require a pitch or even a goal. All you need is a partner or a wall.

▶ *The short-arm throw is the best choice for moving the ball at speed over short distances, and is ideal for setting up quick attacks from the back. Here Belgium's Jean-Marie Pfaff is seen executing the 'flicking' motion at the moment of release. This is the most difficult of the three basic throws in terms of technique. You take the ball back just over your shoulder with a bent arm, and the opposite shoulder and leg move forward in preparation for the throw. Then you bring your throwing arm forward quickly from the shoulder as you fling your forearm forwards and downwards. Don't give the ball unnecessary 'air'; throw it hard and direct from your shoulder to the target so that it gets there as fast as possible. You can get the basic idea by throwing the ball against a wall, but to practise finding a moving target you'll need a couple of team-mates, each with a ball. They dribble towards you, one at a time, and when they get to about ten yards away they pass the ball to you and move off quickly. You field the ball and return it with a short-arm throw so they can run into the space and control it easily without checking their stride.*

29

► A basic practice of rolling a ball against a wall or to another player, though helpful, can get a little monotonous, and this three-man routine introduces the elements of passing and shooting for two outfield players—enabling the keeper to improve his handling as well as his distribution. With just two of you, of course, the second player could also play the ball back in at body or head height, but with three it's easier for the receiving player to be moving onto the ball and therefore test the accuracy of the keeper's throw. The technique is similar to that used in bowls or tenpin bowling, starting with the ball held with both hands in front of the body at hip height. With the palm of your hand supporting the ball and your fingers well spread to give maximum control, move forward onto the leg opposite that of the throwing arm and take the arm slightly behind the body to gather swing. Transfer your weight to the front leg and swing your arm forward, releasing the ball with your hand at right-angles to the ground.

of occasions he has possession. He may be crowded in and have a restricted view of players' positions; he may have made a difficult take or save and need a little time to recover; many of his side may still be in defensive positions following a set piece or a period of sustained pressure; and while players should always be looking to make themselves available, in the lower echelons of the game they will often plead with their keeper for a few seconds' respite from their toils.

Over the past couple of decades—and especially so at the higher levels of the game—the throw has gradually ousted the kick as the main method of distribution. Many continental keepers, in fact, very rarely kick at all. The three main techniques are featured here (underarm, short-arm and overarm) though the professionals often evolve their own special styles for particular situations. Two examples are the double-handed overhead, a sort of shortened, flicked throw-in for finding a teammate when a player is standing in front, which was used regularly by Sepp Maier; and the wide-arm throw, a technique where the throwing arm is swung round parallel to the ground and the ball released at hip or waist level; this has always been a favourite for Pat Jennings of Northern Ireland.

Even within the conventional methods keepers develop their own small adjustments to gain extra power, swerve or accuracy. But aspiring goalies must start with the basics and take things slowly. Remember, too, that despite the huge progress made in this department of the trade that the first priority is still the same: safety first. No side can afford to give away the ball so close to their own goal, and the keeper's prime concern is security. If he can't see anyone available in sufficient space, he should go for distance; he must never risk a throw that puts the receiver under pressure—and of course he should be aware of the limitations and weaknesses of his defenders in this area. The big boot may be out of fashion, but it gets the ball out of the danger area. And if your side has forwards able to judge the flight well, to be aggressive and put pressure on the opponents' back four, then the old way can still be the best. There is a good chance of 'second phase' possession, too, from the resulting clearances.

► *Alan Rough, the most-capped keeper in Scotland's history, rolls out an underarm pass for left-back Frank Gray as Welsh striker John Toshack looks on. The underarm is the simplest of the three main throwing techniques, but it has severe limitations—notably that of distance. It's also best avoided on muddy days; because the ball hits the ground early and stays there it's likely to get stuck before it reaches the target, or at least put the receiver under pressure—a sin with any pass, and particularly from the keeper, who is not under any pressure. Here, at Ninian Park, on a sunny day in May 1979, Rough has no such worries. While the relatively poor power of the underarm throw hardly makes it a natural choice for the swift counter-attack down the middle, it can be used over short distances to find defenders in space . . . and in this instance Rough, aware of the space on the left flank, is actually telling Gray that the move is on rather than waiting to see someone making himself available. Because it comes to the receiver along the ground it is the easiest of the throws to control.*

Kicking

For today's keepers kicking means far more than the place-kick and the big punt upfield, and he must give it the same tactical consideration and attention in practice as the throw. In addition to the goal-kick itself—the keeper should be the best dead-ball kicker in the side, and is at a psychological disadvantage if he has to rely on a defender to get the necessary distance—there are three main techniques: the long punt, the short punt and the half-volley, or drop-kick.

The big punt goes higher and usually further than any other, but accuracy is sacrificed to distance and opponents as well as teammates will have time to get into position. The low flat trajectory of the short punt, a stab volley played from the hand, means that it's ideal for achieving speed and accuracy over medium distances, for finding a player unmarked on the flanks or in the defensive part of midfield. The techniques for the two punts are described below.

The drop-kick is the one in vogue; done well it combines the low trajectory of the short punt with distances almost as great as the big kick. It can be very effective for setting up players in space in midfield, and is particularly useful for the longer kicks into the wind or on gusty days. As with any half-volley (see page 98) it requires perfect timing, so practise it before trying it in matches, getting the technique right before going for distance. Because the contact is made near the ground, use it cautiously on muddy or slippery pitches.

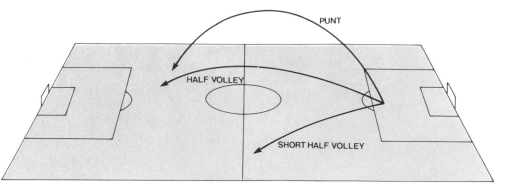

▲ For most keepers the main factor governing the choice of kick is distance, but for the experienced player the long half-volley can be a real alternative to the big punt for reaching the opponents' half. And while defenders can get into position for the higher kick, the drop-kick stands a better chance of still finding your team-mates unmarked in midfield.

▼ With goal-kicks your chief concern is to prevent your opponents gaining possession in the 'danger area'. Aim at the area between the centre-half and his full-backs, and go down the middle only with the big punt, where you can be sure of distance. The tap kick to a defender gives you all the options—but make sure you've both got plenty of time.

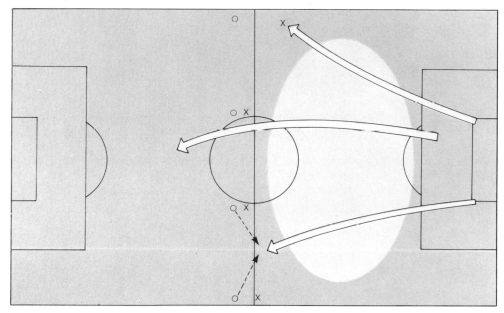

◄ The key to both types of punt is controlled power. It's no good trying to thrash the leather off the ball with the big kick if there's no accuracy. So work on the basics first—timing, rhythm and coordination—before you gradually increase the distance. For obvious reasons it's best to work with another player, preferably a keeper, and on a pitch. With the big punt you can easily introduce a simple competition by kicking back from the point where you catch the ball: if you drive your friend back behind the goal-line you score a point and he starts again from, say, the penalty spot. The pros who almost casually kick the ball 50 or 60 yards began by practising their style over half that distance. You need to give the ball plenty of 'air' on the big punt, leaning slightly back and following through forcefully and rhythmically after contact. Your foot should hit through and under the ball rather than across it. The technique for the short, straight-on punt is more restrained. The backlift is shorter and you drop the ball onto your foot from a lower position for a shorter follow-through, your knee pointing forward.

BIG KICK

STRAIGHT-ON PUNT

31

TECHNIQUES

BALL CONTROL

Basic technique

▲ It's not just target men who must be able to bring the ball under control quickly and cleanly. Here Tampa Bay midfielder Wes McLeod has to master an awkward bouncing ball under pressure from Vancouver's Carl Valentine during Whitecaps' 1979 Soccer Bowl win. Every outfield player must take this kind of control for granted—every time. That means practice to learn the basic techniques . . . and more practice to keep them in fine fettle.

▲ The 'wedge trap' is a neat way to control the falling ball, especially on the move. The trapping angle is made by turning the body slightly sideways to the oncoming ball; the 'trap' is formed by the inside of the foot and ankle and the ground. Exact timing is crucial, the ball making contact with the foot and ground at the same moment. The controlling surface is kept firm, not withdrawn. The 'wedge' technique can be used to control the ball and change direction in one touch, with either side of the foot.

Ball control is the ability to dominate and govern the ball. It is the ability to master a pass quickly and cleanly, in all conditions, even under pressure, time and time again. And you can't participate constructively in a game until you've mastered the essentials of that control.

It is not, however, an end in itself. Control is not about keeping the ball in the air a hundred times; it is about doing the basics well every time. 'Trapping the ball' is a platform for movement.

There are many match situations in which, whether by choice or not, you'll play the ball first time—a shot or pass, an interception, a clearance—but there are far more in which you'll need to bring the ball under control before your next move. The criterion is simple: the ease and speed with which that move can be made. If your control is good, the first touch will be enough and the second will be the positive move; if it's weak, taking several touches, you've lost the initiative. Opponents have

gained time at your expense. And in today's game, where speed of thought and action are so vital to create and exploit space, you can't afford to be let down by poor basic techniques.

Ball control centres on 'touch'—a player's sense of touch when coming in direct contact with a football, played into him at varying heights, speeds and angles. He must develop it in his feet, thighs, chest and head.

Touch brings confidence to take the ball on any part of the body, and this in turn brings vision and perception. You cannot assess the possibilities open to you while your mind is occupied solely with the actual problem of controlling the ball. And the longer you need to control the ball the less time you have to assess and make your next move.

The ball is the footballer's friend. It's rarely going to do anything really unpredictable, like a rugby ball can. Welcome it rather than fear it. You should be alert and poised, literally on your toes. After mastering the basic techniques, learn to apply them on the move, taking the ball and using it without breaking your rhythm; it's not often in matches you can just wait for the ball to arrive. The top players make it look easy, automatic, but they have acquired that ability through countless hours of practice.

▶ All you need for practising basic receiving techniques is a ball and a wall. Strike the ball at varying heights, speeds and angles in order to create different 'passes' off the wall. Learn to move into position, in line with the ball, before bringing it under control with one touch. Balance is vital: if you're in the right position your head, knee and foot will be in a vertical line. With a friend you can kick to each other, but throws will also produce more testing 'passes'.

Volley control

As the game of football has become faster and the marking tighter, the time a player has to receive the ball and bring it under his command has decreased. The quicker and better the initial control, the more the time available to a player to make his second touch count.

This trend has put an increasingly high premium on a whole range of controlling skills and techniques to 'kill' the ball in the air, using the chest and thighs as well as the feet. Most of these skills, considerably refined over the past two or three decades, are now automatically included in the curriculum of football training. Indeed, many coaches would argue that they are in fact among the very basics of modern ball control.

Forward players are expected to make difficult off-the-ground balls into subtle lay-offs to colleagues and half-chances for themselves; defenders are expected to use any 'legal' part of their body if the occasion demands to cut out danger; and midfielders are expected to have several options in mind before collecting yet another pass. Despite this, and even at professional levels, potential passes are

wasted because of clumsy or inadequate initial control.

There are three basic principles which apply to all aspects of receiving the ball on the full. First, decide early and positively which controlling surface you are to use to stop the ball. The earlier you decide—and act—the more time you have: time to become composed, time to carry out the control well, time to assess and execute your next move. The greater the scope the level of your skills, of course, the more

▼A marvellous moment of volley control finally buried West Germany's slender hopes in the 1978 World Cup. It came in the 66th minute of the clash with Austria at Cordoba. The score was 1-1 when Josef Hickersberger put over a harmless looking cross to the far post. Centre-back Rolf Rüssmann not only misread the flight of the ball but also seemed unaware of Hans Krankl behind him. Krankl altered his position as the ball came down to him about ten yards out and cushioned it at knee height with the inside of his left foot—and then readjusted his stance to rifle in a left-foot volley past the despairing dive of Sepp Maier. The Germans recovered to 2-2, but Krankl scored again to give Austria their first win over their neighbours in 47 years.

▲The side-volley trap is a safe and economical way of controlling the harder types of pass coming at you at thigh or knee height. The key to this technique is getting into a good balanced position early with the controlling surface behind the line of the ball, and withdrawing it on contact. With any type of volley control you can't adjust your basic stance, once your controlling foot is raised, so it's even more important than in other areas of receiving to judge the speed and flight of the ball perfectly as Hans Krankl did for his stunning goal (right).

you'll be equipped to make that decision pay, the more options you'll have at your disposal. The choice will probably be all the easier if it is made with the end product already in mind—to hold, pass, shoot, turn or move off with the ball—because you're not worrying during the trapping action about what happens next. On some occasions, of course, you are not granted this luxury; by its very nature control of the volley can often be simply a forced reaction, particularly with passes coming at you at speed.

The second principle behind trapping is to move into position. Whenever possible this should be towards the ball, but it must mean getting your body in the line of the ball as quickly as possible, with the controlling surface squarely behind the line of flight. It's the same idea as a goalkeeper using his feet to get his body behind a shot, and it can require the same sort of quick thinking and nimble footwork. Only in this way can you be sure of being correctly balanced and completely in charge as the ball arrives. Your arms

can be a great help here, and especially if you're in a hurry. Don't worry too much in this area of the game about style; if it feels right, and it works, then that's what counts. Some players are great 'killers' of a ball yet they can look quite ungainly. You'll develop your own little variations within the basic techniques, while in matches the actual situation can demand a slight adjustment to a 'model' skill for any given ball.

Third, relax the intended controlling surface before contact—this applies as much to the foot as to the chest or thigh—and withdraw the stopping area in the direction of the ball as it arrives. These two factors combine to take the pace off the ball, to 'cushion' it. If you adopt the right position and are well balanced, but just stick your foot there, the ball will almost certainly bounce away on impact. The faster the ball is travelling, the quicker and greater the movement of the foot must be. Only practice will enable you to gauge precisely how much 'brake' is needed for any particular ball on a

certain part of the body. Sometimes, when you're taking a ball in your stride, or intending to turn, you will purposely adjust this cushioning effect, or perhaps not apply it at all, in order to direct the ball the way you want to go. But for 'killing' the ball, for 'standing' control, it's absolutely vital to retain possession.

Receiving the ball will always be that much simpler if you are mentally relaxed, too. If you are tense or apprehensive your movements become jerky rather than smooth and rhythmic. This ability to relax is a product of confidence, of the assurance that comes with the knowledge that you can cope with just about any ball that comes your way. And that, of course, can only develop with the kind of control borne of serious and regular practice.

It is worth reiterating that no form of ball control is an end in itself, however neat or inventive. It is a means to an end, and what that end is can dramatically amend the basic principles of trapping; they are guidelines which apply rigidly only if a player wishes to, or indeed can,

▼ *Of the three main contact surfaces used in volley control the outside of the foot is the least effective for simply stopping a ball, but in situations like this one, with a falling ball and a man marking tight, it can be a devastating weapon for a controlled turn. Welsh striker Ian Walsh, in action against the USSR in the goalless World Cup draw at Wrexham in May 1981, is shielding the ball and, more importantly, disguising his intention from his marker. There's no giveaway movement in his body as he alters the position of his foot at the last possible moment to take the ball to his right. He in fact turned well enough across his man to steal a yard on him and get in a left-foot shot on target.*

ALLARDYCE

bring a ball under control as near his standing position as possible. Changes in technique are required, for example, if the intention is to set off at an angle to the flight of the ball, with the stopping surface turned towards the proposed direction and not withdrawn so much or so quickly, if at all, with some of the force on impact being used to send the ball on its way. More will be made of this 'directional control' in the later chapters on turning.

Adjustments will have to be made, too, for controlling a ball in your stride. It may not be possible to get your body right behind the ball, while the last thing you want is to 'kill' the ball completely and so slow you down. There are further areas—interceptions, for instance, where getting a stopping surface to the ball at all is your main target and where you'll be content to secure a second touch of any kind.

There are three contact surfaces used in volley control: the inside of the foot, the instep and the outside of the foot. Each is discussed with the appropriate illustration on these three pages.

▶ 'Killing' the high falling ball on the instep can be a useful alternative to the chest, thigh or the 'wedge trap'. The advantage over body control is that you can move off with the ball more quickly—you're not waiting for the ball to drop. The advantage over the wedge trap is that you meet the ball earlier and there's less chance of it squirting away, especially on wet ground. But it's not an easy technique, requiring exact positioning, perfect synchronisation of the downward movement of the foot with the speed of the ball and precise placement of the ball on the foot as you 'catch' it. In practice (you can simply throw the ball up for yourself) move off a few yards with the trapped ball.

Ball control is not an end in itself: it must be a platform for movement—a pass, a dribble, a holding operation—or a shot. Normally it's fairly predictable when a shot is on, but occasionally a player produces a goal 'out of nothing', after receiving the ball in a position where the attacking possibilities on his own seemed virtually nil. Pelé did it perhaps more than anyone—a superb example follows overleaf—but such delightful digressions from the everyday can happen anywhere. And it happened at Burnden Park on 21 April 1979. Bolton Wanderers, holding on to 17th place in the First Division, were playing hosts to Ipswich Town, seventh in the table and in the middle of a purple patch that had seen only one defeat in the previous 13 League matches. In that time their one-time suspect defence had conceded just eight goals—but now it was in for a real shock. This tale of the unexpected began with a Bolton throw-in well up on their left. Centre-back Sam Allardyce put in a fairly long one, and striker Alan Gowling stole a yard on Russell Osman to reach it out from the near post. He was running diagonally towards the touchline and tried to flick it on to Frank Worthington. But he couldn't get the right touch

and the former England player, policed by Terry Butcher, had to move away from goal to reach it. He got his head to the arching ball to slow it down and, still retreating, controlled it as it fell by 'juggling' it a couple of times on his left foot. With a magnificent combination of perceptive play and the skill to execute it he looped the ball over his head on the next touch and turned quickly, leaving Butcher and the closing Mick Mills marking the space behind him. Retaining his poise, Worthington completed his wizardry with a low left-foot volley (above) just past the astonished Paul Cooper into the right corner of the Ipswich net. Five touches 'off the floor'—and an apparently wasted set piece converted into a score. It wasn't merely a dazzling display of volley control; it was also an exhilarating example of quick-thinking, of an attacker's awareness of the situation. It's not possible, of course, to teach this kind of flair—but it's possible to learn the elements of control that make it feasible, to master them and gain the confidence needed to even contemplate such audacious and magical moves.

GOWLING

COOPER

WORTHINGTON 1

BUTCHER

MILLS

Thigh control

▲ *Karl-Heinz Förster uses his thigh to master a difficult ball and guide it away from a Finnish player during West Germany's 4-0 World Cup win at Lahti in May 1981. While the thigh is usually a 'positive' choice for controlling the ball, it is also a valuable ally in awkward situations such as this, and defenders as well as target men should be confident enough to employ it. Notice how Förster is using his arms for balance.*

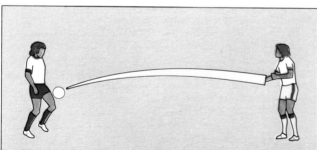

◀ As with any technique, there's no substitute for simple repetition—taking the ball on the thigh time and time again until you've got a feel for the skill. If the ball doesn't fall neatly to the foot, get into the habit of moving to it quickly after contact.

◀ You can practise 'directional control' with the thigh using two players, but it will be far more realistic if a third man puts pressure on the receiver, either from in front or behind him. In all routines don't try to take the ball on the thigh if the pass isn't right for it; it will be self-defeating. In the case of 'inaccurate' balls use the appropriate form of control to trap and return or, in the case of a three-man exercise, to beat your opponent or shield the ball. Here the receiver is using his thigh to beat his man.

The more parts of the body you are able to call on for receiving and directing the ball and the more ways you can use them the better player you will become. You have increased your options available for control, and therefore the possibilities for using the ball when you do have it—new angles for the pass, new turns, new holding techniques. The two main areas for such consideration are the thigh and the chest—both 'growth areas' of control.

Apart from passes into your path at that height or 'emergencies', when it is the nearest or most convenient contact surface, the thigh is a 'positive' choice. Nearly any ball that you can take on the thigh can be controlled with another part of the body—with the chest, volley control or a wedge trap. But being able to use the thigh without thinking twice about it brings another dimension to your play. It simply makes you a more all-round, more equipped player.

The thigh has, too, some distinct advantages over the chest. First, it gets the ball to your feet more quickly and 'economically'. Second, trapping the ball on the chest, with its necessarily exaggerated stance, is telegraphing your intention to opponents. When you use the thigh to control a falling ball the action is altogether more compact, with a minimum of effort and your arms near your sides, and it can therefore be a late movement, keeping your marker guessing. Third, it needs only a small adjustment of the angle to change a trap to almost a turn, again an aid to beating or dummying a defender. In short, the advantages of the thigh are increased mobility and the element of surprise.

Thigh control, however, needs constant practice. While it's soft compared to the foot, the thigh has neither the natural cushioning effect of the chest nor its relatively wide margin of safety.

The basic principles of receiving the ball, as discussed in the previous section, apply again here. Decide early and positively on the controlling surface to be used; get into position in the line of flight with that surface behind the ball; relax the controlling surface before impact and withdraw it on impact. As always, you should be looking to make a constructive movement with your second touch. If the ball is not falling nicely for that, you know that the control is not good enough.

The actual technique for trapping the falling ball on your thigh is best practised simply with a friend lobbing passes to you. Move your non-contact foot in line with the path of the ball to adopt a balanced position. Lift your leading leg up to make contact just before or when your thigh is parallel to the ground, withdrawing your thigh on impact to take the pace off the ball. Take it well up on the 'meat' of the thigh. It is a short, sharp skill using economy of movement.

Remember to keep your eyes on that ball until after it drops; only then look up. It's very tempting to glance around to see what's on as the ball arrives on your body, but while you may get away with that on the chest the thigh has a far smaller margin of error.

Taking the ball in your stride requires a different approach, angling the controlling surface down and adjusting the cushioning effect to ensure you don't have to break your rhythm. After getting a really good feel for the basic trap and using the thigh for moving off at an angle, as shown on the previous page, practise taking the ball on the run. Again, as in those exercises, don't try to get it on the thigh if the pass isn't suitable; use another

form of control and return the ball to the 'server' for the next pass.

Controlling the ball on the thigh is still often regarded as a little 'showy', and many players find themselves reluctant to use it in matches. Yet it is, sensibly, increasing in importance at every level as players realise its value, and it should have a prominent role in your practice sessions on ball control.

Nevertheless there are reservations. Some coaches encourage players to use only their 'better' leg, arguing that the skill has to be precise to be effective and that after trapping the ball it falls to be played with that same foot. While in most areas of control it is logical to foster a high degree of skill 'on both sides', trapping and receiving on the thigh may be a notable exception.

▼Pelé was still only 17 when he startled football with this goal in the 1958 World Cup final at Stockholm. It came in the 55th minute, when a high pass from Zito found him near the penalty spot but guarded by three Swedish defenders. There seemed little danger—until he controlled the ball on his thigh, hooked it over his head and then turned to volley a shot past the keeper. It virtually finished the contest: Brazil, down at one stage, were leading 2-1 when he scored, and they went on to win 5-2, with Pelé claiming the fifth from a header. While it's tempting to say that only great players can score goals like this, Pelé too practised often and hard, during as well as before his long reign at the top, keeping every facet of his control at concert pitch. Stunning moments like this and the one on page 37 could be within the scope of any player who follows that example, developing the confidence to try the unusual.

Chest control

The chest is a 'growth area' of ball control. More and more players are using it more often, and in an increasing number of ways—for turns and passes as well as for basic trapping.

It's remarkable that, in Britain at least, it should be so long in coming, and perhaps even stranger that so many players, particularly at the more modest levels, still shy away from control on the body. The chest, after all, is the largest and safest part of the body on which a ball can be controlled.

For a front player, particularly, chest control is now bread and butter stuff. He could barely perform his functions without it. He is expected to cope with balls that come at him at varying speeds, angles and heights, and when that chipped pass or flighted ball comes in and there's nobody available for a first-time flick-on, or knock-back, or lay-off, he has to hold; and his greatest ally in trapping and holding the high ball is the chest.

The first thing to remember here is not to 'wait' for the ball, especially for the higher passes. The chest trap is a fairly 'telegraphed' technique, easily read by defenders, and it's important to make sure you get to the ball first.

The actual technique for the basic trap, though fairly simple compared to a thigh trap or volley control, requires excellent balance and positioning: legs apart, one a little forward of the other; knees slightly bent and arms out enough for balance; leaning slightly back to present a wide platform for the ball to land on. Your stance should both make a safe area for the ball and shield it from your opponent. Use your arms and legs for balance as your body meets the ball, relaxing and withdrawing the chest away a little on impact to cushion the ball. Though it sounds obvious, it's crucial to watch the ball right onto your body: it's so close to you that your natural reaction is to glance away on contact, and while the chest usually provides a wider safety margin than most other forms of control it will never come off right if your concentration wanders onto your next move.

If the technique is good the ball drops neatly for the second touch—on the thigh, for a volley, or more often simply to ground for the next movement.

Trapping the ball on the move involves a quite different approach and a wide variety of techniques, depending mainly on whether you're stealing away from a marker to get to the ball (facing your own goal) or literally aiming to take the high ball in your stride (facing your opponents'

goal), but also on other factors such as the exact trajectory of the ball. The main difference, however, is that you present a rigid rather than a relaxed controlling surface, amending the cushioning effect to suit each situation. If you're coming off your man and want to hold the ball, you'll still want to take a little pace off the ball; if you're intercepting a high ball or taking it on the run you'll be looking to knock it forward to maintain your rhythm.

Chest control on the move, then, is often a question of improvisation, of mastering and creating angles. And there's been no better exponent of it than Pelé, whose chest seemed at times to be like a shock-absorber. A fine example came in Brazil's opening match of the 1970 World Cup, against Czechoslovakia

As forwards find themselves with less and less time and opportunity to control and use the ball, the first-time lay-off to players in close supporting positions becomes an increasingly vital component of attacking play. The chest pass can be a great friend here, and the trend was well illustrated during the Division 1 derby between Wolves and WBA at Molineux in December 1978 with the last goal in Albion's 3-0 win. Derek Statham played a lofted ball up to Cyrille Regis and the big striker, aware of Bob Hazell's tight marking and the astute movement of teammate Tony Brown, swivelled as he took the pass on his chest to send it into Brown's path. The Albion veteran (it was his 535th League appearance for the club) took full advantage, moving quickly towards the Wolves area before squaring the ball to namesake Alistair, who kept his head under pressure from George Berry and Derek Parkin to place a left-foot shot past Paul Bradshaw into the corner. It was a simple and incisive strike—made possible by a cleverly conceived and neatly executed piece of chest control.

STATHAM

TONY BROWN

REGIS

in Guadalajara. As he drifted across the Czech defence Gerson curled a 40-yard pass up to him and Pelé, at an angle to the goal, leapt to take the ball high on his chest, yet twisted his torso to direct the ball down and towards goal. As the ball came off the ground he pounced on it and, in one smooth movement, struck a right-foot volley past Ivo Viktor.

For Pelé, as much as for lesser mortals, the road to that level of control begins with basic practice. To start off, combine chest control with receiving the ball on the thigh—the principles are the same and the passing at that stage will not always be sufficiently accurate. This can easily be accomplished in a competitive game, using a volleyball-type court or any area with an improvised high net. You can play with two or four people, allowing two touches and one bounce (either before or after the control) and playing the ball only with volleys.

For practising chest control on its own make the exercise realistic: play the ball carefully after trapping it; use a marker to put pressure on the receiver; vary the type of pass played in; try to gain a yard on the defender before going for the ball. Move on later to passing with the chest. Though power is obviously restricted here (compared, say, to the side-volley), this can be a surprisingly effective technique under pressure, and more and more strikers are discovering its subtle value against tight-marking defences.

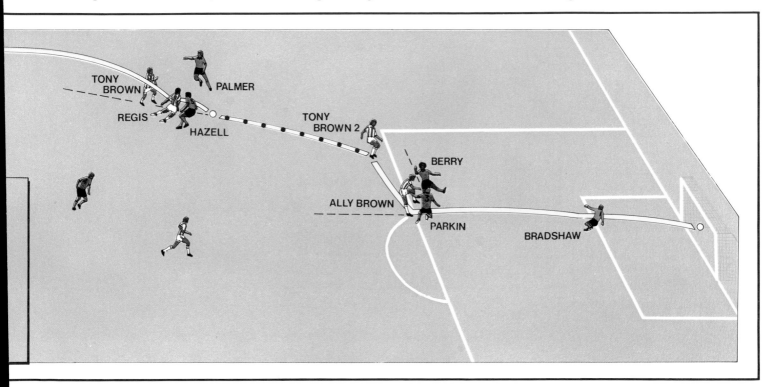

◀ *Rather than break his rhythm in order to control the ball on an easier contact surface Trevor Brooking adjusts his positioning and twists his body to meet it with his lower chest and maintain his forward movement as England break out at Hampden in 1980. Scottish skipper Archie Gemmill and David Johnson are both convinced that Brooking, renowned for his excellent control, will have no problems here; Gemmill senses the danger and Johnson turns to look for space upfield. While all control is based on 'model' techniques applying to certain parts of the body, every player has to amend and improvise on those techniques in match situations. The more you practise and develop a feel for the ball, the more equipped and confident you will be to control it and capitalise on moments like this; if Brooking had needed to check to take the ball on his foot the momentum of the attack would have been lost.*

▶ *England full-back Kenny Sansom uses the wide, 'safe' area of his chest to control an awkward rising ball during the game at Wrexham in 1980. Note the exaggerated stance to create an angle with his body, both to trap the ball and to direct it away from Welsh striker David Giles. The three illustrations on these pages reflect the versatile nature of chest control.*

▼A model example of masterful control and passing set up the goal that retained the European Cup for Liverpool in the match against FC Bruges at Wembley in May 1978. The move that finally broke the goalless deadlock came after a Kenny Dalglish overhead flick was headed out by Vandereyken. The high clearance fell to Graeme Souness just outside the area, and the Scottish international coolly trapped the ball on his chest, 'killing' it perfectly. As it dropped just in front of him he beat the challenge of two Belgian defenders to push a superb pass through into space for Dalglish. His fellow-countryman ran onto it and chipped a neatly placed shot over the diving Jensen inside the far post (see picture page 81). Souness, signed from struggling Middlesbrough for £352,000 the previous January, had practised a basic tenet of Liverpool play: do it simply, do it well, do it quickly. Like Cyrille Regis in the example illustrated on the previous page, he had both the perception to see the possibility and the skill to exploit it. It reinforces, too, the most essential consideration behind all ball control —that it is a means to an end rather than an end in itself, a platform for constructive movement.

The basic practice with two players can be simply a throw for the control and pass, but obviously the exercise will gain valuable rhythm if you use the chip (below). You're looking to get the ball to your feet here, so you can judge the success of the technique by the ease with which you're able to make a pass with your second touch. For three players the answer is a chip, control and pass to a third player, but a fourth man marking the receiver and trying to get in a challenge (right) will help simulate the pressure you'll get in matches.

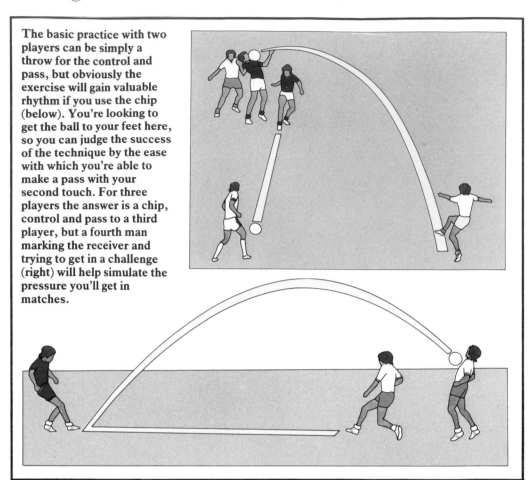

Shielding

There are several courses of action open to you after you have brought a pass under control: you can take the ball on, turn, pass or shoot. That decision will rest on a wide range of factors, including your distance from goal, the space and time available to you, the positioning and movement of opponents as well as team-mates and so on.

When you are facing your opponents' goal, going in 'the right direction' as you control the ball, this choice is usually simple enough. But in the modern game more and more players, and especially front men, find themselves taking pass after pass facing their own goal, often isolated and outnumbered by defenders. A positive move is frequently out of the question: you are closely marked, there's no obvious pass to a colleague and it may not be the time to try a dribble or even less a turn. It's then that you shield the ball, protect it from your opponent until help arrives, usually in the form of team-mates finding space to take a pass.

This decision-making process happens at speed, of course. Good players are aware of the options, or lack of them, before the ball arrives; they will also take the earliest opportunity after the ball is under control to look for new possibilities.

It's not so long ago that shielding, or 'screening' the ball, was seen as a continental skill, part of the ball-playing indulgence of Latin forwards who loved to dwell on the ball. Now it's an integral aspect of our game at all levels, a skill that requires careful thought and patient practice for all outfield players.

With possession the watchword, the attitude towards shielding has switched from reluctant acceptance to positive encouragement. Rather than hold the ball because there is nothing 'on', target players learn to hold unless there is something on. It's a subtle change of emphasis, but one which reflects the new priorities of modern tactics.

Though shielding has developed into something of an art it is, like all aspects of ball control, not an end in itself. It is a delaying tactic, a way of retaining possession under pressure until a positive move is possible. It should never be done longer than necessary. The earlier you can lay the ball off, and be looking for a new position, the better. Holding the ball for the sake of it will be self-defeating; it merely allows defenders to cover the moves made by your team-mates—and any gains you may have made with your initial control can easily be lost.

The most basic rule of shielding is liter-

▲ Scotland's Asa Hartford displays some of the finer points of shielding to fellow midfielder Brian Flynn of Wales in the 1979 home international at Cardiff. He is keeping the ball as far away from his opponent as possible by turning side-on to him and playing the ball with his 'front' foot. His problem now is to find the time to glance up, while retaining balance and control, to see what's on; shielding is very much an enforced delaying tactic, a holding operation under pressure to keep possession until team-mates make themselves available for a pass—or until the man on the ball finds himself in a position to turn.

ally to keep control, to stay 'cool'. While it's vital to get to the ball first, it's all too easy to rush the movements and lose your poise when you have an awkward ball to take, there's a man right behind you and you know you have no obvious or safe pass to make. Try to approach the ball at 'optimum' speed, retaining your balance and control but still making it difficult for the defender. He has to remain goalside of the ball, so if you get to it first, placing your body between your opponent and the ball, you retain the initiative. You, not your marker, must dictate the situation. The better your initial control, of course, the easier the task will be.

There is no set technique for shielding the ball. A whole array of factors will limit and determine your precise course of action on the ball—the sort of pass you receive, where you are on the pitch, the position of your marker, the movements of your colleagues—and it is a mobile rather than a static skill. Nevertheless there are basic guidelines which, if followed and practised, will maximise the chances of maintaining control and keeping possession.

First, always place your body between your opponent and the ball, if necessary moving across his 'line'. Second, while keeping the ball within playing distance try to keep it as far away as you can from your opponent. This means playing it with your 'front' foot as you turn almost side-on to your marker. If you present a 'square' back to him, he is closer to the ball and has a better chance of nicking the ball away through your legs or even getting in a sweeping tackle or touch round you. If the ball goes out of your reach, on the other hand, you could well be penalised for obstruction.

Next, stay relaxed and balanced, with your knees slightly bent. This not only eases the possible impact of a challenge; it also helps you keep your options open since you can switch direction or angle a pass more quickly. Fourth, use any legal tricks to throw your opponent or encourage indecision in his mind. Spreading your arms wide creates a wider physical barrier and restricts his vision; by being more side-on you can 'feel' behind you for the position of your marker (as in the picture above); dummies and feints with **43**

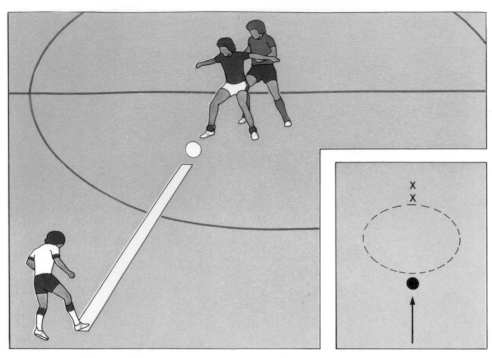

◄ Shielding practice needs confined space and limited time to make it effective, and a simple idea is to play the ball in to someone marked inside one half of the centre-circle. The receiver, making sure he gets his body in line with the ball and is first to it, should control and then try to hold the ball for say 20 seconds (timed by the 'server' or a fourth person) as his opponent attempts to nick the ball or go for a tackle. If the defender does commit himself, turn him and then shield the ball for another 20 seconds in the other half of the circle. The passing player should vary the service he provides, putting in plenty of awkward bouncing balls and chips at body height to test the control of the receiver under pressure. You can expand this theme to two-or even three-a-side in the full circle, with each player in possession holding the ball for 20 seconds before laying it off to a team-mate looking for space away from his marker. The receiver should regard any ball in the area in front of him (inset) as his to control, and he may have to take and shield passes that come at an angle.

your body may unsettle him or commit him to going the wrong way.

Finally, don't think solely of the pass. You may be able to send him the wrong way or steal a yard to the side for a turn or a run, and the movements of team-mates may have put him in two minds about staying close to you. All these, of course, are only pointers: shielding is a subtle, fluent, cat-and-mouse skill which has no rigid rules for every particular situation.

As we've said, screening is very much a means to an end, a stalling device. All through the shielding process—even though it may only comprise a second or two—you should be looking for the chances to glance up and take in what's happening around you, to assess the possibilities for a pass. You must never become preoccupied with holding the ball.

The dividing line between shielding and obstruction is inevitably blurred. So too is that between a genuine attempt to play the ball and a foul tackle from behind. Skilful exponents of screening are adept at gaining free-kicks for reckless tackles—often induced by the frustration of a less endowed defender—but a good shielder will probably have already released the ball.

► Front men and midfielders in attacking positions constantly find themselves receiving passes from defence or midfield with little or nothing 'on' for them. They have a man marking tight and are on their own, their backs to their opponents' goal. If he misses the rare chance of a telling first-time ball into space and is unable to use the pace of the ball for a turn, the player has little option but to hold the ball, shielding it from his opponent. As the player here receives a ground pass, under pressure from a defender, he has no real option; aware of the two covering players and the lack of space for his four team-mates, he must control the ball well and screen it from his opponents until a course of action is open to him—almost certainly when one of his colleagues moves to make himself available. They, of course, should be only too aware of his isolation and must look for space away from their opponents, in this case either with runs for the square ball (A and D) or with movement into close supporting positions for the simpler lay-off (B and C). The passing player should then look for space behind the defence. He may, however, decide to take it on himself if the movement of his team-mates has created a little more space for him on the ball. The art of shielding is to retain control and balance on the ball—able to move or pass quickly in any direction—while still being aware of movement and the various possibilities that develop from it.

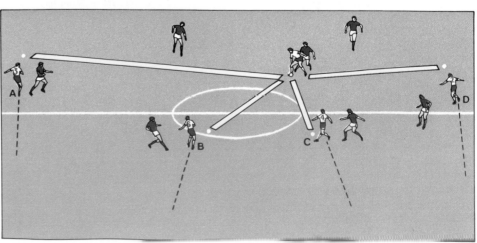

Turning

The ability to receive a ball facing one way and set off with it in another is a crucial part of control. Unless you are moving onto a through ball or taking a square pass, you will be facing your own goal when a ground pass comes to you—and that means in the majority of cases.

Youngsters tend to neglect this area of control when they start playing. They waste the chances of a neat turn by stopping the ball first, by taking the ball round in a time-consuming arc, or by not turning at all. The earlier a young player learns to turn well, the quicker his overall game will improve.

Turning in space should be neat and quick—a smooth, compact, economical movement in which the ball sticks close to you. While the basic turn is not performed under pressure—it would not be workable if you were marked tight—time is still the vital consideration.

The key is to take sufficient pace off the ball to control it while maintaining enough to steer it in the direction intended. You should be relaxed and balanced as you move to meet the ball. Decide early which foot you are going to use and position yourself accordingly, your weight on your non-kicking foot. Welcome the ball onto your controlling foot, cushioning the impact of the ball on contact, and coax it round on the inside of your foot as you 'draw' it across the ball, pivoting on your anchoring leg. Dropping your 'leading' arm will help with balance as you turn. As the ball continues at a slower speed in the direction you have determined, transfer your weight to your other foot to face forward.

After mastering this basic technique you can learn to 'roll' your foot round the ball after drawing your foot across it—that is, keeping the ball 'glued' to the inside of the same foot as you move off.

▲ *While turning with the ball is the staple diet of the midfielder, who constantly receives the ball in space facing his own goal and needs to switch the direction of play, all outfield players should be totally on top of this area of technique. Here Manny Kaltz, the SV Hamburg and West Germany star, sets off after receiving the ball from his keeper. Perfectly balanced—notice how his head is virtually over the ball—he has the option of playing it with his turning foot (his right) or planting his right foot and using his left for the next move. Any manager's dream defender, Kaltz is equally effective as a sweeper or full-back, in either case capable of fine attacking runs from the back (see page 79). He epitomises the new breed of back-four player: adaptable, perceptive and as skilful as any midfield player.*

▶ It's possible to practise turning on your own if you can find a suitable space between two walls, but this has the obvious limitation of predictable passes. The best simple exercise is 'piggy-in-the-middle' with three players. To begin with the two 'servers' should play in easy-paced balls so that the receiver can learn and master the basic technique. As the turning improves, the ball should be hit more firmly, with the odd bouncing ball to shin or knee height, while the player taking the pass can move about to create angles for the turner to aim at. He calls 'turn' to the man in the middle, both to let him know where he is and to develop the habit for matches, when any player receiving a pass appreciates the advice that he has the space and time to make the turn.

Turning against defenders

▲ *The combination of good initial control and a neat dummy enables Bulgaria's Georgi Bonev to turn Mick Mills during his country's European Championship defeat at Sofia in June 1979. Bonev has shielded the ball well from the attentions of the England left-back, and now begins to transfer his weight from his right foot to his left in order to move up the flank. Once seen as an exceptional skill, almost as a trick, turning against opponents is now a basic part of the front player's game on the ball. As well as his distributive function, laying off balls first time or after holding, the forward is expected to turn his marker when there's a chance. He must develop a sense for when it's on, for when the odds favour him, and as well as mastering the first-time turns, using the pace of the ball and the element of surprise, he should always be looking for the way past when shielding the ball as an alternative to the pass to a team-mate in a good supporting position.*

For a front player, turning with the ball is very often a task performed under great pressure. The modern front man must work hard for the space to turn with the ball and take it goalwards. More often than not he is marked tight, forced to make quick, difficult decisions and execute demanding, precise skills. Forwards who can think perceptively and act fast can set up chances not just for themselves but for others, and are now the most sought-after players in the game.

When a target player receives a pass, facing his own goal and closely marked, there are various alternatives open to him. Sometimes a factor outside his control —the nature of the pass, his location on the pitch, the position of defenders, the movement of colleagues, even the condition of the ground—will help determine his course of action. In theory at least he has these options, or a combination of them: he can pass the ball first time with a flick or a lay-off; he can control the ball before passing with his second or third touch; he can control the ball and shield it purposefully, waiting for the chance to find a team-mate in space; or he can turn and try to beat his opponent.

There are basically two methods of turning against a defender. One is the 'first-time turn', using the pace of the pass and the element of surprise to direct the ball past or across the defender. The second is the 'controlled turn', trying to beat your opponent after you have received the ball and used several touches to retain possession: in other words when you are screening the ball.

In the right circumstances turning with the ball and taking it past your opponent in one movement can be among the most devastating skills in football. Played well against a square defence it leaves you with a clear run on goal or, if you are close enough as you turn, a chance of a shot.

Skilful and experienced forwards are adept at using almost any contact surface for first-time turns, including the chest, thigh and even the head, and can steer knee- and thigh-high balls 'round the corner' with the inside or the outside of either foot. But the majority of chances for them, as for players at every level, come with the firmly hit pass 'on the floor'.

There are three basic rules that apply when setting yourself up for, and executing, the first-time turn. The most obvious, as in any area of receiving, is to get to the ball first; there is no way you can produce a convincing turn if you are not in command of the situation. Move towards the ball wherever possible rather than

► In their remarkable quest to win the European Cup at the first attempt, Nottingham Forest were never closer to failure than in the first leg of the semi-final against 1FC Cologne at the City Ground in April 1979. Banking on a decent lead to take to Germany, they found themselves 2-0 down to goals from Roger Van Gool and Dieter Müller. A spirited fight-back produced goals from Garry Birtles and Ian Bowyer to make it 2-2 and then, in the 63rd minute, came the best one of the night. The splendid move began with a throw-in from John McGovern. When the ball reached Tony Woodcock, closely marked by Herbert Zimmermann, McGovern ran into space for the easy pass. The Forest skipper had plenty of time to assess the next play—a run goalwards, perhaps, a cross to the far post, or a little pass towards the bye-line for Martin O'Neill—but he spotted Birtles' diagonal run. Though tracked by Bernd Schuster, who a year later would make such an impact in the European Championship finals for West Germany, Birtles was half a yard up and held the initiative as he beat his man to McGovern's angled pass to the line. His tight turn was a killer touch, keeping his balance in the treacherous conditions to take it on the outside of his left foot and sway round Schuster before firing in a low first-time cross with his right to the far post. There John Robertson, who had plagued Harald Konopka all evening with his wing play, stole in front of his market to dive full length and head the ball firmly into the Cologne net. It was a high-class goal in every sense, combining McGovern's oblique pass, Birtles' textbook turn and Robertson's fine positioning and brave header. It also illustrates the point that the best way to penetrate defences isn't necessarily direct.

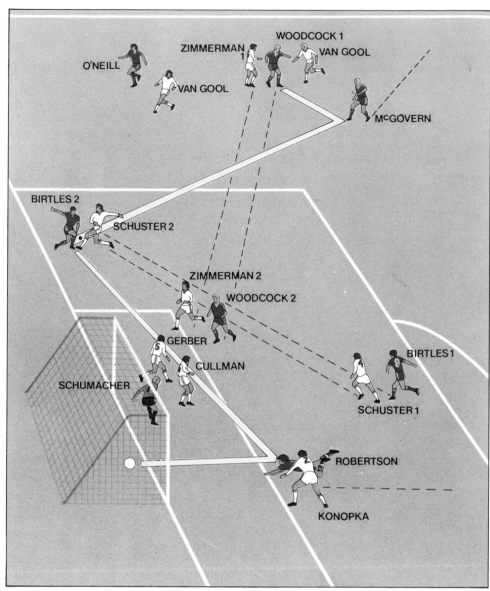

'wait' for it, just as though you were going to control the ball and shield it. Put yourself on the defender's line to the ball to prevent the chance, however slight, of his getting a touch or seizing the initiative.

The second rule is to try anything you can to disguise your intention and fool your close marker. A quick-thinking, fast-moving forward can make space by threatening to get behind his marker before the pass is made. As the defender checks to cover his move, the front man moves back towards the ball, gaining that bit more time and space to make it his and execute the turn. Good understanding between midfielders and the target player will obviously help in this: team-mates in supplying positions can anticipate the types of movement associated with a particular player, and adjust the timing, weight and direction of their pass according to his particular skills.

If the defender follows your movement too closely, the turn itself can beat him. If you can lure him into thinking he can reach the ball and you then turn with it, he will have come 'too tight' and you are away with the ball.

You can always dummy as you actually go for the ball, too, pretending to go one way before 'recovering' to go the other. Sometimes a sidestep motion with the legs or a sway of the body will prove enough. Any hesitation on the part of the defender, however slight, will gain you precious time. Remember, though, that there is little point in trying such tactics at the cost of losing your poise or your control of the situation. Such techniques, by definition highly individualistic in style, should be developed during the training routines for turning.

The third basic rule is to keep your options open. Remain alert and balanced, ready to move either way or change your mind completely. As in shielding, you are in the driving seat and you decide the course of action. Various factors may lead you to choose a certain way at the last moment, including the exact nature of the pass and movement on the part of your marker. You may sense he has drifted a little to one side in anticipation of a turn that way, so you adjust to go the other. You may abandon the turn altogether; a team-mate may have made a neat run into

a close supporting position and you may go then for the first-time pass, knowing that he is moving forward in space while you are moving away from goal and under pressure.

Turning first time with the ground pass can be done with the inside or outside of the foot. The inside turn, using the 'leading' foot to move the other way (right foot to go to your left) is the simpler to use—and the easier for the defender to read. It is more difficult to disguise and, because your foot takes the ball round in a shallow arc, it gives the defender that little bit of time to counteract it.

The outside turn is the more effective yet more economical of the two: using your left foot to go to your left. Because the foot you 'lead' with is not the one used for contact, it is easier to disguise your intention. As the ball approaches you go to meet it and plant your left foot (for a 'left turn') with your weight on that leg, dipping your right shoulder and leaning slightly to your right just before contact. This will help give the impression you are going right—or at least sow some doubts in the defender's mind—and provide a **47**

▶ Three essential elements of the striker's game—turning, close control and finishing—came together to give Liverpool's Kenny Dalglish a magnificent individual goal on the Maine Road mud in March 1979. The contest was just perfect, too: the FA Cup semi-final against Manchester United in a clash of the Lancashire giants. The move that was to put the League leaders in front started with a long ball from Phil Thompson to Jimmy Case, wide on the right flank. As Case cut inside, tracked by Arthur Albiston, United had seven or eight outfield players behind the ball, so there seemed little danger when he played the ball through to Dalglish. Midfielder Sammy McIlroy, always quick to cover, had got goalside of Dalglish, but the Scottish striker, moving slightly away from goal, let the ball run under his left foot and turned sharply to his right round McIlroy to pounce on it past his man. He took the ball forward but Martin Buchan came across to shut him down . . .

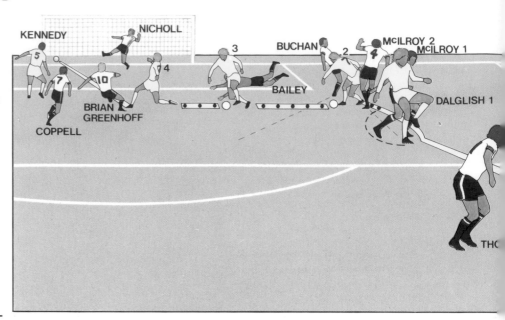

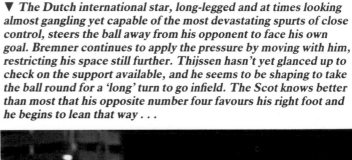

▼ Aston Villa's Des Bremner closes down his midfield opponent Frans Thijssen of Ipswich in the classic pairing of the FA Cup's third round in January 1981—the League leaders against their closest rivals at Portman Road. There seems little danger for Villa as Thijssen, still inside his own half, dwells on the ball, well watched and giving the defenders time to recover after their attack had broken down. Yet this innocuous, static situation was to be a prelude to the only goal of the game, a marvellous moment in a seven-man move that produced one of the goals of the season . . .

▼ The Dutch international star, long-legged and at times looking almost gangling yet capable of the most devastating spurts of close control, steers the ball away from his opponent to face his own goal. Bremner continues to apply the pressure by moving with him, restricting his space still further. Thijssen hasn't yet glanced up to check on the support available, and he seems to be shaping to take the ball round for a 'long' turn to go infield. The Scot knows better than most that his opposite number four favours his right foot and he begins to lean that way . . .

'spring' for the planned movement of the body to the left.

The key to the turn is to 'catch' the ball on the outside of your left foot, at its widest part, and steer it round, transferring your weight to your left leg as you push off in the intended direction. Unless you've really 'sold' your marker this is unlikely to be anything like 180°; it will be nearer to a right-angle in fact, but if the turn is successful you have gained that crucial split-second on him and can quickly adjust to a more forward run. If the ball has come at an angle to you, of course, a restricted turn may leave you on course for goal.

The whole action should be controlled and rhythmic. Do not rush the approach and the contact; the speed should come as

you move off with the ball. The importance of this 'explosive' action cannot be overstated; small compact players, with their low centre of gravity, get the thigh of their controlling leg almost parallel to the ground and the knee almost over the ball as they prepare the swivel and change direction. Simple adaptations of the exercises shown on page 173, with a turn before the run, can help sharpen up this critical factor in the turn.

Practice for first-time turning needs to involve limits on time and space to be effective, and that means playing in a small area against a marker, as illustrated on page 50. The defender needs to be trying hard, too—otherwise the receiver will get a false impression of his prospects on the pitch. Try the four variations,

using the inside as well as the outside of each foot. You should have all of them at your disposal in matches.

Turning against a defender and beating him after shielding the ball, from a 'standing start', is a far less definable area of control. Here we are talking about taking the ball past your marker when you are facing the same way, yet without the great ally of the first-time turn—the pace of the ball. The answer, then, is to create your own pace.

This kind of inventive control comes only with the confidence that derives from total familiarity with the ball. There are no set techniques. The turn demonstrated above by Frans Thijssen is a classic example of waiting, holding, feinting, working an opening—and then exploding.

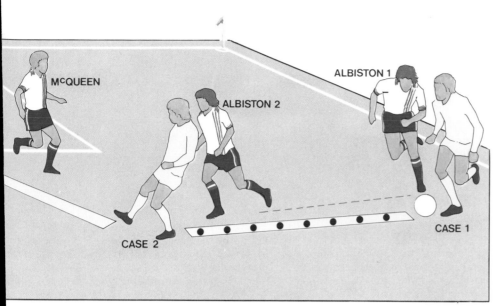

Dalglish turned again, this time taking the ball sharply to his left, leaving Buchan stranded and beating the pursuing McIlroy for pace. The next obstacle was keeper Gary Bailey, coming quickly out of his goal and spreading himself wide to block the run, but Dalglish dragged the ball away from his lunging arms with his right foot. Then, before Brian Greenhoff could get in a despairing tackle, Dalglish kept his head and his balance to steady himself for a stretching left-foot shot into the corner of the net. Two fine examples of turning against defenders and superb close control had produced a chance from nothing—and Dalglish had the experience to finish it off. Unfortunately the goal would in the end count for little; United grabbed a 2-2 draw and won the replay at Goodison to repeat their 1977 final victory over Liverpool. Dalglish's turning ability always makes him dangerous, with defenders having to mark him tight and his team-mates benefiting from the resulting space.

▼ *This knowledge seems of little benefit as Thijssen, after taking the ball back even further, suddenly swivels his body and turns to play the ball to his right with the outside of his right foot. Bremner has been more than a little distracted by the presence of Arnold Muhren, making himself available so close that he's suggesting a swap or a scissors. Thijssen's move takes full advantage of the indecision in Bremner's mind, however slight it is. The Villa player's weight is firmly on his left foot as Thijssen sways back the way he came, cradling the ball on his right foot . . .*

▼ *Using the vital half-a-yard he's gained on Bremner, Thijssen bursts forward as his opponent desperately tries to recover. But the damage is done. Muhren, now in more space and further forward, receives a square ball; a high, hanging cross to the left corner of Villa's area is well won in the air by John Wark, who knocks it down to the feet of Alan Brazil; turning it away from his marker, Brazil takes it on to the bye-line before screwing a low hard cross just out from the near post—and there is Paul Mariner to sweep it into the net a fraction in front of his man for the decisive goal.*

At the same time certain special moves, 'discovered' as a response to the close-marking pressures of the modern game, have become almost mobile set-pieces, often associated with or even named after the player who adapted and refined them. One of the best-known is the 'dragback' technique, perfected if not invented by Johan Cruyff, where the ball is flicked behind one foot by the other, and the player in possession turns a half-circle across the face of his marker.

Another is the 'inside' turn, where the player goes even further, towards a three-quarter turn, to take the ball across his opponent with the foot that was at first farthest from him—an ambitious, twisting movement worked with surprisingly frequent success by Kenny Dalglish. In

Turin Franco Causio for years fooled full-backs and thrilled the Juventus fans with a flick up and across his marker with the outside of his right foot near the touch-line, often running out of play to collect the ball on the other side. The variations are almost endless as front men constantly strive to shake off their shadows; on page 83 Tony Woodcock is seen bringing off one of the cheekiest of all, a 'nutmeg' and turn with a subtle backheel.

All such skilled turns with the ball rely on three vital factors: the dummying of the defender to gain time, a precise execution of the contact, and an explosive burst of speed to make it pay. It's as well to mention, too, that such players also have the overall awareness to conceive such ploys, the perception to realise when they

are possible, and the ability to carry them through to fruition.

That should not deter lesser players—and that means just about everyone—from trying. But the basic first-time turns should be mastered initially. A player must possess a high level of ball control and feel very much at ease with a football at his feet before trying the static turns. Turning, after all, is a risky venture: the dividends are high, but the penalties of failure, psychological as well as practical, can be severe. While a turn should always be in the forefront of a forward's thinking, a good pass is hardly a weak alternative if it is on.

Turning involves other kinds of risks, too. Front players have to be prepared to take not just the niggling taps and shirt-

▲ *The skilful midfield play of Giancarlo Antognoni was a big factor in Italy's win over Hungary in the 1978 World Cup finals. Balanced and alert here, he's only too aware of Karoly Csapo's approach . . .*

▲ *Fiorentina's 'golden boy' moves forward, with Csapo still closing. But as Antognoni plants his left foot the ball is well behind it as he shapes for a pass; the angle of his right leg suggests otherwise . . .*

▲ *With Csapo committed in one direction, Antognoni executes his angled version of the 'Cruyff turn' by pivoting on the ball of his left foot and flicking the ball left with the inside of his right foot to beat his man.*

pulling of frustrated defenders, but also the crunching tackle from behind and the scything foul that so often mars the spectacle of a fine turn. It takes a special kind of player to walk coolly away from trouble after his skill has gone unrewarded, when bruised legs and a free-kick are the prizes for beating your man. But in the game of marking, that's just what the defender wants—to see the front man rattled. It's important for players to keep their poise and their concentration; the more a forward worries about the knocks, the more likely he is to get hurt.

Because of the fluent circumstances and inventive styles possible with controlled turns, it is not an area of technique that lends itself easily to prescribed practices. The answer is to be constantly looking for the chance to try new ways out in training sessions, particularly in five-a-side games. But do not worry about the problem if there is a good alternative, and remember that what may work against one player in training may not come off against another in a match.

▶ Because the turn has been refined to beat the close marking of the modern game, any practice for it must have a player in tight on the receiver to be meaningful. It's possible to do it with three people but it's even more important than in the competitive exercise shown below for the marker to really restrict the receiver and go for the ball when there's a chance, since there's no end product. The passer should play the ball in with pace, varying the exact direction and knocking in the odd bouncing ball and pass to the body to keep both receiver and defender on their toes. The first-time turn relies heavily on the element of surprise, so each move should be different from the last. You can go to your left or your right, and use either side of the foot. Try to sharpen the techniques of dummying your marker (it's not something to do for the first time in matches), but if the one-touch turn isn't on, hold the ball and then try to turn your man.

◀ Ideally a practice for the turn needs an end product as well as limited space. In this simple three-a-side example one side attacks and then the other. The 'keeper' should be a covering defender rather than a shot-stopper, trying to close down the player in possession after he has turned his man before he can get a shot in. A good turn rarely means much in itself, and as in the example on the previous page you may well find that it's a turn into a pressure situation. If the marker robs the receiver, he should feed his team-mate with a pass; it all helps to make it more realistic and competitive. Make sure everyone gets a chance at marking and at receiving—just as today's front men are expected to know how to defend so players in the back four should have a good idea about how to turn against opponents.

Dribbling

▲ *Dribbling doesn't mean constantly watching the ball. While remaining beautifully balanced and in complete command of the ball, WBA midfield man Gary Owen still takes time out between touches to assess the play as he uses the space in front of him to move quickly forward with the ball. Not looking up is often a fault in younger players—and they run into trouble or waste passes as a result.*

With the growth of the 'functional' approach inside the English game, a trend heralded by the World Cup success of 1966, running with the ball and trying to beat defenders quickly drifted out of fashion or last least slid down the list of tactical priorities. The emphasis came to be laid on teamwork and possession, on workrate and support play. First Leeds, then Liverpool and Forest embodied the essence of this collective ideal—and it worked. At its best it could be breathtaking, with a side seeming to have 15 rather than 10 outfield players; at its worst it was

a dour diet, a not-give-anything-away attitude that seemed to be content with 0-0 away and 1-0 at home.

There would be little room in this midfield-dominated method for the ball player, let alone the winger, you would think. Yet while many coaches saw the 'dribbler' as an unaffordable luxury, a barrier rather than an asset to drilled team play, Leeds and Liverpool and Forest all boasted a recognised winger: a man whose prime role was to collect the ball, take it forward and beat opponents if necessary, and get in telling crosses. Eddie Gray,

Steve Heighway and John Robertson may often have been far more than this, and rarely were they allowed free reign, but they were in because they could 'take people on'—and win.

While dribbling faded away in England (and some parts of Europe, too) the rest of Britain, and Scotland in particular, kept encouraging and producing the traditional ball-playing forwards and midfielders. A sample of players who regularly put on the blue shirt between 1965 and 1981 illustrates the point: Jimmy Johnstone, Willie Morgan, Charlie Cooke, Tommy **51**

Hutchison, Willie Johnston, Arthur Graham and Gordon Strachan as well as Gray and Robertson. It's a theme that is nurtured at the very roots of Scottish football.

In global terms the art of dribbling and the value of close control was given a massive boost by the 1978 World Cup, when Mario Kempes and to a lesser extent other members of the Argentina side proved its value at the top level of the modern game. England's new manager Ron Greenwood, always an advocate of skill, encouraged the emphasis in his teams, and at times the form of Steve Coppell, Kevin Keegan and especially Trevor Brooking during the qualifying games for the 1980 European Championship and the 1982 World Cup warmed the heart of even the most romantic supporter. On the continent and in South America, of course, the tradition has been maintained throughout the 1970s; the spirit of Alfredo di Stefano, Raymond Kopa and Garrincha has been kept alive by a host of crowd-pullers from Pelé and Johan Cruyff to Diego Maradona and Karl-Heinz Rummenigge.

Whatever we choose to call it—running with the ball, close control on the run, mobility on the ball or just good old-fashioned 'dribbling'—this aspect of football skill holds a very special place in the game. The feeling of somehow being apart from other aspects of technique is rein-forced by the fact that it's the one area of control you can practise meaningfully on your own, without special props or partners. All you need is space and a ball. This in turn accounts for some of the confusion and argument it generates: the idea that it is a separate component of the game, difficult to merge into a team approach.

As so many clubs have shown, the opposite can be the case: that harnessed and incorporated into a wider scheme (indeed often dictating it), a player's high level of ability on the ball is a golden asset, not an indulgence that may occasionally deliver the goods.

The key to all this is the realisation on the part of players—and not just ball-playing midfielders and speedy wingers—that like any area of control dribbling is not an end in itself. A run with the ball, whether past defenders or not, must end with a shot or a pass. The player in possession must always be aware of what is happening around him, of the options that are closed off or opened up while he has the ball. A player who draws the attentions of more than one defender, pulling an extra man out of position to cover the danger, and then makes a good pass to a colleague in space is of far more value to his side than a greedy player who beats three men and is then robbed by a fourth, or wastes a telling pass, or blows an easy scoring chance. In short, a good dribbler always knows when to part with the ball.

There are, nevertheless, some commonsense guidelines. You are rarely going to risk running at opponents near your own penalty area, for instance, or indeed perhaps anywhere in the defensive third of the pitch, unless it's practically unavoidable. The most advantageous place to beat an opponent, on the other hand, is around and inside his area, since success so easily sets up a chance for a shot—and if you are dispossessed your side should be able to cover any threat on the break.

The other main area where dribbling against defenders is most valid is on the flanks, in the attacking third of the pitch. Even in this era of sophisticated defensive techniques and organisation at the professional levels, a remarkably high proportion of goals still comes from players beating opponents on the wings and getting in their cross.

Confident and talented ball players can perhaps afford to break these rules—and rightly so if they can make it pay and are aware of the alternative. But a defender who tries to beat his man on the edge of his own box, and fails, giving the opposition a gift goal, is hardly likely to receive a chorus of consolation from his frustrated team-mates.

We have implied already that, by its very nature, dribbling is impossible to teach in the conventional way. But it can be learned within certain limits, and that learning process can draw on three useful

▼ *Following what appeared to be a fatal split-second of delay or indecision—but which probably secured his chance of scoring—Ricky Villa prods the ball past Joe Corrigan to give Spurs their remarkable victory in the replayed 100th FA Cup final. Like most great individual goals it almost defies analysis, with intuition, instinct and luck playing as big a part as skill, control and technique. But good dribbling ability was the key, and if luck favours the brave, then Villa deserved every bit that was going.*

▶ For Spurs' Argentinian star Ricky Villa the 1981 FA Cup final brought the depths of despair and, with this goal, the heights of elation. At 4.15 on 9 May he trudged round the Wembley track, heading for the dressing-room after a tepid performance against Manchester City had brought substitution. He was halted by the roar as Glenn Hoddle's free-kick screwed in off Tommy Hutchison, and Spurs saved the day. The following Thursday he was back again for the kick-off; and manager Keith Burkinshaw's faith in his ability was to pay off with a jackpot. First, Villa scored simply but well from close range to put his side ahead; then, after Spurs had gone behind to a penalty and then pulled back to 2-2, he produced the goal of his career. A second bout of extra time seemed likely when Tony Galvin picked the ball up on the left. As Nicky Reid came out of position to close him down, Galvin squared the ball to Villa. The bearded figure surged forward, first past a perplexed Garth Crooks and then, with a neat body swerve, beating Tommy Caton. Next it was full-back Ray Ranson's turn, and then the switch that made it all possible—an angled turn away from the retreating Reid, wrong-footing Caton. A shot seemed on, but Villa kept going, across the face of Ranson, as Caton battled bravely to recover. Out came Joe Corrigan as Villa shaped to shoot . . . and let the ball roll another yard before poking it home.

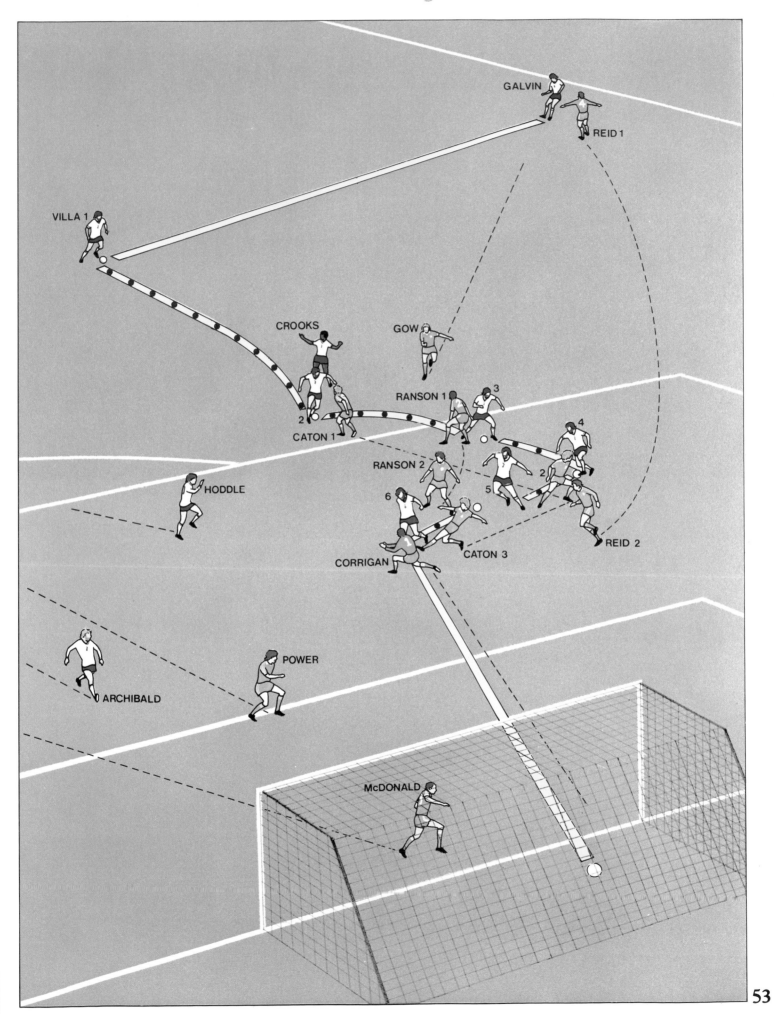

GALVIN

REID 1

VILLA 1

CROOKS

GOW

RANSON 1

2

CATON 1

RANSON 2

HODDLE

6

5

2

4

CORRIGAN

CATON 3

REID 2

ARCHIBALD

POWER

McDONALD

▲ Change of direction is a crucial element of beating defenders on the move, and together with acceleration and a change of contact surface it can produce devastating results. Though this picture from the 1981 FA Cup final, taken behind the Wembley posts, shows Alan Devonshire 'blocked' by David Price and Pat Rice, the West Ham midfield star already has them beaten. Receiving the ball wide, he has moved down the left flank and Arsenal right-back and captain Rice (2) has come to close him down. When midfielder Price comes across to cover Devonshire feints to move down the line and with the inside of his left foot takes the ball inside at an angle. Rice is still transferring his weight to his left leg in an attempt to follow; Price is still applying the brakes in order to recover. Meanwhile Devonshire, a 'ball carrier' in the best Hammers tradition, is heading off infield and to new pastures, pushing off with the ball of his right foot to make the most of the precious time he has already gained. He will now be in a position to readjust his run to a more goalward path past Price or lay-off a telling pass; either way he has in one swift movement taken out a back and a defensive midfielder from Arsenal's rearguard. Being two-footed in such situations as this is perhaps less important than the ability to use a second contact surface. Devonshire could well have played it with the outside of his right foot to get the same result.

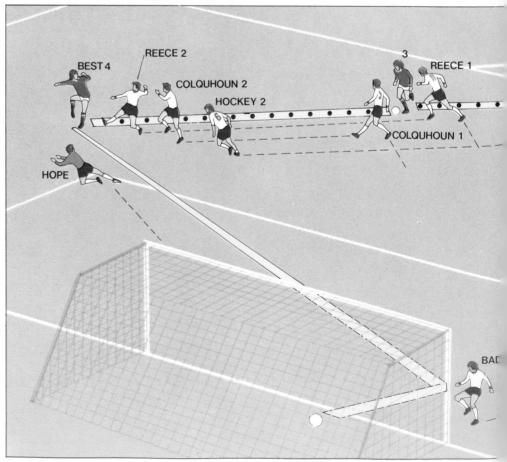

▲ A simple practice for developing and sharpening the close control and balance required for dribbling well. All you want is a start/finish point and four obstacles to 'circle'. You can vary the exercise any number of ways: for example, using only one side of one foot, or alternate sides of one foot, or, as here, all four contact surfaces—inside then outside of right foot followed by inside and outside of left foot. You can make this competitive, against the clock, either with just two of you or with teams operating in relay; in this case you can leave a free choice of controlling surface or stipulate a certain order as above.

▲ Dribbling is the one major area of technique you can practise constructively on your own. All you need in theory is a ball, but with simple props you can devise your own tests. The 'snake dribble' on the left, using a line of skittles or other markers at appropriate intervals, can be used for one-footed control: using the outside of your right foot with the skittle on the right, the inside with the skittle on your left. Start off at jogging pace and gradually increase the speed (and perhaps also reduce the spacing) as you acquire that vital 'feel' for the ball. The exercise on the right, moving along a line tapping the ball from one foot to the other, helps develop two-footed 'mobility' on the ball. Again, get the touch right before speeding up.

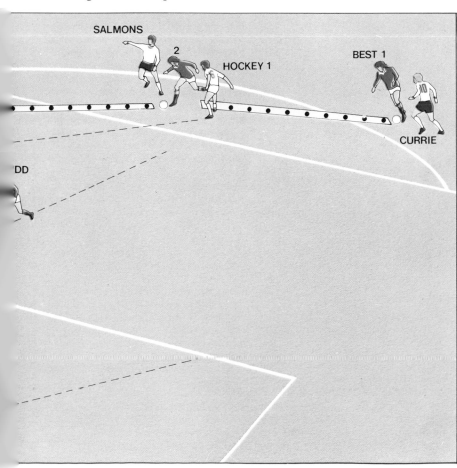

◀ In a career that blossomed early but all too briefly before sliding into sadness and recrimination, George Best produced a bookful of brilliant moves on the ball. Many were two- or three-touch plays, some were Houdini-like escapes from corporate close marking. Others still were tantalising, stop-start runs that often seemed destined for a dead-end before Best somehow found space to fire in a fierce shot. One of the finest examples came in what proved the autumn of his Manchester United days, in October 1971 at Old Trafford, in the middle of a purple patch that brought him 11 goals in as many League games. The visitors were Sheffield United, riding high at the top of the table after their promotion with eight wins and two draws from their ten matches. Best certainly brought them down to earth with a bump, breaking the goalless deadlock after half-time with a typically individual goal having picked up the ball well into the Sheffield half. At first the defence appeared safe, with Trevor Hockey shepherding the Irishman across the area. Best, in fact, seemed to be running into trouble as Hockey continued to track him and first Gil Reece (a winger on as substitute for full-back Ted Hemsley) and then centre-half Eddie Colquhoun joined in the cover. But Best's close control and little bursts of acceleration kept him in command—though for how long? Suddenly there was another spurt and an angle for the shot. Best, apparently without glancing up, whipped in a shot and the ball cannoned in off the far post. John Hope had rightly come off his line to cover the near post, but to no avail. Best knew instinctively there was a line to goal—and his final piece of control and his shot had combined to find it.

◀ Placing a number of obstacles in a limited space—the centre-circle of a pitch is ideal—makes a dribbling practice more mobile and creative. The key here is to exercise your imagination as well as your control, really taking on and beating 'opponents'. You can do this on your own or with two or three players, but almost a whole team can mill about constructively if the markers are removed. This type of practice not only sharpens your ability with the ball; it also encourages you to take those important looks between touches.

basic principles. The first is not to do it 'blind'—to receive a ball and set off without being aware of the options at that moment. That's not to imply that dribbling is in any sense a resort; it's just that it may be the weakest of several courses of action open to you.

The second guideline is that once moving with the ball to keep it within a comfortable playing distance—one determined by the ease with which you can change pace and direction without sacrificing control. There may be exceptions to this, such as pushing the ball well in front to beat a sliding tackle or if you are trying to beat someone solely by pace and there is plenty of room to move into, but it holds true for most. Good dribblers, in

fact, seem to have the ball almost on strong elastic.

Third, despite keeping the ball under control you must take time out to assess the changing shape of the play around you. Not looking up tends to be a basic fault in young players, who by continuously watching the ball not only stumble into trouble but also miss the chance of a good pass. Your eye should be on the ball during contact, but between touches look up to see what's on. With a teammate making an overlapping run close to you this may be little more than a glance to check where he is; if you are confronted by two defenders across your path it may mean slowing right down and taking a longer, harder look. All the time you have

the ball your colleagues will be looking for good positions in space and making runs behind defenders, and their efforts deserve attention.

Dribbling is a very individualistic aspect of ball skill, and there is no 'set' style. Basically it breaks down into two broad areas of controlling the ball on the run in space, with no direct pressure, and beating opponents. Beating defenders is basically divisible into the close-quarters work, where tight control and balance are the crucial factors, often with the use of the sole and various turns; and the strong-running approach, 'taking on' opponents, either deep into their danger area or down the wings, where change of direction is allied to pace. Certain physical attributes

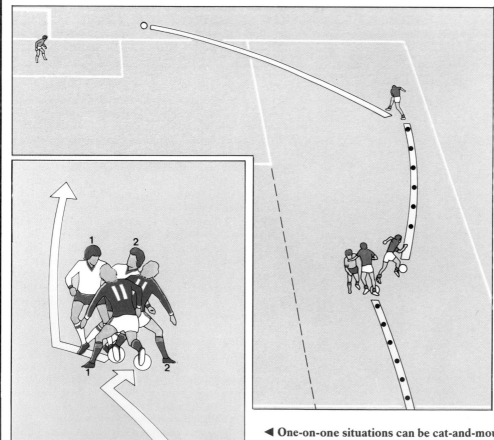

◀ This three-man practice tests the body swerve technique by simulating the pressure of match conditions with limited space, a defender and an end product—a cross if you beat your man on the outside and a shot if you go past him on the inside. A change of pace and direction is rarely enough to succeed in a one-on-one situation: you also have to gain that extra yard or two by fooling the defender, creating a false impression of your move by feinting, wrong-footing him completely or at least sowing doubts in his mind. He will be jockeying, retreating perhaps, but sooner or later he has to make a move, and the body swerve ensures it's the wrong one. Basically it's a simple technique, but it's open to great variation. In the example shown here you dip your left shoulder and plant your weight momentarily on your left foot. As the defender moves onto his right leg you accelerate away to your right, using either the outside of your right foot or the inside of your left to take the ball past him. Timing is the key to success: move too soon and he has time to recover, move too late and he can get in a tackle.

◀ One-on-one situations can be cat-and-mouse affairs, especially in the classic confrontations between wingers and full-backs, and the basic body swerve can be adapted and embroidered in an attempt to beat good defenders if the forward has sufficient skill and speed. This 'double swerve' uses the outside of each foot, but it can also be completed with the inside of the foot that finally takes the ball past the opponent. Such ploys must be self-taught and developed in practice games.

and qualities make players particularly suited to exploiting each type of control —Glenn Hoddle and Trevor Francis, for example—though this no way means that Hoddle cannot glide past opponents or that Francis, as he demonstrates on page 60, is not adept at fine control in restricted space. It's a matter of strengths.

While good close control is the basic ingredient in the art of dribbling, there are other elements. For one thing there are the psychological factors—having the confidence to try in the first place, for instance, knowing that failure can bring recrimination, and being brave enough to risk fouls and possible injury. And there are the crucial physical aspects, notably balance and pace, or rather the ability to change pace: acceleration.

To dribble well you need to be able to switch direction, to accelerate and to use both sides of your 'best' foot—preferably of both feet. Combined in one move and preceded by a feint to help fool your opponent, they provide the nearest you can get to a guaranteed way of beating your man.

There have been great players whose name was made with just one basic movement, but because it was done so well the defender would be beaten time and time again during a match—and then again the next time the teams met. The best example was Stanley Matthews, who was still leaving full-backs on their backsides and sending over pinpoint crosses in Second Division matches when he was pushing 50. He would shuffle up to his adversary, tap-tapping the ball from foot to foot before cradling it in the curve of his right. The defender *knew* he was going on the outside; but when Matthews dummied left, he was drawn, just long enough for the winger, with one flick of the outside of his right foot and a burst of speed, to be away. Occasionally he would vary the pattern with a square ball, an early cross or a run inside, but nine times out of ten it was the same old ploy. That it worked, and worked so well for 33 years at the top, merely serves to illustrate the point that in dribbling even the predictable will succeed if done superbly—and if that little seed of doubt can be planted in the defender's mind.

Matthews liked to receive the ball wide, in space, and to his feet. Other 'dribblers' may like a different kind of service. The rest of the side, and particularly the midfield, can help their ball-players with a lot more than just the right sort of pass. By sensible positioning a team-mate can put pressure on the confronting defender by putting him in two minds, or he can take covering players away from the space behind the defender for the man on to the ball to go into, or indeed simply move into space to 'make himself available' for a possible basic pass.

It all comes back to dribbling being part of the team effort. It works both ways. The player on the ball should be aware of the alternatives to his run; colleagues should help maximise the potential attacking power of that run.

▼ *Forest's John Robertson seems at first an unlikely model as a great dribbler, yet his chunky figure has tormented the best defenders in the game over the past few seasons. As he shows here against Chelsea he has the ability to keep the ball almost glued to his foot as he bursts into action, and it is this control and acceleration, allied to a superb dummy and a rare ability to cross the ball accurately at speed, that makes him one of the best wingers playing today. It's noticeable that while the Chelsea players are watching the ball intently Robertson is looking to that tempting gap between them. He is sufficiently in command of the situation, the ball cradled by his foot and ankle, head and knee over it for complete balance, that he can afford to look up and spot his chance.*

Riding the tackle

When Keith Burkinshaw and Tottenham Hotspur stunned English football by bringing over Osvaldo Ardiles and Ricardo Villa in 1978, the gates swelled wherever the two Argentinians played. And while various aspects of their play drew attention—as well as the overall change in Spurs' style—one area was a revelation to thousands of spectators: their ability to ride the tackle.

In addition each player seemed to have his own special technique, based as much on physical attributes as on the way he played the game and moved with the ball. Ardiles, light and wiry, relied on timing that little push ahead and on an amazing knack of avoiding the scything legs of desperate defenders; Villa, six inches taller and nearly three stone heavier, was at times inseparable from the ball, opponents almost bouncing off him as his control and immense strength let him plough furrows into their territory.

Their comparative mastery of this aspect of dribbling had been acquired in an environment where running with the ball was actively encouraged—and where defenders are not noted for their reticence in the challenge. It was personified by their countryman Mario Kempes in the 1978 World Cup finals, when his ability to

◀ *One of the many assets of Tottenham's World Cup star Ossie Ardiles is his ability to ride the tackles of opponents. He seems to know precisely the right moment for the vital touch past his man, and he has the pace and balance to leave him beaten or, as here with Gary Gillespie of Coventry, forcing him to clutch the trailing leg. Even now the Argentinian could well whip his foot away and keep moving forward—but all runners have to be prepared to pay the price of technical superiority and take the knocks and late tackles. Ardiles probably 'wins' more free-kicks than anyone in Britain.*

▶ It was partly as a result of his fine displays against Spanish League rivals Valencia that Real Madrid, in the club's first ever British signing, paid out £900,000 for Laurie Cunningham in June 1979. The previous November, in the third round of the UEFA Cup, the black winger had capped a magisterial performance in the Mestalla Stadium with a well-taken equaliser that gave West Bromwich Albion a draw and a valuable away goal. For the return leg two weeks later at The Hawthorns, and in front of what was to prove Albion's best gate of the season, he turned it on again to bundle Bonhof, Saura and Kempes out of Europe. Albion were hanging on to a 2-1 aggregate lead when in the 79th minute Cunningham combined with the veteran Tony Brown to produce a killer goal of clinical simplicity. The move began when John Wile intercepted a long ball from Botubot and hit a long pass to Cyrille Regis. As Regis chested the ball down full-back Carrete challenged, but the ball bounced away from him. First to it was Cunningham, who headed down the wing . . .

REGIS BROWN BOTUBOT

take the ball and more importantly himself past opponents paid rich dividends.

As an aspect of ball control riding the tackle falls into two main areas: moving away from defenders in semi-static situations, possibly even shielding, and moving past defenders on a run. The actual techniques involved, much the same in essence but highly individualistic in nature, must be developed by each player. They must be evolved in practice and adapted to meet the build, qualities and style of play of each person. And of course every tackle and every challenge to some degree presents some variation on the basic theme.

The key to keeping possession in these situations is to retain balance, keeping an upright stance whenever possible. And while balance is to a large extent an innate gift, it can be cultivated by constant attention and the right approach in every aspect of ball practice.

Thinking quickly can be as important as moving quickly: assessing the strength, speed and timing of the tackle and sensing precisely when to make that touch to take the ball past the challenge. The emphasis is on the 'protecting' leg, since it both hides the ball from the opponent and provides the push to move forward.

► *Diego Maradona's debut in Britain matched his 'wonder boy' tag as he scored once and set up two goals for Leopoldo Luque in the 3-1 win over Scotland at Hampden Park in June 1979. As at Wembley the following year, it was his scintillating runs that caught the eye—his close control at speed, his bewildering changes of direction, his ability to go through the smallest of gaps—and this exceptional talent, aided by his low, powerful build, enabled him to resist challenges and ride tackles both fair and foul. This time Paul Hegarty is the luckless pursuer.*

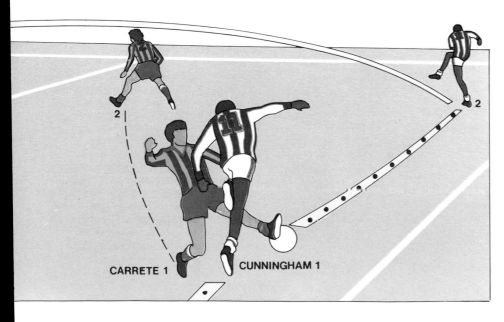

CARRETE 1   CUNNINGHAM 1

Cunningham had beaten Carrete with various ploys all evening, and this time a combination of the winger's skill and the full-back's vulnerability once again took the Albion star past the challenge. Instead of jockeying, holding up his man and looking for an opening, Carrete rushed in with his tackle; Cunningham, alert and balanced, timed his push of the ball perfectly and then skipped over the defender's lunging leg, leaning slightly forward and left to retain his balance and leaving him completely beaten. On he went towards the bye-line and, with time to spare, hit a low hard cross into the area out from the near post. Tony Brown didn't wait for the ball; he made his move early across the box, losing his marker, and sent a rasping right-foot volley on the turn past Manzanedo in the Valencia goal. It was a stunning score that put Albion 3-1 up on aggregate and sent them comfortably into the quarter-finals. And the following season (as Valencia found success in the Cup Winners Cup), Laurie Cunningham was riding tackles for Real as he helped them to their 20th Spanish League title.

Control with the sole

Although far from being a new skill—as the example below illustrates—the use of the underside of the foot for retaining control, and more particularly for beating opponents, is very much a growth area of football technique. With the increasing pressure of defenders who mark tight on front men and close down wingers near the line, ball-playing forwards are finding that 'sole power' provides another neat alternative in the quest for getting past opponents and finding space.

It is, however, rarely an optional extra in such situations. While the sole can be used anywhere by a player with time—Franz Beckenbauer is often seen rolling the ball gently forward under his boot as he seeks a target for one of his long raking passes—it only works for beating a man if he is in very tight, within playing distance of the ball. The circumstances have to be right. It can be a good ploy, for example, for a winger closed down near the touch-

◄ In England's rude awakening at Wembley in November 1953, when their unbeaten record at home against opposition from outside the British Isles was torn up in shreds by Hungary, there was one moment that highlighted the difference between the teams. It wasn't so much the fact that the goal made the score 3-1 and virtually sealed the hosts' defeat; it was more the manner of its scoring. England had plenty of cover when, in the 23rd minute, Zoltan Czibor took a pass from Sandor Kocsis. Beating left-back Bill Eckersley with ease, Czibor almost reached the bye-line before cutting a hard low pass back to the edge of the six-yard area and towards Ferenc Puskas. The Hungarian captain seemed to have gone too early, receiving the ball wide of the near post, as England skipper Billy Wright closed in on him. Wright, renowned for his speed and timing in the tackle, pounced on Puskas . . . and found himself on his backside, flailing at air. Puskas had checked, pulled the ball back with the sole of what would become the most famous left foot in football, watched Wright sail by—and then before any defender could blink had hit a fierce rising drive into the top of the goal. The nature of the goal and the sight of Wright, the epitome of the English professional, groping around in confusion, cruelly exposed the massive gap that had grown between England and the best in Europe. It was that one flash of quick thinking and merciless skill, every bit as much as the result itself, which left the home of football floundering in disbelief. Six months later, in a return fixture in Budapest, the Hungarians won 7-1 against an almost new England side to reinforce the lesson they had handed out to Wright and his team at Wembley.

◄ *A fine example of 'sole power' from Forest's Trevor Francis as he rolls the ball back to beat the sweeping tackle of Nacional captain Victor Esparrago during the World Club Championship game at Tokyo in February 1981. The pictures aptly illustrate the point that the defender has to be in tight on the man with the ball to make the skill feasible and successful. Like most ways of beating an opponent, using the sole has to be adapted to meet the situation; here the England forward, side-on to his marker, pulls the ball back with his right foot and then switches it to his left as he transfers his weight to his left leg to go past Esparrago. Notice too the position of his body in relation to the ball as he prepares to move. When facing an opponent, the ball is pulled back and then taken on with the same foot, either by dragging the foot back over the ball to move it onto the inside of the foot or, in a slightly quicker and more cultivated technique, taking the foot more across the ball to push it past the defender with the outside of the foot—a skill which Brazil's Roberto Rivelino used to great effect in tight spots to give himself just enough room for his explosive shots. Whatever method is used, it can be a great psychological as well as physical weapon if it comes off.*

line, where there is little space to exploit. But it can also be a valuable way of switching play; a tightly marked forward moving across the box looks up, sees little on, and uses the sole to turn and face the other directon, hoping to wrong-foot the defender in the process. The sole is also a useful addition to the armoury of the player shielding the ball, especially when he wants to keep it well away from the defen-

der as he grabs the chance to look up and see what options are available.

Sureness of touch and good balance are essential before the sole can be used to effect in matches, and practice to get the feel of the ball under the foot is vital. It is, after all, a rather special controlling surface to employ, and has very limited application in terms of power and mobility, so the control must be precise. It's not

surprising that we see it most often exploited by skilful but strongly one-footed players. While all aspects of practising ball control should involve both feet, players can expect to confine themselves in matches to their better side in using the 'bottom of their boot'. Still thought a little 'flashy', sole control can be as embarrassing when it fails as it can be uplifting when it succeeds.

▼ It needs a good deal of confidence to use the sole in a game, and this comes only from acquiring a good 'feel' for the ball in what is a fairly unorthodox and static position with the foot. You can do this simply by taking the ball gently along a line—perhaps the centre-circle of a pitch—and now and again stopping to pull it back. Gradually make the movements faster as your touch improves and you learn the knack of rolling the ball onto the inside of your foot to go forward; in match situations the technique has to be done at speed to be effective, with the motion of the ball linked to a sudden transfer of your weight from the anchoring foot to the controlling foot.

▼ Using the sole to beat an opponent is only valid and effective when the space you have to work in is very limited. It's also important to remember to see such skills as part of a move rather than as isolated incidents. This three-man practice reflects both considerations. The defender moves in tightly on the receiver as he takes the square ball near the touchline, and the man in possession tries to pull the ball back with his sole and then transfer his weight from his right leg to his left to go past the defender on the outside. To make the practice realistic don't plan for it every time; the defender should occasionally stand off or dive in more quickly for the ball to keep the receiver guessing.

The 'nutmeg'

In Britain it's called 'the nutmeg'; in the United States they have dubbed it 'the small bridge'. Whatever the name, beating an opponent by slipping the ball between his legs and collecting it on the other side of him enjoys a special position in the realm of football skill.

The operative word here is special. First, because it can happen only rarely; second, because it's something you pick up rather than set out to learn; third, because it is invested with remarkably strong undertones of 'oneupmanship'.

If it comes off—and it should be if tried at all—the nutmeg can be a very effective psychological weapon, a boost for the individual and his side. It is telling the opposition that he is not worried by their close attention, that it will take more than tight marking to stop him. This aspect of the skill, and the minor humiliation it provides for the defender and his team, is often accentuated by the fact that it is far more likely to be tried by a player whose side is two or three goals up than when the match is in the balance.

It is not a skill that you can practise for its own sake. The nutmeg is a quick-thinking response to a particular situation. If the opportunity presents itself, it may be exploited. The best time to pick up the knack is in five- and six-a-side games, where the emphasis lies with fast action 'on the floor'.

◀ *Even the greatest of players can leave themselves vulnerable to the nutmeg. In this NASL clash of the giants, Johan Cruyff tries to shut down a break for Cosmos by Franz Beckenbauer as a Los Angeles Aztecs team-mate scuttles back to cover. But the Dutchman, hardly renowned as a defender, leaves an inviting gap between his legs and Beckenbauer knocks the ball through, clipping the inside of his right calf. The former West Germany captain, open-mouthed with amazement, for once seems to lose his poise and awareness, marvelling at his accomplishment rather than nipping round his opponent to collect his prize. The nutmeg, if done at all, should be a means to an end, however neat.*

◀ The basic version of the nutmeg is played as you go forward against an opponent who has tried to close you down. As you move towards him he adopts the classic 'barrier' stance—body slightly hunched, arms out wide, knees bent in order to move quickly in any direction for the tackle. But he's got a little too close . . . and his feet are well apart. With space available to run into behind him you knock the ball through the gap and accelerate round him (on the opposite side to the foot that played the ball) and collect on the other side. Done quickly and well, it leaves him stranded. He can only turn and chase or, as happens all too often, resort to a foul tackle or obstruction.

▶ The nutmeg 'through the stride' is a less indulgent skill and an even more instinctive response to a given situation. It happens most often when a defender comes across and commits himself. As you clip the ball between his legs you check as his momentum takes him past—and then collect.

KICKING
THE
BALL

Basic technique

On average, eight times out of ten that you receive the ball you will pass it to a team-mate. Passing is the lifeblood of a football team, the link between its components, the only collective means a side has of achieving a common goal. And just as a measure of a good team is how well they find each other, even under pressure, so poor passing is the most common cause of attacks breaking down—and the quickest way to destroy confidence as well as any chance of success.

Good passing is knowing where and when to place the ball, with the right weight and accuracy. It can only come with the correct techniques and an understanding and appreciation of where and when to apply them.

A pass does not just involve the player making it but also the player receiving it. The quality of a pass is not measured by the way it is struck; it's measured by the ease with which the receiver can control it or lay it off first time.

Passing boasts almost endless variety of types and permutations of them: long and short, high and low, straight or curled; played with the inside of the foot, the outside of the foot, the instep, the heel or even the toe. Each may suit a certain player in a particular situation, and within limits individuals will always develop their own style.

But there are a few pointers to those limits, a guiding framework. The first point is to practise long and hard, not so that you can do the unusual but so that you can do the simple thing well. Good control and good passing means keeping possession; add the touch that comes with total familiarity with the ball and you get confidence and vision. There is a temptation to take passing, especially its simpler forms, for granted. Yet the higher the level, the greater the degree of control and accuracy required.

As a very general rule, play the way you are facing. While it is an obvious precept of the game that you should go forward wherever possible, this isn't always on. The backheel and the reverse pass have their place, but most often you will want to pass to a player you can see. Pass along the ground unless there is a reason not to

do so; it is the quickest route and is easier for the receiver to control.

Passing involves an understanding of the problems of receiving the ball as well as mastering the techniques of kicking it. This means you should give a pass when the receiver is in the most comfortable position to take it rather than when you are in the most comfortable position to make it; it means aiming for the side farther from his nearest opponent; it means responding to your team-mates' strengths, knowing how they like the ball played to them.

The three main factors in passing are accuracy, weighting and timing. Accuracy, which does not automatically mean playing the ball to feet, comes first because wayward passing is the prime cause of moves breaking down—at every level of the game. Weighting is the strength or speed of a pass. If it's too strong, the ball

will be difficult to control or run out of reach; if too weak, it will be intercepted or leave the receiver with the so-called 'hospital pass'—the one which puts him in a 50-50 situation with an opponent and the obvious problems that causes.

Timing, the art of when to release the ball, is a more demanding aspect, one which is not possible to master with simple practice. It is a skill acquired only in fluid situations, simulated or competitive, and no matter how good the accuracy and weight of a pass it will be ineffective if released at the wrong time.

To these three basic elements we can add two further ingredients of passing. One is the vision and perception to see balls other than the obvious ones, to spot subtle runs by team-mates, especially on the blind side, to play angled passes into space to set up chances and so on. The other is a degree of disguise. This does not just mean the surprise moves like the backheel, the reverse pass or playing off the front foot; it also applies to the basic passes. Try not to telegraph your intention and keep your opponents guessing.

PASSING AND SUPPORT
Support play is the hidden key to good passing and team-work. Before you can make a pass, after all, there must be someone available to receive the ball. Team-mates should help the man on the ball, running into space to make themselves available, taking opponents away to make space for others, getting in on the blind side of defenders. After giving the ball the passer should in turn be looking for space, often for a return from the receiver with a wall pass. The simple, fast, fluent 'push and run' approach, full of first-time passes, one-twos and nicely weighted through balls, is almost impossible to contain if played exceptionally well. So the basic maxim of passing is 'give and go'.

▼ Behind every good pass in a match there are thousands of passes in training. To get the 'feel' of the ball, you can't beat a solo practice, preferably with first-time passes, against a wall (below right). It's not so easy as it looks: try marking a target and hitting it with, say, ten consecutive passes. Keep moving and keep on your toes—no pass should be played flat-footed —and use both feet. Gradually increase your distance from the wall, but bear in mind that the push pass is geared for accuracy, not power. Practice with a partner is more fluid and mobile, but simply kicking a ball back and forth can get boring. Try a player receiving short passes as he runs gently backwards—that tests the ability to adjust and weight the pass correctly—or play first-time returns in front of your partner as you move round the centre-circle. With three players you can move about a lot more and create angles; remember to use both feet.

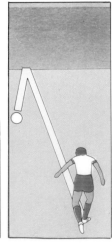

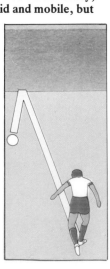

◄ *The sidefoot or push pass is the game's basic ball, the most reliable method of shifting the ball accurately over short distances. Here West Ham captain Billy Bonds is pictured just after contact, having struck the ball quite hard but lifted it just a little in an attempt to gain distance while retaining maximum control. His kicking foot is turned outwards at right-angles to the direction of the pass to secure safe contact on the largest available area of his foot; his kicking leg is at full extension after follow-through; his non-kicking leg is bent at the knee for stability and balance as he leans back; his head is steady, eyes still on the ball. Bonds will have placed his non-kicking foot level with the ball, almost alongside it. He will have struck the ball through the mid-line, measuring his aim carefully before stroking the ball with the inside of his foot. Though a bread and butter technique, exaggeration in the push pass is better than sloppiness. You can never take this kind of skill for granted: at the higher levels of the game a far greater percentage of passes are played short (under 30 yards) and along the ground than at the lower levels. While the amateur takes risks, the pro usually follows the maxim 'keep it simple, make it quick, do it well', concentrating his efforts on erasing unforced errors from his play. And he will still practise this pass in training.*

◄ After an absence of nearly four years from Wembley, it took Alan Ball just 16 minutes of the 1979 League Cup final to make his telling mark with an example of what had always made him such a good player—doing the simple thing supremely well. In this case it couldn't have been easier in theory—a first-time sidefoot pass—but its accuracy, weight and timing opened up the Nottingham Forest defence and enabled Southampton to take the lead. Phil Boyer began the move, out on the left, with a flick to Nick Holmes. As the Forest defence regrouped the ball went back to Boyer. A fine supporting run by left-back David Peach gave Boyer options: beat the defender or feed the ball inside to his team-mate. He chose the pass but Peach, closed down by John McGovern and then David Needham, was forced across the area. He stabbed a pass to Ball, as ever making himself available in space, and in a marvellous example of 'give and go' the full-back set off for the space now behind centre-back Needham in the danger area. He found it, and Ball's perfectly struck push pass found him. As Peter Shilton came off his line to narrow the angle, Peach steered it away from his spreading body with his left foot on the run before coolly slotting it home with his right. Peach, who as the Saints' penalty taker was no stranger to pressure in the opposition box, had shown that it's running off the ball and support play that provides the framework for a good pass; 33-year-old Ball, who unfortunately would receive his third club loser's medal at Wembley (with three different teams), had shown how to take advantage of it with the most basic pass in the book. As a young player at Blackpool, Ball had once been removed from a practice match on the insistence of Stanley Matthews after playing the ball into space for the veteran winger instead of to his feet, and then yelling for him to move to it. All right for the 'wizard of dribble' perhaps, but not here.

65

The front-foot pass

Coaches and coaching manuals used to encourage players always to play off the 'back foot', to put their non-kicking foot alongside the ball. The only accepted technique for the short ball was the side-foot or push pass. Now playing the ball off the front foot on the run is increasingly in evidence at all levels of the game, both for the little lay-off pass and the more forward through ball.

The reason is time. Striking a ball on the run with the inside of your foot means checking your stride to readjust your stance, taking a valuable fraction of a second and telegraphing your intention; striking it with the front foot means making the pass in your stride, using no extra time and surprising the opposition by playing it 'early'. It is a skill of limited if important scope: the number of situations which actually benefit by it are few, and both distance and direction are proscribed by the nature of the technique.

Playing off the front foot seems to come instinctively to some players, and it may even be argued that it is a prequisite of the great footballer. Matthews, Kopa, Di Stefano, Puskas, Netzer, Cruyff and Beckenbauer are among those who played a high proportion of their game that way, whether dribbling, screening or, most often perhaps, when passing.

In the front-foot pass the ball is played with the leading foot as you move into the next step. The ball is kicked from a central position, with the toes turned inside and a firm ankle, in a flicking motion. Because the ball is taken in your stride there is virtually no backlift or follow-through. Although power is limited, the pass has the assets of natural swerve and surprise: the angle of the pass is determined only after the ankle has stopped turning—and by then the ball is away. It's the perfect ball for the little bending pass down the line for the player on the overlap or for a quick 'give and go' short ball where you can keep moving for a return.

▼ A three-man practice for developing the knack of the front-foot pass, based on a one-two move. The player on the ball is confronted by an opponent but allowed to pass, and the receiver takes it on before curling it back to the first player past the closing opponent. Do it at a gentle pace until you have a feel for the technique, and then learn to play the ball first time in your stride (as shown here). Don't try to play the ball in either case if the pass isn't right or the defender has covered that realistic option; the essence of front-foot play is a response to a certain situation, and if the pass isn't on then cut inside the defender (as shown). With the squarer lay-off ball, contact is made later but still in front of your non-kicking foot (inset).

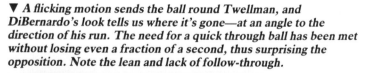

▼ *Cosmos' US international Angelo DiBernardo demonstrates the technique and value of the front-foot pass to Tim Twellman (20) and Bjorn Nordqvist of Minnesota Kicks. The passing foot is well in front of the non-kicking foot as he makes contact in his stride, the toes turned inwards to kick 'from the knee' . . .*

▼ *A flicking motion sends the ball round Twellman, and DiBernardo's look tells us where it's gone—at an angle to the direction of his run. The need for a quick through ball has been met without losing even a fraction of a second, thus surprising the opposition. Note the lean and lack of follow-through.*

The long pass

The further the ball is kicked, the greater the chances of inaccuracy and the more time the opposition has to intercept or to cover. The longer passes thus demand a high level of skill if they are to be creative ploys rather than merely hopeful ones. This applies as much to the receiver as the passer, and especially for front men taking balls under pressure from defenders and often on a run.

Apart from the goal-kick (where the kicker, usually the keeper, always enjoys the advantage of a stationary ball), there are four main areas of application for the long pass: the crossfield ball to near the touchline, usually for a winger or full-back moving forward, and played either to feet or into space in front of the receiver; the target ball to a front player from defence or midfield, most often played in the air; the longer type of through ball into space behind the defence; and the cross or centre, particularly to the far post. The tactical aspects of the last two are dealt with in later chapters; here we are concerned primarily with the actual technique of striking the long ball.

This breaks down essentially into two types—the low drive and the lofted drive. The low drive, struck with the instep and the foot pointing down, keeps the ball near or on the ground; the lofted drive, using the instep to get under the ball at an angle, gets height to take the ball over opponents to its target. Both involve a significant change in approach from the push pass, which while reliable because of the wide contact area employed has a very limited range and by its nature is restricted to being played along the ground.

The low drive, designed to get power on the ground ball, involves using the instep, the top of the foot, to hit the ball 'off the laces'. The foot is arched and the toe pointing down so that the instep makes contact through both the horizontal and vertical mid-lines of the ball to keep it low and straight. Though you should begin practising with your foot in a vertical position, to get the feel of the technique, passes are usually made with the foot at a slight angle, depending on the direction.

Placing your non-kicking foot is as important in kicking the ball as it is in controlling it. No amount of striking skill can compensate for the lack of balance that comes from poor positioning of the standing leg, and judging where to place that foot in relation to a moving ball is a central art in passing (and shooting), especially

for a first-time contact. In the case of the low drive it has to be alongside the ball and a few inches from it.

The low drive is like a golfer's shot off the tee. The backswing (or backlift, in the footballer's case) and follow-through are generous; the eyes are fixed on the ball and the head kept down both during and after impact. And, like the golfer, the footballer's key to success is timing. So many young players try to hit the leather off the

▼ There are few more devastating weapons for the counter-attack than the well-hit, well-placed long through ball. Wrexham found out as much on their visit to Brighton in November 1978, against a side who under Alan Mullery were shaping up as promotion candidates. The move that gave Brighton a 2-1 lead and two valuable points (they eventually finished second to make Division I for the first time) began deep in their own half. Centre-back Mark Lawrenson intercepted a Mel Sutton pass intended for Bobby Shinton (inset), went past his man and pushed forward before steering a ground pass to Teddy Maybank just inside the Wrexham half. Maybank laid it off first time to Peter O'Sullivan, who controlled the ball, took it left, looked up—and hit a high raking pass between Gareth Davis and full-back Joey Jones for Brian Horton to run on to. The Brighton captain saw the ball early and caught up with it after the second bounce, beating the closing dive of Dai Davies with a superbly judged lob played with the outside of his right foot.

ball when they would get greater distance—and accuracy—with a more subtle approach. The best exponents of the long ball, high or low, seem to make their passes with almost casual ease, just as the great batsmen can stroke rather than lash the ball through the covers. You don't see Ray Wilkins, Trevor Brooking, Glenn Hoddle, Graeme Souness or Liam Brady thumping their 40- or 50-yard passes; they have all developed a smooth, rhythmic approach and a clean, crisp contact.

The low drive is inevitably a technique of limited use, even for the most astute

and accomplished of passers. There just aren't that many occasions on which a long pass can go forward on the ground and find its target without being intercepted, and its useful employment is increasingly restricted to the crossfield ball played in deep positions. The technique, however, also serves well as the basis for learning the art of shooting.

The lofted pass is the more common long ball, an obvious way of taking out defenders by playing the ball over them to, or into space for, the front men. Unless the ball is intentionally swerved, using the

inside or outside of the foot (see next chapter), the contact surface is the lower part of the inside of the instep, where the big toe joins the body of the foot, striking through the bottom half of the ball.

Again, the approach is crucial. The last stride should be a long one and at a slight angle to the intended line of flight, with the non-kicking foot placed slightly to the side of the ball and just behind it. You pivot from the hips to produce a powerful but controlled and rhythmic leg swing, your body leaning slightly back as the swing develops.

◄ *A pass master as well as ace dribbler and scorer, Johan Cruyff gets his foot under an angled lofted drive for Aztecs on his way to winning the NASL's 'most valuable player' award in 1979. Note the sweeping motion of the foot as it is turned outward to hit through the bottom of the ball for height. A great example of rhythm and timing to produce controlled power.*

▼ Cruyff had already played for an NASL team before his surprise move to Los Angeles, 'guesting' for Cosmos against Chelsea at Stamford Bridge on the American club's 1978 tour of Europe. And among many memorable moments, one of the best was a beautifully played long ball. Cruyff began the move with a confident one-two on the edge of his area with Franz Beckenbauer. He controlled the ball on the run, took it a few yards, and then suddenly adjusted his stance to hit a superbly weighted 50-yard lofted pass over the Chelsea midfield and just in front of Giorgio Chinaglia. The Italian international, pursued by David Stride, raced on with the ball, but what would have been a classic score was foiled by the dubious lunge of reserve keeper Bob Iles.

◄ The low drive is a difficult technique to master because a relatively small part of the boot strikes the ball (the centre of the instep) and a relatively small part of the ball (approximately the middle of the vertical and horizontal mid-lines) must be hit accurately. A simple starting tip is to place the ball with the maker's name or an appropriate mark in the correct position to make sure you hit through the ball and 'off the laces'. This also helps in the crucial positioning of the non-kicking foot in the last stride—level with the ball and a few inches from it. Get the contact right before graduating to a moving ball.

◄ Rhythm and timing are more important elements of hitting a good long pass than sheer power, and before trying to build up distance (even before kicking a ball at all), young players should try the movement to get the feel of it, rather like golfers take a few practice swings before teeing off. When it comes to actual practice, making the long pass interesting does present problems, simply because the distance factor means it's difficult to weave it into a game situation. Two inventive trainees, however, will soon develop a competitive exercise. When you have the basic idea, build up the power and distance, but never at the cost of control and accuracy. Learn later to vary the approach and the angle of your foot on the ball: the lofted drive can produce an array of different passes and you'll quickly see how slight adjustments will affect the height and distance of the kick. Using the lines of a pitch as targets will help in gauging the right distance.

Your ankle should be extended and firm on impact, with contact made through the middle of the bottom half of the ball. The direct result of power with timing, distance is achieved by the pivoting of the hips, the forward movement of the thigh, the straightening of the knee on impact, good contact and a smooth, full follow-through in the line of the pass.

The exact angle of your foot on the ball and the precise point of contact will be determined by the angle of approach and the distance and direction required. For a wide-angled approach the non-kicking foot is placed further from the ball and the kicking foot is pointed outward, sweeping through the bottom half of the ball. This technique, imparting backspin and sacrificing distance to height (though not necessarily in ratio) is often used to produce the 'hanging' ball at the far post.

The lofted pass can be a difficult technique for youngsters to master, more particularly with a moving ball, but it is too easy to put it down to lack of strength. As we have said before, rhythm and controlled power are the keys, not sheer energy. If the height and direction are there but not the distance, you are probably kicking at the ball rather than through it, not transferring your weight through the movement and thus the ball; if there is too much height but not enough 'carry', you have probably made contact too low on the ball, converting the kick into a kind of chip and wasting horizontal force. By the same token, if you have not achieved sufficient height, it may be because you have made contact a little high, perhaps lifting your head and thus straightening your body too early.

When there is distance and height but no direction, the chances are the ball has been pulled, like the golfer's 'hook', because your foot has wrapped round the ball slightly. This may be due to a straight run up, or lack of control on the follow-through, with the leg swinging across the body and the intended line of flight too early. It may also be because you are 'opening up' too soon, facing the required direction before the full movement is completed. A good deal of practice, and some helpful advice from a friend or coach, will soon sort out the problems—and then mastery of the longer passes will make you a far more rounded team player.

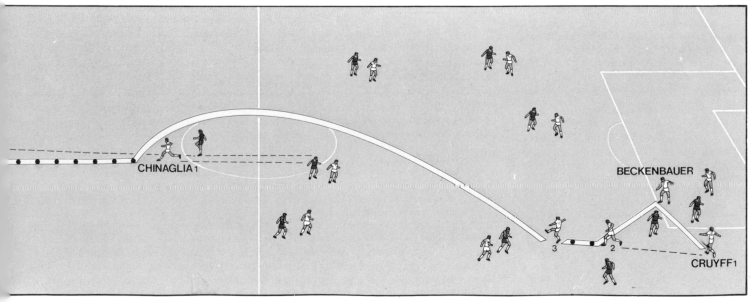

CHINAGLIA 1

BECKENBAUER

3   2   CRUYFF 1

The swerving pass

▲ *With Alfredo Quesada in front of him, Poland's Grzegorz Lato strikes a front-foot pass round an opponent and into the path of a team-mate in the game against Peru at Mendoza in the 1978 World Cup. The outside of the foot provides far less security than the inside for the swerving pass, but it can produce more power on the ground ball and, as here, capitalise on the element of surprise—though in all the swerving techniques the intention can be disguised by the experienced player.*

Once seen as something a little special, the swerving pass is now a basic football technique employed at every level of the game. It is an important facet of control to master, providing a whole range of options from merely adding safety to a crossfield pass to a devastating through ball round a defender and into the path of a team-mate.

The skill, often also called the bending or curling pass, enables you to reach parts of the pitch other passes cannot reach, or

can make it possible in circumstances where an alternative, say the chip, could be difficult or risky. It can avoid interception, take out opponents and exploit space. But it is not easy to play it precisely, especially with the outside of the foot, and because it is both curving and spinning it can be a tricky ball to receive compared to a 'straight' pass. These factors combine to ensure that it is still a relatively rare method of passing, one usually and advisedly retained for when it can really do some damage.

Though there is almost infinite variety in the swerving pass, depending on exactly how and where you make contact with the ball, the technique divides into four main areas: the ground ball and the lofted pass played with the inside of the foot, and the ground ball and the lofted pass played with the outside of the foot. All of them are governed by the principle that the ball swerves in the direction of the spin imparted on impact.

The starting point for learning the curved pass is the ground or low pass hit with the inside of the foot. The approach is the same as for a straight pass—the element of disguise is a great bonus in all forms of swerving pass—but your foot actually moves across the ball from inside to outside with an outward 'rotation' of your kicking leg. You strike the ball with the forward part of the inside of your foot, in the area around the joint of your big toe with a strong brushing action, wrapping your foot round the ball. Contact is through the horizontal mid-line of the ball, but to the right of centre for a right-footed pass. This will generate anti-clockwise spin and swerve the ball from right to left. You should hit the ball firmly with a good follow-through to be sure of imparting sufficient spin and swerve.

The main difference for the swerving lofted pass is the point of contact on the ball, as shown below. To get height, the ball must be struck well below the mid-line, and the lower the point of contact, the higher the ball will go.

The use of the inside of the foot can provide swerve and is a fairly safe technique. Using the outside of the foot can

◄ **A simplified representation of the contacts required for the four major variations of the swerving pass, though it's important to remember that small adjustments to the angle of the foot and the point of contact on the ball will produce significant changes in direction and the degree of curve. For the pass with the outside of the foot (A), the boot is moved across the ball from outside to inside at an angle to the intended 'direction' of the pass. In the case of the ground ball, contact is made with the foot angled down on the horizontal mid-line of the ball and, for the right-foot pass, to the left of centre; for the lofted pass, contact is made lower in that same quadrant. The ball spins clockwise, and the swerve is from left to right. The further from the centre the ball is struck, the more the spin and the greater the swerve. For the pass with the inside of the foot (B), the boot is moved across the ball from inside to outside, generating in this case (with the right foot) anti-clockwise spin and swerve from right to left. The lower the point of contact, the more the ball will rise. The inside of the foot can't produce the degree of curve that the outside can, but it is a 'safer' technique for passes which require only a small amount of swerve because the brushing motion of the foot can be effective almost anywhere along the forward side of the boot.**

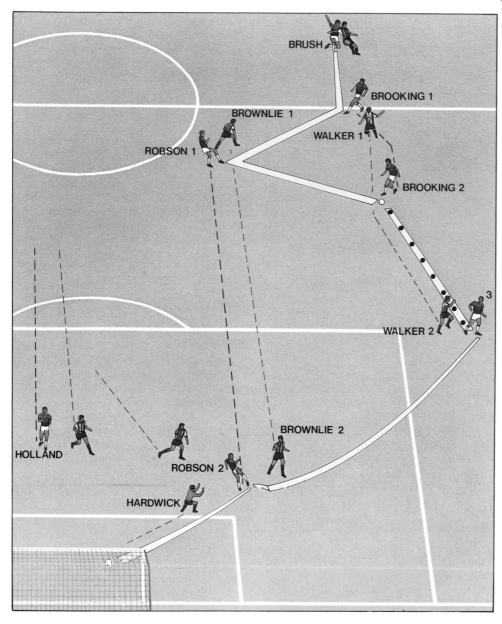

◄ In a frustrating season that saw them always just outside the top three, West Ham's brightest spot of 1978–79 came with their biggest win, a 5-0 victory over Newcastle which rekindled hopes of a first-time return to Division 1. And on that March afternoon at Upton Park one incident stood out, even in all that good football—a goal conjured up in true Hammers style. It was their second, and it started when left-back Paul Brush's timely challenge steered the ball to Trevor Brooking on the halfway line. With Nigel Walker coming in quickly to try to close him down, Brooking slipped a first-time pass infield to 'Pop' Robson and nipped round his man for the return. Young Walker was as quick to recover as he had been to close, and though Brooking was away he did manage to keep him off a direct route to goal. It mattered little, however; the England star was never really pressured and a swift look up to see what was on was followed by the telling pass—a curling left-foot ball into the area out from the near post, safely round John Brownlie and into the path of Robson after the first bounce. Robson, in his second spell with West Ham and playing against his old club, timed his strike perfectly, capping his 40-yard run with a left-foot volley past Steve Hardwick to notch up his 207th goal in League football. It was a neat variation on the near-post theme pioneered by Ron Greenwood at Upton Park, centring on a beautifully weighted swerving pass hit with the inside of the left-foot, played away from a retreating defender and into the stride of a team-mate renowned for his clinical finishing. An enviably two-footed player, Brooking may well have had the option of playing the ball with the outside of his right foot. Certainly the 'inside' pass enjoys a greater degree of control over the direction of the swerve.

▶ A 'frozen' moment from the opening game of the 1978 World Cup finals, between West Germany and Poland in the River Plate Stadium at Buenos Aires. Polish captain Kazimierz Deyna, with opposing midfielders Rainer Bonhof and Heinz Flohe holding off, launches a swerving pass towards the edge of the German penalty area in the hope that their fast-moving striker Andrzej Szarmach can race onto it. More often the curling pass is used the 'other' way round against square defences—through the gap and into the path of the forward; and while Rolf Rüssmann appears to have been pulled out of position by Wlodek Lubanski (whose movement has produced the chance for the pass), the holders still have plenty of cover with Herbert Zimmermann, skipper Berti Vogts and sweeper centre-back Manny Kaltz. In fact Deyna's touch and accuracy combined with Szarmach's reactions and speed to produce what was nearly a very good chance, one foiled by the tackle of Zimmermann. Unlike Vogts and Kaltz, who were caught out by movement behind them, the left-back had been able to spot Szarmach's run and get across to cover. The incident emphasises the fact that passing is a combined skill, relying on receiver as much as kicker.

◄ *The swerving pass can be a useful ploy for keeping the ball away from a possible interception but still finding your man, as Aztecs' Dutchman Thomas Rongen shows while under pressure from Diplomats' Hungarian international Joszef Horvath in a 1979 NASL tussle. He has to steer it past the challenge of Horvath yet keep it in play and on target; so he has hit across the ball with the inside of his right foot, making contact in the 'bottom right' quadrant to secure lift as well as swerve.*

produce more spin and more swerve, but the margin of error is far smaller and the contact has to be precise to be effective.

For the ground pass, your foot is held at a downward angle as it moves from outside to inside across the body and therefore the ball, making contact partly on the instep and partly on the outside of the foot. For a right-footed kick, you strike the ball to the left of the centre of the vertical mid-line, thus imparting clockwise spin and making the ball swerve from left to right. Your non-kicking foot should be placed a few inches to the side and slightly behind the ball (to allow for the swing of the kicking leg) and the ball should be in the centre of the stance.

The further from the centre and the nearer the 'edge' of the ball that you make contact, the more the ball will spin and swerve; the steeper the angle of your foot, the quicker the ball will travel. For the lofted curved pass you must strike the ball below the horizontal mid-line, and to the left in the case of the right-footed pass. In all these approaches, keep your eye firmly on the ball and your head steady until the follow-through is complete.

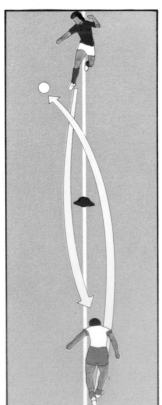

◄ The first thing in practising the swerving pass, as with all the kicking skills where the point and nature of contact on the ball are so vital, is to get the 'feel' of the ball on your foot. You can practise on your own with a wall, using a line to the wall or an obstacle as guide to your progress, or as here the same markers can be used with a friend. Don't try to bend the ball in a big arc; at first you're just after the touch and control with the simple inside-foot ball. When you have this well taped, with moving as well as stationary balls, move on to doing it with your weaker foot and, later, practise the outside pass with your better foot. This is a very exact skill, and most top players rarely risk a swerving pass with the outside of their weaker foot. Precise contact, and therefore touch, is even more important here than with the inside pass, so once again get the feel of it right first, aiming for a gentle curve, before really trying to bend it. The outside of the foot also involves more variations of flight and curve because of the adjustments possible to the angle of the foot, from almost upright to nearly flat.

► With a friend you can easily make the practice for the ground passes competitive by placing coats or other markers to create gates to aim through from a central position on the ball, with each gate worth a number of points according to the amount of swerve required. You could agree to score an extra point for hitting the ball first time, another bonus point for using the outside of your foot, and perhaps double the basic or add more points if you are successful with your weaker foot. If the markers are canes or posts, you can also practise the lofted passes.

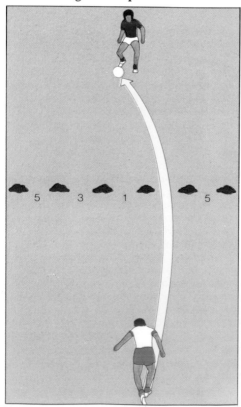

Crossing the ball

When it is not possible for them to gain possession by intercepting or winning the ball, defenders try to deflect attacks down the centre to the wings, diverting the play away from the danger area to what are thought to be the areas of least danger in the defensive third of the pitch—the flanks. Yet well over 60% of all goals scored come directly or indirectly from passes played from such positions.

The cross is thus one of the most important of all attacking techniques. It was once the domain of the winger, the specialist player whose main function was to 'get it over' for the centre-forward to head home. In today's fluid football, however, every outfield player must be able to make telling, intelligent and varied crosses: overlapping full-backs, supporting midfielders and front men moving out wide are all expected to play their part on the wings, and where appropriate to supply the final pass.

That pass, the cross (or centre), has been the subject of huge tactical change over the last three decades. Until the 1960s the winger would wait near the touchline for the ball, take it forward, beat his man if necessary using classic dribbling skills and pace, go towards the bye-line and then sling the ball over. The cross was most often aimed at the area out from the far post, and the bustling centre-forward (his duties almost prescribed by his number nine shirt) would do battle with the opposing centre-half and quite probably the goalkeeper as well in order to 'get on the end of it' and score. It was a central feature of the British game, and continental powers envied and feared it; several generations were reared on it, marvelling at the aerial power and heading ability epitomised before the war by Dixie Dean and after it by Tommy Lawton.

There were other methods of crossing the ball, of course. Two great Wembley goals from the year 1953 illustrate the point: Stanley Matthews pulled the ball back on the ground to the area out from the middle of the goal for Bill Perry to score the winner for Blackpool in the FA Cup final; and six months later Hungary's Zoltan Czibor did the same for Ferenc Puskas on the near post (see page 60). But the high, far-post cross was easily the most common course of action. Forwards, defenders and keepers all positioned themselves from it, simply because that was the norm—and because it is easier to meet a ball when moving forward than when moving back. Since more balls are going to be hit a bit short rather than long, this was the logical approach.

▲ *Despite the pressure of an imminent lunge from Rumanian right-back Tilinhoi, Italy's young star Paolo Rossi remains calm as he shapes to cross a moving ball during the 1980 friendly at Naples. His head is steady and his body has begun to turn to get the angle on the short cross (made a few yards from the goal-line and just inside the penalty area). But with his non-kicking foot already 'committed', he looks to have planted it too far from the ball, which is still moving away from him, for an easy centre; conscious of the rapidly decreasing space between his opponent and the line he has been forced into playing the ball too far from him. It's interesting to compare this picture with the one of Des Bremner on page 77, where the position of the non-kicking foot, tucked in just behind the ball, enables the passer to be completely in control before impact.*

It now seems extraordinary that the almost naked near-post area should have been left unexploited for so long. The Hungarians of the 1950s sometimes played the ball there, as did the great Brazilian side which followed them, but it was left to an Englishman to fashion it into a tactical science, or more accurately an art. Ron Greenwood, then manager at West Ham, was the first man to recognise the massive possibilities there in the mid-1960s, and though all his players were encouraged to look for it he was fortunate in having two who were 'naturals': Martin Peters and Geoff Hurst. For more than two seasons their apparently telepathic understanding baffled opposing defences,

and not just for West Ham: the goal they created for England against Argentina in the 1966 World Cup (see page 120) was one of their best ever.

Other clubs followed suit and by the end of the decade the near-post cross, refined and embellished with flicks and lay-offs, had become an accepted basic of the game. But it somehow did a lot more than that; it opened the doors to thinking in general about crosses. Since then the whole approach to where and when the ball is centred has been re-evaluated. The vast range of crosses available—high and low, long and short, straight and swerved, 'early' and from the bye-line—is now being tapped in the constant struggle to

73

find ways of breaking down tight-marking and crowded defences and setting up scoring chances from every possible angle.

Each one is suited to a particular need; and each requires a different skill to produce it. Most are based on the types of kick covered in the previous two chapters, but one facet of crossing the ball, centring from near the goal-line on the run, requires special attention as a technique.

The most dangerous position from which to play the classic far-post or the mid-goal cross is near the goal-line; played properly, it leaves covering defenders having to turn to follow the ball while the incoming forwards always have it in their sights. It means that the ball is moving away from their players (including the keeper) and towards your players. In recent seasons there has been no better example of the advantages of the cross from the bye-line, and the problems it causes for ball-watching defences, than the John Robertson–Trevor Francis goal that won the European Cup for Forest in 1979 (see page 162).

A special type and level of skill is needed for these crosses, and few players seem to possess that ability—or at least the capacity to display it under pressure—even at the highest echelons of the game. Many who do are able to 'screw' the ball across (some, like Steve Coppell, are easily capable of turning the ball more than 90°) but most are 'tumblers', forced to roll over after contact with the momentum of the move.

The players who keep their balance while still crossing good balls at sharp angles are rarer still—Peter Barnes and John Robertson are two examples—but

▶ The key to good crosses lies as much in knowing where to put the ball (and why) as it does in acquiring and developing the techniques needed to get it there. Crosses can be aimed at players (especially on the break, when there may be only one team-mate in support), but more often than not you aim at designated areas. A good cross is one which can be met in a danger area by a player going forward; a perfect cross is simply one which produces a score. It is the movement of the receiver, even more than the nature of the pass, that determines the ultimate value of a centre. Essentially there are two main areas at which to aim high crosses: the far post and the near post. Three or four decades ago the far-post cross, frequently played from near the bye-line (A), was the accepted ploy for wingers; played away from the keeper and his defenders and into the path of big forwards coming in, it remains the classic cross and players are still encouraged to 'stretch defences', to 'get round the back'. In the mid-1960s the near-post ball (B), pioneered by Ron Greenwood at West Ham, revolutionised the thinking behind crosses, leading to a far greater variety of placement and trajectory and putting more emphasis on the receiver and his role. Today the men in the middle are expected to learn how to judge their angles and time their runs, often diagonal ones, to meet the cross, and to use a range of contact skills to put the ball in a particular part of the goal.

▶ 'If someone had written it in a book no-one would have believed it.' That's how Arsenal coach Don Howe described the ending to the 1979 FA Cup final against Manchester United, a game which produced the most dramatic finish in modern times. Yet the move that gave the Gunners their last-gasp victory could have been taken from a book written by Howe himself it was so well conceived and executed—and it revolved round a perfect cross. Arsenal had been coasting to a 2-0 win in a rather mediocre match when with four minutes left Gordon McQueen stuck out a foot to poke the ball home and give United a glimmer of hope. Then Sammy McIlroy capped a fine dribble by squeezing the ball past Pat Jennings for a sensational equaliser. With less than two minutes to go everyone girded themselves to the thought of extra time. United, having celebrated the leveller as though it were a winner, relaxed. Liam Brady, socks rolled down but still full of running in the May sunshine, went on a final sortie, and his characteristic ride over the tackle took him past the tired challenge of Micky Thomas. Then, confronted by Martin Buchan and tracked by Lou Macari, he took both players out by releasing a beautifully weighted pass for Graham Rix, seemingly without even a glance. The Arsenal winger, behind Brady when the Irishman played the pass, ran smoothly onto the slowing ball and, keeping balanced and cool under pressure from the tenacious Macari, put over a looping cross that climbed to beat the groping hands of the inexperienced Gary Bailey—but dropped sharply just outside the far post and a couple of yards from the line. Alan Sunderland had read it well, and he summoned the last reserves of energy to beat the desperate lunge of left-back Arthur Albiston and send a slightly miscued half-volley into the United net for an astonishing finale. Just as United had shown character and coolnees in coming back from the dead, so Arsenal had been the great professionals: keeping their heads after blowing a two-goal lead, continuing to play thoughtful controlled football based on good habits and solid technique, still playing for each other and linking well and, perhaps above all, playing to the final whistle.

▶▶ *Graham Rix, shadowed this time by right-back Jimmy Nicholl, sends over a cross from an identical position earlier in the 'four-minute final'. Note how he has leaned slightly back and bent his right knee to get height for the comparatively short centre but still kept his head down and eyes on the ball.*

The 'early' ball is usually wasted if played to the far post, but played in to the near-post area during fluid play (C), before the defence has time to organise, and especially if it curls round behind the defenders, it can be the most devastating ball in the game. The ball is played into the space at the near post area so that the receiver can move to attack it in that space at speed. The crossing player isn't looking for the receiver to be waiting for the ball in the space, or indeed even near it; the attacker will often move from a position well outside the goal area, possibly from an original location out from the far post. The near-post cross becomes decreasingly effective the closer the crosser gets to the goal-line, but if the player in possession is near that line the near-post ball is still valid—as a ground pass pulled back to a team-mate just out from goal; a good example, from way back in 1953, is the Ferenc Puskas goal featured on page 60. In addition there are diagonal crosses, but these are covered later under the through ball. Any of these centres can be made, of course, from positions further infield, and to a certain point the basic principles still apply. Indeed many youngsters find it difficult to get the power for the full cross; if the technique and timing are right, it will come.

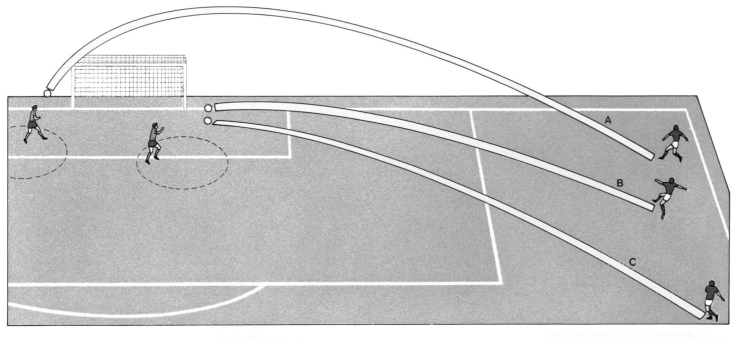

THOMAS

BRADY
1

MACARI
1

▲ *A fine example of making space for the cross from Brazilian winger Ze Sergio during the Gold Cup at Montevideo in 1981. As we pick it up (1) he already has the retreating defender, Wolfgang Dremmler of West Germany, in all sorts of trouble after feinting to go inside and then going on the outside with his right foot. Ze Sergio now has that vital little bit of space as he powers away from his recovering opponent (2), winning enough time to steady himself for the cross. Dremmler is well beaten as the Brazilian whips in a high ball towards the danger area (3). Though the sequence shows all the elements of classic wing play—close control, beating a man, getting in a telling cross—every outfield player must be able to supply a centre under pressure.*

1 while few youngsters can ever attain their special brand of skill all players can learn to cross on the run from deeper positions.

The first rule is to make the cross easy on yourself. If you have time and space, use it: look up, pick out the target area, adjust your run and stance to improve (that is reduce) the angle of your body to the intended direction of the pass. Stay relaxed, too; tightening up is probably the biggest single cause of poor crosses.

The second point is to be positive and confident about the cross. Centres that go limply behind the goal, or float gently into the keeper's hands, or are miscued just a few yards to a defender, or are sliced over the goal-line, are not just wasted passes; 2 they are also among the great moraaale-sappers of football. But do not be afraid to play the ball in firmly. Early crosses give front players a chance of losing their markers, while defenders do not enjoy the pass played in quickly before they are set to deal with it. Such balls can easily get behind them and forwards can take advantage on the blind side. The swerving pass can of course be a great ally in this type of attack.

Crossing on the run is all about balance. You are, after all, moving at speed in one direction and aiming to steer the ball with some force in another. The placing of the non-kicking foot is vital here, since with the ball travelling away you have to judge 3 how exactly to chop or more often stretch that final stride. The foot must be close enough to act as a fulcrum but still leave enough room for the swing of the kicking foot across it. The more you can turn your body to face the intended direction of the pass, the easier this aspect of crossing technique becomes.

For a right-footed cross from a square position, your left foot is planted just inside the ball and slightly behind it. You use both arms (and particularly the left) for balance, and you keep your head steady throughout, with your eyes fixed firmly on the ball. You bend your non-kicking leg and lean in slightly as your right foot begins to move down and across. On impact your right leg is extended and your right foot hits under the ball. The point of contact will vary a little with the nature and circumstances of the cross, but it is basically the inside of the foot around the area of the big toe. This enables you to get the necessary angle on the centre with a clipping motion as your kicking foot ends up almost at right-angles to the direction of your run. Your head stays well down until after the ball is on its way.

This is the approach for the 'bye-line cross', the centre pulled back square or behind square from near the goal-line. The movements are similar, though not quite so pronounced, for any cross played at speed, and practice will tell you which adjustments produce which results. By

The Watford goal that put Manchester United out of the League Cup in October 1978, scored at Old Trafford, made nonsense of the two-division gap between the sides and proved that you can do good things against any opposition if you do them well. The move that gave Graham Taylor's team a 2-1 win started from an apparently 'dead' situation—striker Ross Jenkins having to run wide to pick up a Brian Pollard pass. Big centre-half Gordon McQueen, however, left the middle to follow him. Jenkins found support from full-back John Stirk, who had made good ground to help out, and in turn Stirk, quickly closed down, played a first-time ball to Dennis Booth, also sharp in making himself available in space. Booth hit a curling first-time cross to the far post, where Luther Blissett ran in to beat Martin Buchan and Arthur Albiston and score.

▲ The perfect picture of poise, style, balance and concentration for the cross: Aston Villa's Des Bremner gets it all right as he prepares to send the ball past Shaun Elliott of Sunderland. The placing of the non-kicking foot (so vital in any pass but particularly important in the cross, where the ball is fast moving away from you) is as close as possible. The whole stance suggests power yet economy—good backlift, body and non-kicking leg leaning slightly in, arms acting like a tightrope walker's pole for balance, head steady. He knows where he wants to place the ball, and he must not take his eyes off it once he's into the movement, either to check on potential targets or the challenge of opponents. With long crosses like this, where you have a little space to play with, it's possible to turn your body towards your target, converting the centre into a form of lofted drive; crossing from near the goal-line and under pressure, however, requires a very special technique few can really master. The game featured here produced a 4-0 win for Villa, their biggest of a season which saw them take the League title for the first time in 71 years. Bremner was one of seven players not to miss a League match, and as the right-sided midfielder he was expected to provide width on that side wherever possible. It was never quite so vital for his left-sided team-mate (Gordon Cowans), since the Villa attack boasted a genuine left-winger in Tony Morley.

► There was a time when the cross was the prerogative of the winger, but in today's fluent game every outfield player is expected to get into wide positions, usually with supporting runs off the ball but also by carrying the ball. This applies particularly to full-backs, who should always be looking for the chance to attack down their flank; but as Manny Kaltz showed in a remarkable display at Wrexham in May 1979, there's no reason why it should be confined to one side. Kaltz, in fact, had already helped to dent Welsh hopes of going to the European Championship finals by providing the cross with which Herbert Zimmermann had given the West Germans a half-time lead. Now, seven minutes into the second half, the versatile Hamburg defender produced the run which would end in the killer goal for Wales. Kaltz picked up a loose ball just inside the centre-circle and began to move menacingly forward on a diagonal run . . .

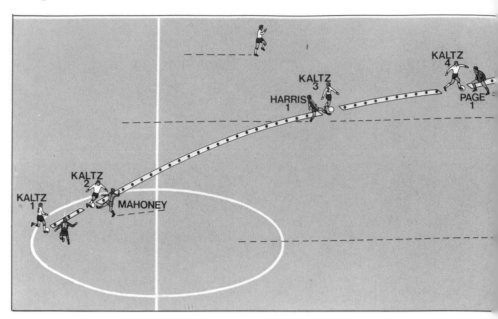

leaning in further and hitting the ball more on the instep, for example, you gain power at the expense of height.

Practising the cross is not easy without several players. Knocking centres in to a friend is useful, of course, particularly in the early stages to get the feel of what to many youngsters is a daunting area of technique because they lack the power to find the far post. The answer here is to start by playing the crosses from inside the penalty area to the near post, gradually building up the distance in both 'directions' as the basic technique improves.

But exercises involving sets of players can more accurately convey the inherent problem of the cross: that it is a moving skill dependent on the marriage of two players. The timing of the run by the receiver is as important as the actual kick

itself. So with six or more players (the greater the number the more continuous and helpful the practice) you can work on the following routine.

One set of players (A) line up well outside the penalty area and level with or just outside the far post; the other set (B) line up the same distance from the goal-line but a few yards in from touch, the exact position depending on the age of the players. A spare attacker (X) stands near the edge of the area, and another man is in goal. Player A1 begins the practice by passing to B1, who plays a one-two with X round an imaginary defender and then crosses the return first time to the area out from the far post, where A1 should have made his run in order to meet it. Players A2 and B2 then move up a little and do the same, again using X for the wall pass.

After all the participants have grasped the basic idea, the exercise can be altered to take in further aspects. First, the runs by the A players can be to the near post; then they can be to either danger area, forcing the crossing-player to glance up before knowing which of the two areas to aim at. The B players can take the ball on towards the bye-line before crossing, or they can be confronted by 'real' defenders who try to block the wall pass and come across to challenge the B player on the ball. Finally you can introduce another defender to help the lonely keeper and put pressure on the receiving player.

It is not a bad idea to physically denote the two main danger areas on the pitch, at least in the early stages. Playing the cross into them should become a habit for any player centring from a wide position.

1. Normal cross

2. Check back and cross

◄ In his efforts to try to tackle you or cut out the anticipated cross, a defender will sometimes 'sell' himself. He can be the man tracking your run or a player coming across at an angle to cover. Either way, if he commits himself he is vulnerable to the 'dummy cross'. This is where you shape to centre (perhaps with a little touch of exaggeration, but not much) and instead check back, wrong-footing your opponent or watching him sail past, taking the ball onto your 'inside' foot. You have beaten your man and have time to work out your next move—a cross with your other foot (as shown here), a square ball to a colleague in space, a simple lay-off or perhaps a dribble towards goal for a shot. It's an easy, almost predictable move, yet if executed well and at the appropriate moment it works over and over again, even at the highest levels. At the more modest levels, it's an invaluable asset for the player finding himself on his weak side and wanting to get the ball onto his stronger foot. It can't be pulled out every time, of course, or even more than once in a game, but it adds another important dimension to the art of crossing.

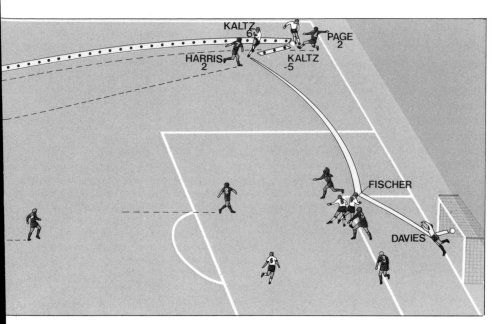

First came John Mahoney, failing with a lunging tackle, and then Carl Harris, trying to tackle back but slipped for pace. Kaltz had Bernard Dietz outside him but he kept going, next beating right-back Malcolm Page with a neat feint. The danger seemed then to subside for the Welsh defence as Kaltz, tracked by Page, was forced to take the ball wide. Page appeared to have him bottled up—until a quick side-step, followed by a hop over the defender's tackling foot, gave the German the room he needed for the cross with his better foot. Over it went, a neatly flighted near-post ball that split centre-backs George Berry and Leighton Phillips and was welcomed by a choice of attackers. Klaus Fischer, one of the best headers in Europe, moved a few yards towards the ball to beat Zimmermann and place his firm downward header past Dai Davies. It would be the first of his six goals in the qualifying games—but the only one delivered by a right-back out on the left wing.

▲ *Nottingham Forest's full-back Frank Gray, watched by Wolfgang Kraus of Bayern Munich, puts over a square, chipped cross. While Gray's head and upper body face his opponent, his lower body and legs are almost square to him, following the direction of the pass; and his left foot, stopping dead after digging under the ball to get height over a short distance, is at right-angles to the camera. His head is still in the same position as before contact (as far 'over' the ball as possible) and again he is using his trailing arm for balance. The pass follows all the rules for the chip (see next page), but is played here as a centre, and a neatly disguised one at that. Like all modern full-backs Scottish international Gray, who later rejoined his first League club, Leeds United, has to be the master of a whole range of crossing styles and techniques in order to fulfil the attacking role demanded of him in today's fluid game.*

The chip

The nature of modern defensive play has given a new lease of life to the chipped pass. The need to get a ball over tight-marking opponents into a restricted space behind them, and to hold the ball up in that space for a team-mate, has taken the chip from something of a fancy skill to a bread-and-butter technique for the outfield player, and especially the midfielder. In addition it remains, in rarer circumstances, one of the most audacious and spectacular ways to score a goal over the keeper who is off his line.

Many young players find the chip difficult to understand and control. The best way to see it, perhaps, is like a chip shot at golf; the golfer needs height to get over a mound or out from under the lip of a bunker, and he therefore needs some

power, but he does not want that power to make the ball run once it hits the green. The chip solves both problems: the chopping action makes the ball rise sharply and also imparts backspin, which enables the ball to 'grip' the grass on landing and thus stop quickly.

The footballer is looking for exactly the same qualities—early rise and fast stop—and achieves it with the same basic principle: striking under the ball, almost digging into the ground with a stabbing action that is more down than through.

The approach here is as important as the contact. Your non-kicking foot should be close to the ball and level with it. You bend the knee of your supporting leg a little and lean slightly back, though still keeping your head steady and almost over

▼ It took a marvellously controlled volley by Jimmy Greenhoff to earn Manchester United a replay against Second Division Fulham in the third round of the FA Cup in January 1979—but the goal was set up with a fine piece of play by his fellow striker Stuart Pearson, playing what proved to be his only first-team game of a season wrecked by injury. Pearson, who had already figured once in the move with a lay-off, took a ground pass from Martin Buchan and, shielding the ball neatly from Richard Money, took the ball to his left, gaining just enough space to turn and hit a long chip to the right of the Fulham area. The home side's defenders were caught out by the depth of the chip: John Margerrison and Ray Evans could only watch and turn too late as the ball sailed over, while Kevin Lock did everything he could to try and stop Greenhoff. The United forward was always going to be favourite on a blind-side run like that—Lock couldn't be goal-side of his man and watch the ball and his opponent at the same time—but the timing of his run and his finishing showed experience as well as skill.

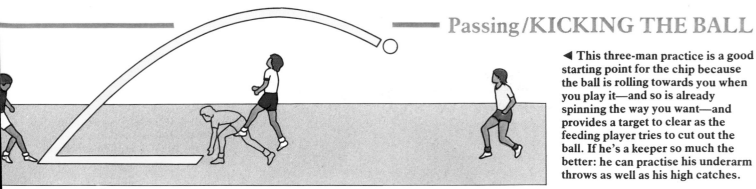

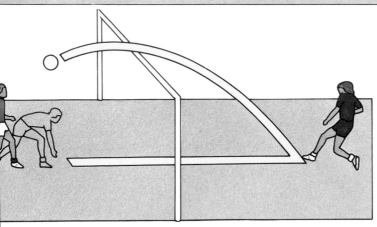

◄ This three-man practice is a good starting point for the chip because the ball is rolling towards you when you play it—and so is already spinning the way you want—and provides a target to clear as the feeding player tries to cut out the ball. If he's a keeper so much the better: he can practise his underarm throws as well as his high catches.

◄ If there are only two of you then the barrier of imaginary defenders can be a crossbar; all you require is something to help you gauge the strength and angle of your kicks. Once you've mastered the approach and contact for the chip, you can play the ball continuously, first by trapping it and playing it through for your partner to chip, and later by trapping the ball and playing a chipped pass every time, without the benefit of 'automatic' backspin. If you are on your own you can use a wall, making a target line on it at six or eight feet. As with the two-man practice start with rolling balls before graduating to a trap and push pass between each chip and then onto a chip every time. All these exercises should be done with a proper football if possible, because the lighter plastic balls deviate in flight, and on grass rather than a hard surface like tar. Later, try working your chips over set heights and onto targets, such as hoops or bins.

the ball. The angle of approach is virtually in line with the intended direction of the chipped pass or shot.

Hardly any backlift is required; the speed of the kicking foot is developed mostly by the quick straightening of the knee, which is not fully extended until after impact. Contact is through the very bottom of the ball, some say 'through the ground', and made full on the instep. Because of the natural curve between the ankle and the instep, and because the ball is struck at its lowest possible point, the line of force is nearer the vertical than the horizontal. Your head should stay steady and the follow-through is minimal, though it may be fuller for a longer pass.

It is not a difficult technique, though it needs a lot of practice to gauge exactly how to strike the ball to produce specific heights and distances. On the basics there are three common faults. The first is that you are too far away from the ball to get your foot properly under it; the second is that you lift your head a shade on impact—your body straightens and your foot comes up, producing contact with the ball alone rather than with the ball and the ground; and the third is not enough of a 'stabbing' motion with your foot, possibly linked to an over-generous follow-through, thus using horizontal rather than vertical force.

The technique for chipping the ball is not as rigid as this may sound. These foundations are essential, but after you have practised and mastered the basic knack the chip becomes a more fluent skill. It can be used for longer balls or adjusted to suit a certain trajectory (as pictured here); it can be used with different parts of the foot at certain angles to produce swerved balls, like the marvel-lous bent chipped pass used to feed players on the flanks by Franz Beckenbauer; it can be, as we have already mentioned, a wonderful way to score.

Two factors help a chip, however basic or advanced in concept. One is soft ground: if the grass 'gives', then the foot can get right under the ball with ease. The other is the ball moving towards the kick-er: it is already spinning in the desired way. By the same token, the chip is an ambitious ploy indeed on a bone-hard surface with a ball that is running away from you. Even so, if the technique is right the chip would still be on.

▲ The chip can be a deadly weapon against the keeper off his line, but it's difficult to play because the ball is spinning and moving away from you. The goal with which Kenny Dalglish retained the European Cup for Liverpool in 1979 was secured with a deft first-time chip from Graeme Souness' fine pass (see page 42). Bruges keeper Jensen had spotted the danger early and raced off his line, and he was already lunging to spread himself across Dalglish's line to goal when the Scot made contact, stabbing down on the ball just enough to send a controlled chip well clear of the keeper but with enough speed to hit the far corner for a subtle, economical goal.

The backheel

Because the ball is played in the opposite direction to the way you are facing, and to a lesser extent because the contact surface is 'blind' and relatively narrow, the back-heel is a rather minor aspect of passing and of control. At the same time its 'reversible' quality makes it unrivalled as a surprise tactic in switching the direction of play and catching out defences.

As the three examples on these pages show—retaining possession, a special turn and a scoring touch—the heel is a versatile ally. But all these instances have one dominating element in common: they are all instant, perhaps intuitive, reactions to certain situations. This is not to say the backheel is an instinctive skill—many a player has deliberately used it to deflate opponents when his side is ahead.

The most common position for a back-heel pass is around the middle of the opposition danger area, when the man in possession is moving across the pitch, tracked by one or more defenders, and by backheeling he can set up a colleague in space behind him for a shot or more direct route at goal with virtually no warning—to either side.

It is a risky rather than difficult or complicated technique. A player may well fool his opponents, but he may well fool his team-mates too. It must be treated as a serious and constructive skill which can help your side, not just something to boost your ego or please spectators.

There are only two basic rules. The first is do it as a positive move, not just to get out of trouble. The second is never try it near your own goal: it could be the most embarrassing pass you will ever make.

► *Tony Woodcock demonstrates what a great friend the heel can be with an inventive 'nutmeg turn' against VfL Bochum's Jupp Tenhagen during a 1980 Bundesliga match for 1FC Cologne. Woodcock has sensed his chance is there, and though the ball catches the Bochum captain on the calf his quick reaction still makes the turn a possibility—despite the tripping foot of the German player.*

▼ *Rumania's Constantin Ticleanu uses a quick backheel in an attempt to stop Bryan Robson nicking the ball away during England's World Cup defeat at Bucharest in October 1980. Even for moving the ball just a short distance, as here, the backheel can be a risky if wonderfully deceptive way to play the ball; you have to be pretty sure what's behind you and with a pass it can be just as easy to fool your team-mates as your opponents. Yet it has a unique role in switching the direction of attack, whether it is played straight back or with the foot making contact on the inside of the heel. In short, it's a high risk skill that can bring high rewards.*

▼ Denis Law was always renowned for his quick-thinking opportunism near goal, but such scores were normally the result of acrobatic volleys and spectacular headers. Yet one such goal, the most ironic (and the last) of an illustrious career, came with a modest backheel. It happened on 27 April 1974 when Law, by then 34, was playing what proved to be the last game of his second spell with Manchester City, against the neighbours who had transferred him in dubious circumstances the previous summer after 11 years' service. For United it was a crucial game: facing relegation in 21st place, they needed full points from this match and from the last, at Stoke, to stand a chance of staying up. Manchester's second best crowd of the season packed Old Trafford to see the derby with a

difference—and to witness just one goal. It came in the second half after a typical Francis Lee run into the United defence. Martin Buchan pushed Lee wide, but as he entered the United box he suddenly hit a low, angled drive across the goal. Law reacted sharply, almost casually steering the ball past an astonished Alex Stepney with his right heel. Five minutes from time some of the United supporters could stand no more; they invaded the pitch and referee David Smith abandoned the game. But the result stood, and while the man they called 'The King' finished his career with an Indian summer at the World Cup finals in West Germany, where he won his 59th and last Scottish cap, his old club dropped into the Second Division after a stay of 36 years.

The lob

Like the chip, the lob is a way of gaining height over relatively short distances; like the backheel, it is an 'instant' skill, used in response to a certain circumstance. And while it is used more often than either of the two for attempts on goal, it remains first and foremost a passing technique.

A looped, often parabolic volley, the lob gives the off-ground ball further height. It is used to clear opponents and find team-mates, usually with a single touch on a ball you have to hit first time—a loose pass you have to really stretch for, an awkward bouncing ball that would take time to control.

It takes plenty of practice to get the contact element of the lob correct. While a fairly generous area of the foot is employed (most of the instep), precise contact and deft touch is vital if the pass is to be accurate. Because of the stance involved the basic forward lob can appear an easy skill, but it is far more demanding and exact than it looks.

This casual air stems partly from the fact that, unlike most ball skills, you lean well back to achieve the right balance. You 'point' your knee at the ball, keeping your toe well down and ankle fully extended and making contact with the upper part of your instep. There is virtually not follow-through, simply because your leg is straight and well forward on impact and you are rarely looking for power. More often, in fact, you will be looking to pull your foot away a little on impact to control the height and distance of the pass.

All lobs, rather like they do in tennis,

▼ *The only way to score with the ball off the ground against an advancing keeper is with the lob. And it's a far more difficult skill than it looks: you're moving at speed, the ball will be rising or must be just right. Here Rangers' Derek Johnstone does well to convert a through ball against Morton at Ibrox in November 1978. As Bobby Russell's pass is played in, Johnstone beats the Morton defence to it and shapes to lob as Denis Connaghan starts to move* out (1). *By the time the ball has come down to a kickable height Connaghan is well out, forcing Johnstone to knock the ball up steeper than he wanted (2); he now knows he can't score direct and the race is on. He evades the keeper and just beats the covering Barry Evans to nod the ball home (3) and put his side 2-0 up. As Johnstone raises his arm in triumph (4) Neil Orr appeals vainly to referee Renton, presumably for offside.*

◀ Because the lob is a first-time volley continuous practice is a simple matter of two players, a ball and a target to clear, such as a crossbar. Repetition will soon develop that vital touch and timing. With three people the 'barrier' can be more mobile and testing; the middle man, preferably a keeper, can feed a player with a throw and then try to cut out his lob.

▶ *Brazil's midfield star Dirceu plays an angled lob over the head of Franco Causio during the third place match of the 1978 World Cup in Buenos Aires. It's a fine example of a time when only the lob will do: he can only just reach the loose ball, but it must be played quickly and accurately past an opponent to a colleague in space or on a run. Note how he is leaning back, poised on the toes of his non-kicking foot, as the knee of his kicking leg 'points' at the ball, with his ankle fully extended and his instep arched on impact, using his arms to keep nicely balanced. Dirceu scored the winner in the 2-1 victory over Italy that gave the former champions third place.*

benefit from a degree of disguise, if it can be done. This is particularly relevant when you are through and trying to put the ball over the keeper; he is aware of your problem and is going to try to make life difficult. You have to learn, through practice and in matches, when it is best to lob early to leave him stranded and when to lob at the last possible moment, after he has committed himself. The choice may well be influenced by other factors, of course, such as the actual direction or run of the ball, the position of opponents closing on you, or a defender's covering run behind his goalkeeper. Many successful scoring lobs actually bounce behind the goal-line, the judgement good enough to send the ball in just under the crossbar.

▶ The lob is all about being controlled and balanced, and this becomes even more important when it's used for a strike on goal. Usually scoring lobs come when a player is through on his own and the keeper comes out, thus narrowing the angle but leaving space behind him, but sometimes players simply sense that the time is right. Andy King did just that at Derby in August 1979 to bring Everton their first points of the season, and his brilliant piece of individualism was enough to win the game. With the visitors' goal under siege, the ball ran to Trevor Ross on the edge of his area. He saw the chance of a break and played a long high ball well into the Derby half for Andy King. Chased by David Langan and Steve Wicks, King jumped to meet the ball in his stride and flicked it on. As he raced for the ball he was aware not only of Langan closing—but also of John Middleton's position, staying put but just still outside his six-yard box. Though moving at speed and under pressure, King conjured a beautifully controlled topspin lob over the surprised County keeper and into the net.

The side-volley pass

Passing on the volley breaks down into four main techniques, each of which merits separate consideration: the angled lay-off with the inside and the outside of the foot, the 'push' volley (as shown left), and the full-face volley, which is a toned down version of the volleyed shot, played with the instep, featured on page 100.

The first and second are skills reserved for the first-time ball, deflections of the pass that comes at you between knee and hip height. Timing and balance are vital here, so it is a question of composure as much as of technique. The ball should be met crisply, maintaining its pace to send it away straight rather than looped or falling—though to a large extent its actual trajectory will be determined by the position and movement of the intended receiver. Slight changes in the position of the foot can produce significant variations on the pass, but with the inside of the foot the area of contact is so generous that control should be of a very high standard.

There is a far smaller area available, and thus a smaller margin for error, using the outside of the foot. But as it requires only a minor adjustment to the basic stance—mainly a more upright position of the body—it can be a neatly disguised move, the foot turning inwards at the very last minute to send the ball in what is almost the opposite direction to the one indicated. If you can play the high volleyed passes with both sides of both feet you are well on the way to becoming the complete one-touch player.

The 'push' type of side-volley is an altogether safer pass, and not necessarily played as a first-time ball. It is not possible to tell, for example, whether Kenny Burns' back-pass is his first touch from the picture here. This is the volley that guarantees retaining possession, but it can rarely create openings.

Most volleyed passes are by definition movements requiring quick thinking and quick responses. But that does not mean they are hurried. Composure, poise and sense for the stylish are needed to cultivate the touch and timing so important in this area—and they begin with the confidence which grows with mastering the basic elements in practice.

▲ The volleyed lay-off is a pass that should feel good and sound good. To be effective it needs to be done with a dash of style, a little bit of poise. With the ball coming at speed at an awkward height, and the deflection having to be exact, it's a technique that must enjoy perfect touch and timing. The contact should make a 'popping' sound, rather like a tennis player's firm volley at the net. In a simple three-man exercise the middle player volleys with alternate feet to the passers, who can throw or chip the ball into him. If you learn the knack quickly, try the outside of your foot.

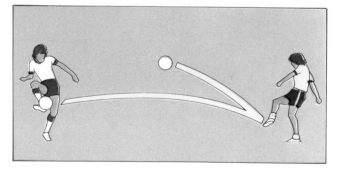

▲ With two players you can try a continuous one-touch practice, setting a target of say ten volleys each, using either one or both feet. Remember to hit through the ball rather than under it and don't 'snatch' at it. Keep up on the toes of your non-kicking foot, with the supporting leg slightly bent for balance. Once on top of that, introduce more players to increase the angles, using the outside of the foot as well as you play a more mobile one-touch practice or play in balls to one person surrounded by a ring of players.

Basic technique

The ultimate objective in football is to win, and that means scoring more goals than the opposition. Over two-thirds of goals come from genuine shots, and even when the all subtle variations are subtracted—volleys, chips, lobs and the rest—the basic ground shot remains by far the most common and important means of finding the net.

However high the quality of the approach work, a team's combined play means nothing if the final touch is poor. Even in an era of sophisticated teamwork, 'sticking it away' is still what it all boils down to in the end. Chances mean little if they cannot be taken. There may be a danger that coaches, in stressing the value of team play, neglect the crucial conversion factors of shooting and heading. It can become an automatic reaction for a player to look for a team-mate instead of for goal—even in a scoring position.

But passing the ball may mean passing the buck. Having a go at goal should be the first choice in scoring positions, a good habit. And it's easy to lose, or to fail to acquire, that vital attacking habit.

While it is not feasible to manufacture the gift of goalscoring that makes a Greaves or a Law, a Pelé or a Müller, it is a simple task to improve basic techniques near goal to a point where confidence is high, where no second thought is needed before action. This confidence, this willingness to try, is essential for shooting from any distance, and is founded firmly on a belief in a person's ability—a belief based on the sure knowledge of skill.

It is not possible to score without going for goal. In the vast majority of cases it is better to miss than pass the responsibility and waste a chance. It would be a strange

team indeed that could be accused of 'over-shooting'. There are also the secondary benefits: there is always the chance of a deflection or the fortunate rebound off the keeper to a team-mate.

This is perhaps the first principle of shooting: the proportion theory. Assuming the chances are genuine, it means having a crack at goal if there is not a viable, constructive, immediate and better alternative. It is, in effect, the first choice up front. This does not mean that forwards have time to look up and casually assess play; shooting is a positive course of action. The Brazilians have leaned towards this philosophy for decades, while in Europe its greatest proponents have been the Ajax and Holland sides of the early 1970s. The approach involved not merely taking the ball forward and having a crack, or banging in the loose ball first time; it also meant a greater preparedness to use the shot earlier and regard it as the natural culmination of combined play, often after delicate one-twos on the edge of the area set up by midfielders and defenders going forward. This policy, almost a 'shoot on sight' mentality,

perhaps reflects the confidence that only the members of really great sides can possess in their own and each other's ability.

The second guideline, linked to the first, is to 'do it early', to strike the ball first time where possible. While this is of far more relevance to the various volleys and to close-range finishing in general, it also applies to the longer shot. The biggest giveaway of a striker out of form is not his missing the target or having his shots saved; it is hesitation, dithering on the ball when the chance was there, blowing it all by trying to make absolutely sure with one touch too many.

Technically, distance shooting is a welding of power onto accuracy. One is useless without the other except when special skills are brought to bear, like a swerve. From close range it is possible to sacrifice a little of either or both and still convert a chance (indeed it is often advisable to tone down the power to help maximise the direction) but from 15 yards or more the ball must have pace as well as precision. Practice for shooting must always reflect this point.

The top scorers, however, rarely strike the ball unnecessarily hard. They do not waste energy in trying to blast the ball when what is required is a subtle combination; they are looking for controlled power, not naked force.

▶ A model of controlled power: Brazil's Eder displays all the prerequisites for both accuracy and force as he shapes up for a shot. His non-kicking foot is parallel with the ball and about nine inches from it; his backlift is high and straight; he is using his arms to balance himself as he prepares to thrust forward; and he keeps his head steady, with his eyes fixed on the ball. As his left foot comes through Eder will make contact with his instep, extending his ankle and keeping his toe well down to hit 'off the laces', offering almost a flat contact surface to the ball. His head and knee will be over the ball and his head will stay down until after the ball has gone; lifting the head, a great temptation as the player seeks to see the result of his strike, is the biggest single cause of inaccurate shooting. The follow-through is low but full—the longer it is the greater the degree of sustained control and therefore accuracy.

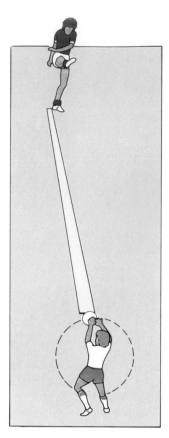

◀Power and accuracy must be given equal thought in any shooting practice. The basic starting point for two youngsters is to shoot so that the receiver doesn't have to move from his spot to take the ball. It's not as easy as it sounds, even from say 12 yards. If you don't have or want a partner, practise with a dead ball on a target area marked on a wall to begin with, graduating to second-touch and then first-time shooting, with both feet if possible, as you increase the distance.

▶A goal in the local park can provide the ideal place for shooting/goalkeeping practice for three players. Once you have the basic technique of kicking the ball the keeper can feed one forward. If the keeper is beaten, the receiver can choose whether to return the ball with a first-time shot or control it first. It's easy to make this a competitive exercise, with say a point for hitting the target (shot saved) and two for a goal, with points doubled for a second-touch shot and trebled for a first-timer. With a netted goal, you can adjust the practices shown on page 102, which provide passes from a wider angle. Make sure you vary the pace of the passes and take them on the move—you'll rarely shoot with a 'dead' ball in matches.

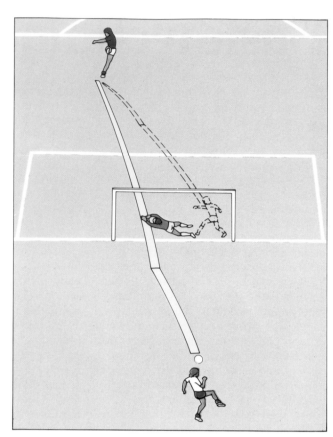

Everyone likes to see the opponents' net bulge upwards with a fierce rising shot, but it is important to remember that ground shots are more difficult to save than high ones, since the keeper takes longer to get down to a low wide ball than up to a high wide ball. And the higher the shot, the earlier the keeper will see the ball clearly, whereas the low shot may well be coming at him through a forest of legs. So shoot often, shoot early—and shoot low.

Psychological factors are more prominent in shooting than perhaps any other area of the game. There is no chance of a reprieve, as there is with a poor pass. But in a way this begs the question; if you don't shoot you don't score goals. You may feel bad about a miss, but you must shrug it off and be determined not to blow the next chance. It must not be allowed to dissuade you or your team-mates from shooting. All players should be willing to shoot, and that means encouragement from coaches and colleagues alike; all players should be able to shoot, and that means dedicated practice. Even experienced players have to keep their shooting skills 'in trim'. Always include a few minutes shooting in training, whether or not the session is about attack.

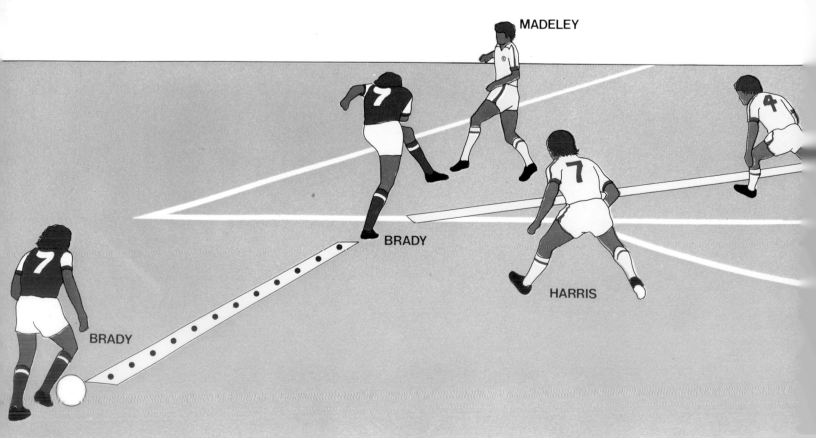

MADELEY

BRADY

BRADY

HARRIS

▲ *Nigerian striker Owalabi lets fly during his country's win over Algeria in the 1980 African Cup of Unity final in Lagos. Notice the way the 'natural' swing of the kicking leg across the body is allayed by pointing the opposite shoulder towards the target.*

◄ It's ironic that there should be a strong 'surprise' element in long range shooting; yet it certainly applies, and especially for players with a quick, short backlift that gives little notice of a shot. It also helps if the player is not renowned for it. Liam Brady has an awesome reputation for many skills—weaving runs, subtle chips, swerving passes, clinical through balls, and so on—but powerful shooting isn't one of them. So he surprised everyone on the opening day of the 1978–79 season at Highbury when he took a Frank Stapleton crossfield pass in space, moved forward, looked up and gestured to Stapleton, who had made a run across the goal—and then let fly. With keeper David Harvey and the whole Leeds defence anticipating other things (perhaps a ball through for Stapleton) Brady had beaten them with a low raking shot into the corner. Paul Madeley had jockeyed him, Brian Flynn and Carl Harris were helping out; but it was all to no avail against a well-hit, well-placed ground shot.

89

The goal with which Nottingham Forest retained the European Cup in Madrid in 1980 embodied the two main considerations in distance shooting—technique and confidence. John Robertson, collecting the ball on his customary position wide on the left, beat Hamburg right-back Manny Kaltz and moved inside. He played a one-two with Garry Birtles and then took the ball on towards the edge of the area before letting go, despite the awkward presence of Ian Bowyer. The shot, from about 22 yards, was low but not that hard; Rudi Kargus saw it late as it began to swerve a little, bounce, and kept bending away from him, clipping the inside post before giving Forest a 20-minute lead they would never surrender. Robertson's pose—head still and facing down, ankle extended, toe pointing toward the target—is a model for the low shot; and the confidence his solid technique gave him enabled him to cut inside and have a meaningful crack at goal with his 'other' foot. The element of surprise was there, too: the Hamburg defence were probably expecting a pass or a crossover with Bowyer. So too, perhaps, was Bowyer.

PLACING THE SHOT

► Scoring with ground shots isn't all (or even mostly) about cracking the ball home from outside the area; it's also about putting away those chances from 10 or 12 yards. 'Tucking them in' from these positions is concerned more with placement than power. The idea is to maximise accuracy while maintaining enough power to beat the keeper. This can mean using the inside of the foot in some cases to get the greatest possible surface area on the ball and steer it home. With simple practice you can learn to direct it to the best part of the goal, most often the near post.

GEMMILL 1

JONGBLOED

◄ Placing the shot can be the cream on a superb dribble near goal, as Archie Gemmill demonstrated in Scotland's 3–2 win over Holland in the 1978 World Cup. While that last game salvaged some of Scotland's pride, his goal helped rescue her reputation for individual skill. It came in the 67th minute after Gemmill picked up a loose ball from a tackle on Kenny Dalglish. Though well outside the box and confronted by several Dutchmen, he headed for goal, beating Jansen's tackle, dummying Krol to go behind him and then slipping the ball between the lunging legs of Poortvliet. After a run like that he may have been forgiven for fluffing the finish on his weaker right foot; but experience told and Gemmill, cool and composed, adjusted his stance to slip the ball home.

The acute-angle shot

While managers and coaches rightly stress the development of 'good habits' and the promotion of teamwork in football, the game would be poor indeed if players always followed the norm, always complied with a prescribed pattern. One of football's most attractive features is that it has the facility for an individual to try the unexpected, to break away at any time from the code of general practice. It's often a gamble: if it comes off, particularly with a strike on goal, you're a hero—if it doesn't you're in for some stick.

Nowhere is this more apparent than with the shot from difficult angles near the bye-line. Other techniques invoked near goal may be more spectacular—the diving header and overhead 'bicycle' kick, for example—but in those cases there is rarely an element of choice; they are usually the only method of getting meaningful contact and little blame attaches to the player who goes for goal and misses.

The acute-angle shot is very different. If the player scores, he is acclaimed for having the confidence and skill to do the wrong thing perfectly at the right time. When the shot is blasted over, or screws harmlessly into the side-netting, there can rarely be excuses—no matter how fast he was moving, where the keeper was positioned or how well team-mates were marked. A player has to be prepared for a good deal of criticism in those situations, and it may not be confined to the moment; a wasted chance when a dangerous cross was on may seem a genuine crime to a tired and beaten side after a game.

Apart perhaps from an indulgent dribble, taking on that one man too many, nothing is more frustrating to a player who has made a long run into an unmarked scoring position than to see a colleague scorn the cross and fail with a shot from an 'impossible' angle.

Yet goals are scored from such positions, when the target has shrunk to little more than a tall door, and even from on the goal-line itself. The failure rate is high, but the successes stay in the memory far longer than the numerous near-misses. And especially when they come at the highest level.

It is not possible to get any higher than the World Cup final, and it was this fixture that produced one of the finest acute-angle goals of all time. It came at Santiago in 1962, in the game between Brazil and Czechoslovakia—and it's perhaps no surprise that it was scored by a player from a country renowned for treating us to flashes of unexpected skill, for producing moments of total magic.

▲ *Dennis Tueart (bottom left) wraps up his first season in the North American Soccer League by scoring his second and Cosmos' third goal in the Soccer Bowl victory over Tampa Bay Rowdies at the Giants Stadium in September 1978. The England international didn't give much thought to the conventional alternatives—a far post cross to Giorgio Chinaglia (9), or perhaps a ball pulled back to a colleague in space—since with keeper Winston DuBose stranded he just had to keep his head and hit his shot well to beat the retreat of Mike Connell. But the viewpoint of the picture, taken beyond the far post, provides an unflattering impression of the ease of the task; from Tueart's position the area to aim at was quite small, and he had to strike the ball while moving at speed. His control and contact were more than adequate, however, and a late curve on the ball (caused by hitting slightly across it) took it safely into the top corner of the net. It climaxed a superb summer for Tueart and helped him win the award for 'the most valuable player of the play-offs'. The ex-Sunderland and Manchester City man had two years before produced another spectacular goal in a final with an overhead kick (see page 106)—a fact suggesting perhaps that it takes a certain type of skilful and confident player to try the unexpected.*

The champions had just gone behind to an early shock goal by Masopust when Amarildo received the ball on the left corner of the Czech area. The teenager, who had played brilliantly since replacing the injured Pelé in the group games, then produced a goal worthy of his idol. Beating a challenge from Pluskal, he took the ball to the bye-line and then along it a couple of yards towards the near post. With the Czech defenders, Brazilian attackers and the Chilean crowd all expecting him to pull the ball back to a colleague, Amarildo unleashed a fierce rising left-foot shot that pierced the narrow gap between goalkeeper Schroiff and the near post.

The astonishing goal, scored less than a minute after the Czechs had taken the lead, not only boosted Brazil's confidence; it also demoralised Schroiff, who after a marvellous tournament then completed a miserable day by being at fault with the goals that gave Brazil a 3–1 victory and another four years as holders of the Jules Rimet Trophy.

Another final, that of the FA Cup at Wembley, nine years later, produced another goal from an acute angle on the left, this time on the ground. Liverpool's ultimately vain attempt to win the trophy (and thus stop Arsenal winning the double) received a spectacular and unlikely boost early in extra time from Eire international Steve Heighway. Moving at speed past the Arsenal defence towards the goal-line in a position similar to that of Amarildo, Heighway shaped to cross as he **91** cut in slightly; goalkeeper Bob Wilson shuffled a yard or so off his line at the near post—and Heighway rifled in a low swerving drive through the tiny gap.

'You have to play the percentages,' explained Wilson later. 'That's what goalkeeping is all about. In this situation you have to assume that the player is going to centre and not shoot. From that angle the odds against him are very, very high. The right thing for him to do is to get the ball into the centre, and I had to adjust my position accordingly. In the same situation I'd do the same, every time. But you have to give anyone who tries it the credit for seeing the chance and having the nerve to go for his shot.'

When a player is taking the ball towards the goal-line the angle on the goal is getting increasingly tight. The usual course of action, the 'right thing to do' as Bob Wilson calls it, is for the player to cross the ball. This will probably be a fully-fledged cross in the air if the player is out wide, but from nearer the goal it may be a little chipped cross to a specific team-mate or a ball pulled back along the ground. Whatever form it takes, the cross will be dangerous simply because it will be moving away from the defenders and into the path of the attackers, who always have it in their sights. These crosses can be played blind to certain areas (most often the near post and far post) or they can be the result of a quick look up by the player on the ball.

It is during that glance that the decision is taken to shoot and not cross, probably as a result of seeing the keeper just out of position. The acute-angle shot is not a preconceived technique: it is an instant response to a particular situation. For many players, lacking the confidence to try it and the skill to succeed, it would

▼Practising against a wall with a goal chalked on it will enable you to keep the routine flowing, in spite of the angles involved. The goal need not be full size if there are only two players: at first you're trying to control the shot and master the various angles rather than pick your spot in a match situation. When you're striking the ball, keep your bodyweight foward, your knee over the ball and your ankle firm. The backswing will be short for a snap shot, but the follow-through should still be as long as possible. As with all such practices it will be more enjoyable if you make it competitive; so keep going until one of you misses, with the winner the first to, say, ten points. A third player as keeper will of course make it both more testing and more realistic. With a 'life-size' goal on the wall, and a good grasp of the basic techniques, you can make the practice more constructive. Pull back to a position outside the penalty area and put a defender in front of you. Practise going past the defender and shooting for goal as you near the bye-line. If you are working in groups, a player from the second group follows up at the near post to put away any loose balls.

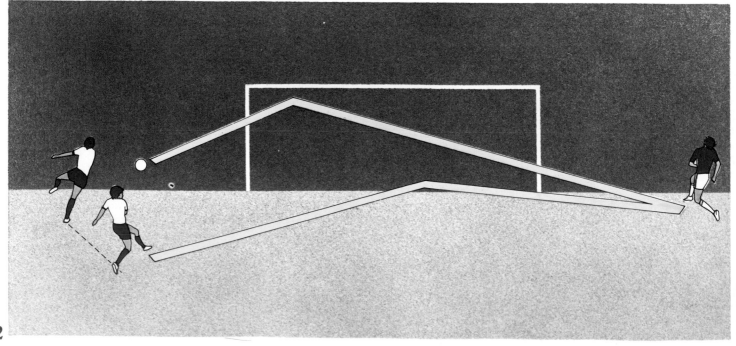

◀The goal scored by Manchester City winger Peter Barnes against Tottenham at White Hart Lane in April 1979 neatly illustrates the circumstances for a possible acute-angle shot as well as one variation of the technique itself. The move began with a Spurs corner being cleared from near the edge of the area by Dave Watson into the stride of Gary Owen—a fine example this of a defensive header, with distance and direction, setting up a quick counter-attack. Owen found Barnes towards the left, and the England man's speed and control took him past first the sliding challenge of Ossie Ardiles and then, just inside the area, the attempted recovery tackle by Steve Perryman, who had been trying to jockey him over the past 30 yards. As Barnes went on keeper Mark Kendall decided he was going for the shot from a tight angle, and he came off his near post towards the forward. But Barnes, poised and composed, found plenty of room to clip it between keeper and post into the far corner. Mike Channon (far post) and Brian Kidd in the middle were both unmarked for the ball pulled back—while Owen, who had made a supporting run of 60 yards or so, may also have had a good case for being aggrieved had Barnes' shot been saved by the keeper, missed the far post or simply screwed into the side-netting, as so many acute-angle shots do. As it was Barnes was the hero, not the villain.

▼ *The perfect finish: Peter Barnes retains his balance and control to clip his shot past Mark Kendall. He has steered the ball using the inside of his foot rather than blasting it with the instep.*

simply not enter their heads as an option. For others, it can be a decision easily regretted. For some, luck may play a part, with a 'go for the far post and it may drift in' approach paying off. For a privileged few, like Amarildo and Heighway, it will mean a place in football folklore.

There is more chance of it coming off, of course, if you have given it some attention in training. Practice for the acute-angle shot can be very static on a pitch, but using a wall can enable you to keep the routine going. Though it is possible to do it with just two players, and make it an enjoyable competitive game, the more people involved the more interesting and constructive the exercise will be.

With a number of players, they stand in two groups, one on each side of the goal about 20 yards away and at an angle. Two footballs are required, and it is best to mark the wall just inside each corner of the goal. One player runs in with the ball and shoots at the mark inside the far post. A player from the other group collects the rebound and runs in to shoot from the other corner. Having a keeper in goal will make the practice more realistic and demanding, as well as thus involving the whole team.

While concentrating on technique—keeping your bodyweight well forward, your head and knee over the ball with your ankle firm and your foot pointing down—stay aware of the keeper's positioning; if he moves too far off his line, try a shot to

the near post at the last moment, perhaps placing it with the side of your foot rather than the more powerful shots to the far post with the instep. Once the practice is going well a player from the other group can run in to support the shot, looking for the rebound.

Introducing a defender will make these exercises more match-like. The two groups move back until they are in an area between the penalty area and the touch-line and about 20 or 25 yards from the wall (or goal-line if you are practising on a pitch). The defender stands four or five yards in front, and the idea is to beat him before getting in your shot. A player from the second group then does the same. At first the defenders should just make their presence obvious, but later they should go

for a genuine attempt to win the ball or close down their man.

The exercise can easily be elaborated to create more pressure on the forwards. One suggestion is a supporting player standing on the edge of the area, with the man on the ball playing a one-two with him to beat the defender and set up the chance for the angled shot on the return pass. In the end you have a totally fluent situation, with the attacker going for the shot and the defender trying to stop the pass or tackle the man in possession.

Such practices will not only help you improve your shooting technique; by making you aware of the angled shot and how to exploit it they will make you a far less predictable and inhibited player when you are on the ball near goal.

The swerving shot

The basic recipe for a good long shot is accuracy plus power. A well-struck, well-placed effort from 20 or 25 yards will need something special to stop a score—and with youngsters this may apply from 15 yards or so. If you then add a further ingredient, that of swerve, and retain the same level of control on impact, then in theory at least you have the nearest thing possible to the perfect one-man strike.

That it is tried so rarely, even at the highest levels, is of course indicative of the degree of skill required to succeed. At the same time, the majority of shots hit from a reasonable distance possess a certain amount of 'natural' curve. It is no easy matter to hit a ball, especially a moving one, in a straight line; and many players, young ones in particular, often bend the ball when they do not wish to, when what they are after is a straight pass or shot.

The shot that swerves simply seeks to harness and exaggerate those qualities in a sort of power version of the swerving pass.

▲ *One of the finest 'benders' Europe has produced is Rainer Bonhof, who is especially dangerous with a dead ball. It took all his set-piece precision to spare the blushes of world champions West Germany in the friendly against England in February 1978, on the Munich ground where they had won the title. The Germans started the second half behind to a Stuart Pearson goal, but (as he had done the previous evening in the 'B' fixture at Augsburg) Ronnie Worm came on as sub and scored. Then, after considerable pressure, the Germans won a free-kick on the edge of the area. Though Mick Mills took up a good position on the end of the wall, Bonhof still went for that side. This picture captures the strike just after impact: he has hit right 'round' the ball with the inside of his foot, leaning well away from it and pivoting on the ball of his left foot. From this viewpoint it seems hard to believe that he has struck the ball with the inside of his right foot, or that the ball will bend to go inside the post. It did, beating Ray Clemence's late dive to give the hosts a 2–1 victory over their great rivals.*

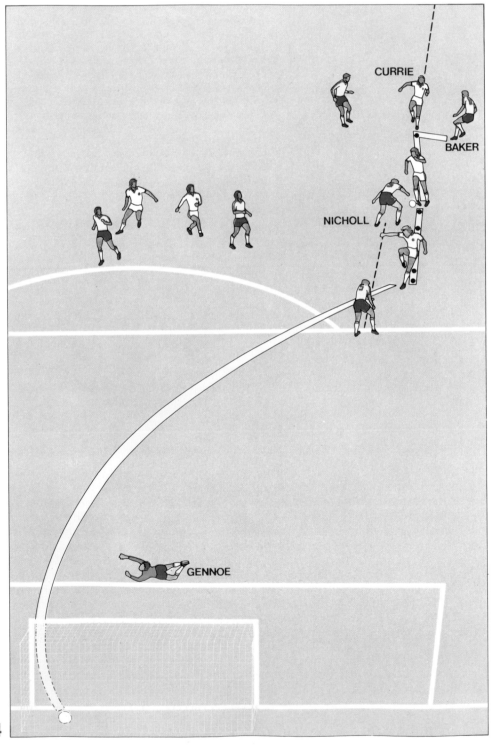

CURRIE

BAKER

NICHOLL

GENNOE

◀The swerving shot played with the inside of the foot cannot generate as much force as that with the outside of the instep. The technique is nearer to an extension of the swerving pass, still relying on placement rather than power. A shining example of when and how to use it came at Elland Road in November 1978 from one of the country's most inventive midfielders, Tony Currie, during Leeds' win over Southampton. Currie gained possession when he pounced on a mistimed pass to Alan Ball from Graham Baker. Taking the ball on, he was quickly confronted by centre-half Chris Nicholl, who backed off to hold him. Just outside the area Currie glanced up, looked down at the ball and then clipped an almost casual shot with the inside of his right foot, following through forwards and with a slightly bent leg rather than across his body with a straight leg. The result was a trajectory that took the ball well wide of Nicholl and then, with a fierce late curve, looping inside the far post, yards from the helpless Terry Gennoe. 'I saw the defender was blocking the keeper,' said Currie later, 'so I knew I could bend it round him.'

▼An outstanding feature of the 1978 World Cup in Argentina was the long-range shooting. Perhaps the most spectacular effort, in terms of context as well as content, was Arie Haan's goal against Italy in what was effectively a semi-final. The Dutch midfielder had already demonstrated his ability in this area three days before, when his 30-yarder made it 1–1 against West Germany—a goal, incidentally, that was the first conceded by keeper Sepp Maier in a record 475 minutes of World Cup action, since the Johan Neeskens penalty of the opening seconds of the 1974 final (see page 97). Now Haan went one better, scoring from fully 35 yards out. The goal resulted from a 75th-minute free-kick not far inside the Italian half. Seeing the chance early, Rudi Krol rolled a short pass to Haan, who took it forward a few paces before letting go. His full-blooded drive, neatly disguised by a characteristically short backlift, flew off low between two defenders—and started to bend. Dino Zoff saw it late—like the rest of his side he was caught by the quickly taken free-kick—and unlike Maier, who had been beaten by sheer pace, he had had the time to take a couple of steps before making the save. As it was he dived desperately at a ball that was on an ever-increasing curve away from him. He got the fingertips of his left hand to it, but it wasn't enough: the shot cannoned in off the post (inset) and Zoff's vision of holding up the World Cup was no more. Holland, 2–1 up and with a better goal difference, were as good as in their second successive final; their 'shoot on sight' policy had paid off yet again.

The same principles apply in terms of where and how you strike the ball, with the swerve operating in the same direction as the spin (see page 70) and that direction determined essentially by which side of the vertical mid-line you make contact with the ball. There is usually less need for height in the case of the shot, so contact is normally on the horizontal mid-line.

For the shot played with the outside of the foot the approach is much the same as for the swerving pass. The gradual increase in power stems from changes to the speed of the foot on impact, the degree of follow-through and the angle of the foot on impact. The more upright the position of the foot, the more power can be generated. At its extreme this means hitting the 'inside' of the ball with the outside of the top of the foot (the instep) rather than the leading 'edge' of the foot. This is the only way to cultivate the kind of power used by Arie Haan against Italy (right).

The same adjustments apply to the shot with the inside of the foot in the quest for power, though since the kicking foot must brush the 'outside' of the ball as the body leans the other way, this technique has distinct limits on the force it can produce. Unlike the shot with the outside of the foot, it also requires significant changes in approach: the non-kicking foot should be well away from the ball (perhaps as much as three ball-widths) to allow the long but lateral leg swing, and the body leans away from the ball before and during impact. For his notorious bending free-kicks Brazil's ace Roberto Rivelino used to approach the ball sometimes almost at right-angles to the intended target.

While most professionals, and certainly all lesser players, cannot hope to get near either the power or the degree of swerve attained by Rivelino (or more recently players like Rainer Bonhof, Michel Platini and Antonin Panenka in Europe), they can and do find that up to a point this technique can afford a high degree of swerve with pace while maintaining the necessary control to make it pay.

ZOFF

HAAN 2

KROL

HAAN 1

▲ *Klaus Fischer has been one of the most prolific scorers in the Bundesliga and for West Germany for many seasons, and here he notches up another goal for Schalke 04 in a game against MSV in Duisburg, drilling home a fierce swerving shot from the edge of the area with the outside of his right foot. Note how he has his body forward to keep the ball down as he has swung across it, and the position of his non-kicking foot, pointing at an angle to the target.*

◄Practice for the swerving shot should be based on the techniques for the swerving pass (see page 72). The idea is to build up power gradually, without sacrificing accuracy. Indeed you should aim to be even more precise here than with the pass, which if played into space allows a certain margin of error. While the shot played with the outside of your foot requires little change in approach, the 'inside' shot entails a significant change of approach, with your non-kicking foot placed further from the ball and your body leaning away from the ball on impact. Even then, there is a definite ceiling for most players on the degree of power possible. You can practise on your own using a wall and a suitable 'obstruction': shown here is a gymnasium box. This has the advantage of being angled; you can therefore practise round the top part first before moving on to the bigger curve needed to go round the bottom part. The lower the better—the keeper sees the shot late and he has further to dive to save it. The shot curling into the top corner of the net is far more likely to come from the flanks than from a straight position.

Penalties

Of the many moments of tension that occur in football, nothing compares with the pressure of a penalty at a critical point of a game. And it is the player who can handle that pressure, rather than the star forward or the best striker of a ball, who tends to be a side's penalty expert.

A penalty is a direct free-kick from 12 yards. There is an area 24 by 8 feet to aim at and the keeper cannot move meaningfully until after the ball is kicked. It is designed to be a punishment, a gift goal—but there are frequent misses and the most talented players are often reluctant to shoulder the responsibility.

There is not really a 'perfect penalty'. There are good ones, which result in a goal, and misses, which do not. The rest is immaterial. Taking penalties is as much about temperament as technique.

Penalties should not just be left to the regular taker. He may be injured, and now many knock-out competitions use them as deciders if extra time fails. So a few small hints may be helpful. Watch the ball and not the keeper; don't change your mind; if in doubt about actual technique,

go for a sensible compromise between power and position, using the inside of your instep, rather than for sheer pace; try to disguise your intention, though not at the cost of rhythm and control; bear in mind that most keepers are right-handed and right-footed and will tend to move that way; practise seriously, but you can only take a few at a time before bad habits creep in: if you have no partner, chalk a goal on a wall and mark the areas shown—a well-struck kick can hardly fail there.

▲ A firm, controlled shot into these areas almost guarantees a goal, even if the keeper guesses correctly, and in general it's preferable to the 'blasting' technique, with its obvious risks. Aim low rather than high—it takes the keeper longer to get to the ball—and 'go for the stanchion'. Every player should be able to take a good 'spot-kick', but don't practise it for too long: a penalty is by definition a one-off. A marked wall may be better than a keeper in a netted goal too—you can never be sure if he's really trying.

▶ *The two dramatic penalties in the 1974 World Cup final between West Germany and Holland—there had been none in the nine previous finals—were converted in very different ways, illustrating the point that a good penalty is simply one that goes in. The first, awarded by Jack Taylor after Uli Hoeness brought down Johan Cruyff, came with the game less than a minute old, and was only midfielder Johan Neeskens' second match touch. Despite his deft skills he went for power rather than position—and just got away with it. From this picture it seems Sepp Maier will save it, but in fact it was hit just right of centre. Had Maier stayed put, he would almost certainly have saved it; like most keepers, however, he moved to his right.*

▶ *Just 24 minutes later the Germans equalised from the spot after a dubious decision against Wim Jansen for a tackle on Bernd Holzenbein. Paul Breitner, left-back but stronger on his right-foot, opted for placement rather than power. Apparently cooler even than the free-kick specialists in the side (Beckenbauer and Bonhof), the Bayern Munich star obliged with a firm, clipped shot to the foot of the stanchion with Jan Jongbloed helpless. It's noticeable in both scenes how loath team-mates appear to be to hunt for the possible rebound off the keeper or the woodwork; perhaps they are transfixed by tension or have perfect confidence in their colleagues—neither of whom was a striker. Taking penalties is as much about temperament as technique—at any level of the game.*

The half-volley

The concept of the half-volley is a vital one in a whole range of ball games. It is the key to front-foot play in cricket, an irreplaceable mid-court ally in tennis, and the very essence of the drop-kick in rugby. In the most popular ball sport of them all it is a somewhat neglected area. In part this is because while it comes easily to 'natural' ball-players, many youngsters find it difficult to understand and even more demanding to master.

The reason for the 'high tariff' rating on the half-volley is twofold. First, the question of timing. A half-volley is when your foot makes contact with the ball as it hits the ground—actually the tiniest fraction of a second after it hits the ground. It must be exact to be effective. Second, the problem of contact. This applies only to the half-volley when it is used for power, nearly always for a shot but sometimes for a long pass, and not to the lay-off technique, where the side of the foot is used. Your foot has to be kept pointing down to keep the ball low, and so the contact area is small, an 'arched' area of the instep round the laces. The contact must therefore be as precise as the timing.

Mastering the half-volley comes down mainly to a matter of experience. Determined practice will create the timing and the touch that will, in turn, breed the confidence to apply the skill in matches without a second thought.

There are two main types of half-volley—the shot and the lay-off. Both are normally first-time reactions to a given situation where it is the only technique able to produce the desired affect in the time available, but both can also be the second or even third touch after control.

First, the 'power version'. The action involved in the half-volley is capable of generating great force (perhaps more than any other shooting technique), but accuracy must of course take priority. Indeed, if the approach is controlled, balanced and rhythmic and the contact good the result will almost automatically be a high degree of power, even without a strong follow-through.

The most important thing to remember is to keep your toe down; the rest—watching the ball carefully, head down if possible, arms out for balance—are simply the other basic principles of shooting. But with the half-volley the ball is actually rising as you strike it, so your ankle must be extended as you hit through or above the mid-line of the ball to ensure the ball stays down.

There are three common faults with the half-volley. The first is to misjudge where the ball will bounce, and therefore not place your non-kicking foot close enough to that point, causing you to stretch and overbalance to get contact. This ability

▲Determination as well as concentration from Poland's Grzegorz Lato as he tries a half-volley shot from just outside the six-yard area during the World Cup qualifier against East Germany at Chorzow in May 1981. The picture is a good illustration of some of the problems that can be involved with the technique. The first-time strike is only a possibility here if the ball is hit on the half-volley, yet at the same time the ball has come a little 'behind' him. So although his non-kicking foot is quite near the ball (a crucial consideration in the skill) he's having to really bend his right leg and swing his 'near' leg wide in order to direct the ball towards goal. This means it's very difficult for Lato to obey the golden rule of the half-volley: to keep the toe down and hit through or above the mid-line of the ball. While he stays well balanced on the ball of his right foot and keeps his head well down, his ankle is not fully extended and he's always going to be striking too low (or too 'late' if you like) on the rising ball. The result, a shot screwed high and wide over the bar, is no surprise. The power half-volley is nevertheless made for such 'instant' situations, a technique which makes anyone a more complete player and far more versatile and dangerous near goal, and Stal Mielec's winger was one of its most adept exponents as he fired his way to the top scoring spot in the 1974 World Cup finals with seven goals.

JENNINGS

RICE

SUNDERLAND

BLAGOJEVIC

PETRO

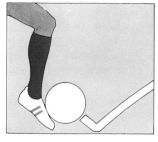

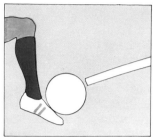

◀The half-volley is when you strike the ball a split-second after it hits the ground, as opposed to taking it 'on the full', or volleying it, as shown below left. As the ball is in fact already rising when you kick it, the most important consideration with the 'power' version is to make contact through or above the mid-line to keep the ball low; this means your toe must be pointing down. Timing is the key to the technique, and if the rhythm and control are there the timing will be right and the power will follow. Practise with a second-touch half-volley against a wall, gradually building up the power after getting the feel of the skill.

▶The half-volley with the inside of the foot is ideal for lay-offs, either first time or after controlling the ball with your chest or thigh. The best practice is a triangle, taking turns in the middle spot, but two players will do.

will only come with practice. The second is not keeping the instep vertical enough; this, like the third fault of lifting your head before contact, will lead to a poor strike, almost certainly with the ball going far too high.

The half-volley lay-off can be an extremely neat first-time ball as well as just another method of passing over short distances. A wonderfully astute example was played in England's victory against Hungary in Budapest as they struggled to make the 1982 World Cup finals. While that game will rightly be remembered for the two goals from Trevor Brooking—he had scored three in 43 previous internationals—the best pass of the evening was the lay-off that set up his second, the goal that restored the England lead.

Phil Neal, on the right touchline about level with the edge of the Hungarian area, was closed down and looking for a target. He found it in the form of Kevin Keegan, making a typically sharp run across the area towards the corner flag and pulling his marker with him. Neal clipped the ball in firmly to the England captain, who instead of taking the ball forward turned towards Neal a fraction before laying it off into space infield on the half-volley for Brooking. The angle of the pass was far more than 90° and it curved the ball into the space vacated by Keegan and his man. Brooking, already moving goalward, took full advantage, taking the ball a few yards before hitting a left-footed drive from 25 yards from just inside the far post. It was yet another reflection of the understanding

between the two men, and a superb illustration of an underrated but devastating skill. Keegan did not kick the ball: he merely steered it. No other technique could have produced that crucial pass.

The inside of the foot is perhaps the more common surface for the half-volley lay-off, and is often used too for the second-touch pass following control on the chest or thigh. It is a safe technique, a sort of half-volley push pass, with the same advantage of a large margin or area and the same limits of power.

Understanding and mastering the half-volley is not merely a matter of shooting and passing, either. A player who grasps the knack can extend the range of his controlling and turning techniques, with both sides of his feet, as noted on page 34.

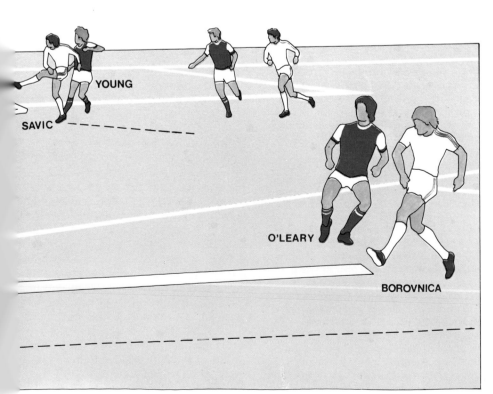

◀Arsenal's hopes in the 1978–79 UEFA Cup were ended at Highbury by one of the best goals seen in Europe that season. It was produced by Red Star Belgrade in the second leg of the third round, and came when they were trailing 1–0 on the night and heading for extra time. Less than two minutes remained when Borovnica received the ball on the left just inside the Gunners' half. He drifted inside, tracked by David O'Leary, and then stopped, put his foot on the ball, and turned to knock a casual pass back to Petrovic on the left. Petrovic wrong-footed his marker by moving away from goal towards the ball but playing a flicked backheel pass into space for Blagojevic, who had made a fine overlapping from behind Borovnica. Despite good covering by striker Alan Sunderland and the presence of full-back Pat Rice the Yugoslav got in his cross—a low, swerving, first-time centre played with the outside of his right foot. Dusan Savic moved to the ball first, coming across Willie Young and doing well to convert the chance past Pat Jennings with a fierce rising half-volley off his 'near' foot. It was a move that, with three examples of model technique and a fine piece of support play, showed how to make an opening; and a move that, with a crisp, confident half-volley, showed exactly how to exploit it and turn a match.

The low volley

1 Volleying is a very precise aspect of kicking the ball, usually an 'instant' response to a situation. The ball is often moving at speed and at an awkward angle, and a relatively small part of the foot is used for contact. There is only a small margin of error with a volley.

While it requires plenty of steady practice to acquire the right touch for the volley, the rewards are well worth the effort, particularly in front of goal. Quite apart from the great feeling that comes from striking the ball well—a thrill at its strongest, perhaps, with a rasping volley—it means that a far higher proportion of passes you receive in the danger area can be considered possible chances. This does not just mean first-time strikes, either: the first three goals featured in the ball control section of this book (by Hans Krankl, Frank Worthington and Pelé) were all remarkable pieces of skill polished off with a volley.

Nevertheless, in none of those examples was a shot on with the initial touch, and the power volley is essentially a first-time technique. Sometimes, of course, there seems little choice, and it can be the only possible decision, but the temptation can often be there to want to control the ball before volleying home. The element of surprise, particularly an advantage with the higher volley, may well have gone; the

◄For Ipswich Town's young striker Alan Brazil the dawn of the 1981–82 season presented a double challenge: to help steer his club to the League title they missed the previous spring and to gain a place in Scotland's World Cup plans for Spain. He began his quest with a typically aggressive performance against Sunderland at Portman Road, and this confident effort was an example from early in the game. As we pick it up, Brazil is making an angled run onto a bouncing through ball just inside the corner of the Sunderland area. The ball is approaching the top of its bounce (1), and he is shaping for the first-time volley. Defender Rob Hindmarch seems to give up the chase early as Brazil sets himself for the shot (2). The positioning of his non-kicking foot is vital; it governs the entire technique of volleying and once it's down you can't change it. Balanced and composed, Brazil prepares to shoot (3). Note how his right foot is already pointing down and how his head is steady. He has to hit slightly across the ball because if the angle of his approach in relation to that of the ball and the goal. In the follow-through picture (4), Brazil is a model of controlled force, using optimum rather than maximum power. Later in the season he scored all Ipswich's goals in a 5-2 win over League leaders Southampton.

keeper might have taken up a good position; defenders could have closed you down and covered your colleagues. Nearly always in scoring positions with a 'volleyable' ball, one touch is better than two. Badly hit volleys do not look very pretty, but missing the chance to shoot is a far worse crime than missing the target.

It is fairly obvious that confidence plays a significant role here, and this comes back to the right feel of the skill built up with patient and regular training. This means that you will not merely be able to volley the 'unavoidable' balls; you will also be prepared to move in and take a ball on the full in order to beat defenders to it. Far from spurning chances to volley, good finishers are always on the lookout for creating them, hoping to catch out opposition defences and keepers by stealing in and taking the ball early.

The first and possibly most important consideration in volleying technique is the positioning of your non-kicking or supporting foot. It provides the stability and balance for the whole skill, and once it is placed and you have begun to prepare for the ball to arrive there is no way you can change it and still get any meaningful contact. The rhythm and the timing so necessary for good contact are governed by this, so in training you should concentrate first on judging where to place the non-kicking foot rather than actual contact, both on through and crossed balls. In general, the earlier the ball is played in flight, the further your non-kicking foot should be from it.

Because a small area of the foot is used in volleying (the central part of the instep), and because this surface is convex rather than concave—that is, arched towards the ball rather that 'with it'—the contact must be very accurate and precise compared to most forms of passing and shooting. This is not difficult to apply to a loose ball in space or if you are moving on to a nicely weighted through pass, but it is far more testing when you are trying to put away crosses and under immediate pressure. And the majority of volley chances stem from the flanks in some form or other.

Begin your training programme with the basics, getting the feel of the straight volleyed pass before building up the power and starting to take and play the ball at various angles. Practise by throwing a ball against a wall from six or eight yards and adopting the right position for a simple return. At this stage concentrate on technique rather than power: correct placement of the non-kicking foot, head well over ball, foot pointing down, instep making contact through the horizontal mid-line of the ball, head still down after impact. While the follow-through is not long, learn not to snatch at the ball—

probably the most common contact fault in volleying as far as contact is concerned. Make the technique crisp yet rhythmic and controlled. Gradually increase your distance from the wall and then introduce a partner; with two players you can create slight angles on the passes and shots to make it more testing.

Another useful and very enjoyable practice for mastering the basic points is volley tennis. This can be two or even three a side and played almost anywhere there is space—in a gymnasium, on the beach, on a hard tennis court. It is touch that counts here, not power. The rules can be for one, two or three touches, with one or two bounces and using various parts of the body, depending on the level of skill of the participants. It is easy to make up simple rules, again according to how many people are playing and how good they are.

The next stage is to build up power, though this an aspect of volleying that is too often overstressed. A well-struck volley from say 12 yards should beat any keeper if it is placed accurately. A screamer may look spectacular, but it can involve unnecessary risks. So you should be aiming for optimum rather than maximum power as a general rule, combining accuracy with force.

The longer your leg swing, the faster your foot will be moving on impact and therefore the stronger the shot. Thus the lower the point at which the volley is played the more powerful the result. The danger is that the longer you delay the strike, the greater the chance of leaning back and getting under the ball—no problem for defenders clearing their lines, perhaps, but certainly one for strikers. With the higher type of front face volley your leg is more bent on impact, so it is easier to keep the ball down.

▼The first-time volley is usually a response to a situation rather than a choice, employed when any delay could be fatal. It is the great converter of half-chances, a skill for making something out of virtually nothing. This can often mean capitalising on a loose ball or punishing defenders' mistakes as well as getting on the end of a pass—particularly if you have the confidence to go in and make the ball yours. A good example came in the first leg of the League Cup semi-final between Leeds United and Southampton at Elland Road in January 1979, with the goal that gave the Saints a deserved draw. It stemmed from a big punt by keeper Terry Gennoe which was headed out long and wide by centre-half Paul Hart. The loose ball was picked up by Nick Holmes, and he crossed an early ball into the Leeds penalty area. Hart, now harried by Phil Boyer, headed out again the other way, but this time there was neither height nor distance on the clearance. The ball fell to the edge of the area where the young midfielder Steve Williams, alert to the chance, darted in between Eddie Gray and Trevor Hebberd to strike a perfectly timed right-foot volley past David Harvey; a powerful yet economical low drive. It was the kind of late, well-timed run more often associated with players feeding off the target man's knock-backs but Williams, quick to see he was in a better position to shoot than Hebberd, made the most of a defender's error. It made the score 2-2, and Southampton went on to reach their first League Cup final.

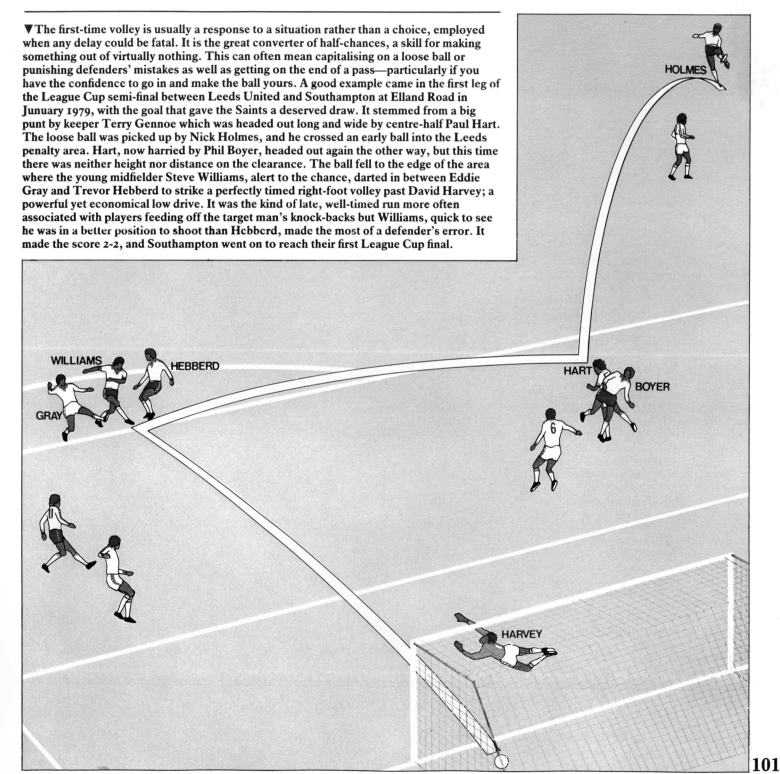

The most subtle and difficult of the frontal volleys is the 'dipper', a topspin lob used for beating stranded keepers or finding team-mates when you want height and a fast run-on. You lean back and the movement comes from the knee. With your ankle dipped down, the left and spin is imparted by a jabbing movement, making contact as high as possible on the ball. To start with, practise by dropping the ball from above your head a couple of yards in front of you; then step forward and strike the ball at about thigh height. A remarkable example of a 'fast ball' variation of the topspin volley, played on the run and at an angle to the goal, gave Steve Coppell a fine score in the incident recalled on page 172.

Finally, a few general tips about training for the volley may be useful. First try to make the practice as mobile as possible once you have the basic feel of the skill, as shown below; 'static' exercises may well give you a false impression of your ability in the fluid environment of a match situation. Second, practise with a leather ball (a proviso for all forms of kicking training, of course, but more particularly for shooting). Third, and again this applies to kicking in general and shooting in particular, try to build up the strength in your legs with simple exercises.

▲ *A marvellous illustration of volleying technique under pressure by Mario Kempes of Valencia during the 1980 European Cup Winners Cup final against Arsenal in Brussels. The Argentinian star has kept his balance and concentration despite the challenge of David O'Leary. No snatching here: the full leg extension testifies to that.*

▶ Once you have a good feel of the volley on your instep—you can learn how to get into the right position and the essentials of the technique itself by throwing a ball against a wall and hitting first-time returns—you should move on to a more mobile practice. The low volleyed shot is rarely an 'on-the-spot' skill like the high volley, and indeed the chance of a strike at goal is sometimes only created by making ground to the ball in the first place. The idea is to start by feeding balls in from the goal-line, either with a bounce (1) or 'on the full' (2), to a player making runs of a few yards inside the box. Contact is made round the level of the penalty spot. Concentrate here on timing and technique rather than power: the margin of error is small in any volley and contact has to be precise to keep the ball on target. A good volley automatically generates speed on the ball, and a well-hit, accurate shot from this kind of distance should beat any keeper, however prepared. These practices will help teach you the crucial art of placing your non-kicking foot as well as the technique itself: head well over the ball, knee pointing forward, toe well down with ankle fully extended on impact. The most common fault in approaching the volley is lifting your head and not keeping your foot pointing down, with the result that you hit under rather than through the ball. Later, as your touch improves, increase the angle of the passes round to take crosses from the flanks (3) and then practise moving on to the through ball (4). With teams or a squad it's easy to create relays using proper crosses.

The high volley

As a general rule, the higher the point at which a volley is played the more difficult it becomes to control. Thus the 'hip-turn' volley, struck around waist or hip height, is among the most testing kicking skills in the game. It can be played by defenders for first-time hooked clearances, or by wingers on the flanks to knock bouncing balls back into the middle; but both its most common and its most dramatic application is by forwards near goal.

Most volleys come from crosses rather than lay-backs, through passes, loose balls or errors by opponents. A small but noteworthy proportion of these will by the law of averages fall level with or slightly behind players rather than slightly in front of them and at waist or hip height. It is possible to convert such passes into chances, but only with a volley using your 'near' foot and a turn of 90° or more unless, as Gerd Müller does here, you are able to move to the ball going across you and use your 'far' foot.

Unlike the low, frontal volley the high turn volley is an acquired rather than natural technique, and to a certain extent adaptable according to the build and the talents of any given player. Scoring with such passes in the danger area is a matter of improvisation rather than style, results rather than appearances—and speed of thought and movement rather than power or even placement.

At the same time as being a very quick skill, it will often provide you with more time than you think, especially if you are confident about your judgment and ability. Where possible you should get into the line of flight early. As with any volley, think about the positioning of your non-kicking foot in relation to the angle be-

▲ *Gerd Müller bangs his waist-high volley past poor Peter Bonetti to complete one of the finest comebacks of World Cup history. Trailing 2-0 to the holders with only 20 minutes left of their 1970 quarter-final at León, West Germany scored twice to force extra time and now came the goal that wrought revenge for the final of four years before. It stemmed from yet another cross put over by substitute Jurgen Grabowski, whose bye-line centre floated over the England defence to the far post. There Hannes Löhr climbed above Keith Newton to nod the ball back across the face of the goal. It looped high over Müller's right shoulder but the stocky figure turned quickly, ran two or three yards and lunged at the still-falling ball. It was the only way he could have scored before Bobby Moore reached the ball—a classic example of the improvisation required with high volleys near goal. There was little style about his strike, but in the six-yard box it's scoring that counts, not appearances; one of the great finishers, Müller was quick to see the chance and quick to convert it.*

tween ball and target. As you are going to take the ball high with your 'leading' foot, and therefore early, the supporting foot should be as far from the ball as can be to allow the extension of the kicking leg.

You should aim to develop a swivelling movement of the body, a sort of 'corkscrew' motion which takes you through 90° or more to make contact—and still stay upright. There is a great temptation to lean back, away from the ball, and while this can generate more power (the longer the leg the greater the swing) it too easily forfeits balance and control. Your head should be as near to the ball as

possible, and the farther you lean away the less the chances of being able to watch the ball onto your foot.

Contact should be with the middle of your instep through the centre of the ball or slightly above it. A big percentage of high volleys are struck too low, with the result that they screw upwards off the top of the foot. If you get slightly on top of the ball then at least there is a possibility it will go in the right direction, and may retain enough pace to achieve the desired result. Another fault is to try to 'take the leather off the ball'; quite apart from being superfluous (the majority of high volleys are

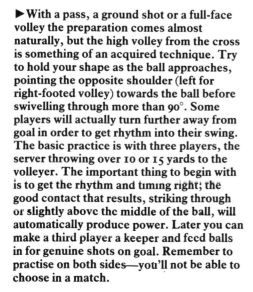

▶ With a pass, a ground shot or a full-face volley the preparation comes almost naturally, but the high volley from the cross is something of an acquired technique. Try to hold your shape as the ball approaches, pointing the opposite shoulder (left for right-footed volley) towards the ball before swivelling through more than 90°. Some players will actually turn further away from goal in order to get rhythm into their swing. The basic practice is with three players, the server throwing over 10 or 15 yards to the volleyer. The important thing to begin with is to get the rhythm and timing right; the good contact that results, striking through or slightly above the middle of the ball, will automatically produce power. Later you can make a third player a keeper and feed balls in for genuine shots on goal. Remember to practise on both sides—you'll not be able to choose in a match.

played only a few yards out and it is speed to the ball that counts, not speed of the ball), it will entail unnecessary risks and undermine your confidence. Many a chance has been wasted because players are not prepared to volley at goal in such situations. Think carefully about your positioning and about your rhythm and the power will take care of itself—the result of proper timing and the correct contact on the ball.

This area of volleying is an 'artificial' aspect of technique. The rudiments of the skill can be learned in training—you can even do the crucial swivel action without a ball—and worked on with a ball in practice. But this is only a framework: every one you try in a game will need some adaptation. As long as that sense of timing and the touch are there, the rest is down to improvisation on a basic theme.

▼Two of the finest touch players in Britain combined to produce a stunning early candidate for 'goal of the season' at White Hart Lane in 1979. It was a warm August evening when Tottenham took on Manchester United in the first leg of the League Cup's star second round encounter; and the goal that made it 2-0 saw the perfect marriage of the skills of midfielders Glenn Hoddle and Ossie Ardiles. It came from a first-half set piece, a free-kick 35 yards out following a foul on Terry Yorath. The Welshman took it himself, pushing the ball firmly to Hoddle just outside the area. Hoddle flicked the ball inside to Ardiles with the outside of his right foot and turned sharply to his left, round winger Micky Thomas, looking for a return. Ardiles, who like Hoddle was tightly marked with his back to goal as he received the ball, obliged with the second stage of the wall pass, into the space for Hoddle. The direction and weight were just right, but as Hoddle pointed out after the game: 'It was a bit high. I wasn't sure whether to take it on or hit it first time. In the split second I settled on the shot, and I'm thankful I did.' He launched himself several feet off the ground and hit a full-blooded volley that cannoned out of Gary Bailey's net off the stanchion. Unlike the swivelling technique used for crossed balls, where you have to use the 'near' foot, Hoddle was able to run on and use the foot farthest from the ball, virtually converting it into a straight volley by fine timing and a superb athletic approach. It looked like a brilliantly planned set-piece play, but in fact it was spontaneous. 'It was an off the cuff goal in every sense,' explained its scorer. 'We work on a lot of set pieces in training but not this one. I shouldn't even have been in that position, really. Normally for free-kicks around the area I stand on the ball, but I decided to stay up this time.' One of the reasons it looked so rehearsed was the movement off the ball, and credit must go to Chris Jones for the early run across the area that dragged Martin Buchan away and created space on the right for Hoddle.

The overhead kick

No player has yet devised a more spectacular way of scoring goals than the overhead kick. Though it can be used by defenders for a dramatic clearance and by wingers for a surprise cross, it captures the public imagination as the ultimate in terms of finishing.

Yet it is not the 'flashy' skill that it appears; a player uses the technique in very special circumstances, in situations where no other approach could possibly produce the immediate result he wants. It is often, ironically, a logical rather than brilliant course of action. Improvised yet obvious, it rarely draws criticism from team-mates or spectators if it fails. It is,

nevertheless, a tricky skill, requiring speed of both thought and movement, demanding a high level of agility and co-ordination, exact timing and not a little courage and commitment.

The overhead splits into two main types, though it should be emphasised that as it is a fairly adaptable and spontaneous skill these tend to blur in practice. First there is the 'over the shoulder' hooked volley, in affect an exaggerated version of the lean-back type of high volley. An example is Giorgio Chinaglia's angled effort shown below.

Then there is what we could call the true overhead, played with your kicking

▼ *Cosmos' superstar Giorgio Chinaglia scored a sensational goal with this looped 'bicycle' kick in the game against a World XI at Meadowlands in 1978, after a season in which he finished top NASL scorer for the second time in three years and set a record haul of 34 goals in 30 matches. It was this kind of commitment—he's gone for an acrobatic strike on artificial surface and in a friendly—that helped make the former Swansea player one of the highest paid footballers in the States and, later, a real force in the Cosmos structure. Notice how he uses his hand and forearm to break his fall on the hard ground, even though this particular kick is more of a high hooked volley than a genuine 'overhead'. The techniques involved are not quite as difficult as they appear; the overhead is largely a matter of patient practice, starting slowly to get the co-ordination and timing required. This in turn leads to the level of confidence displayed here by Chinaglia.*

▶ **Care should be taken with practising the overhead kick. To begin with, do it on soft ground, springy turf or sand. Ideally, start learning with an old thin mattress: this will hinder your take-off but help you to master the knack of landing—using your hands and forearms to break your fall. The approach should be gentle at first, using lobbed throws at head height rather than hard crosses, as you get acquainted with the special physical aspects of the technique as well as the vital co-ordination and timing. For a right-foot shot, you fling your left leg upward and your arms forward, thus pushing your body back. Keep your left leg as high as possible until just before impact, when your right leg, straightening from the knee to make contact at full extension, passes the other in a quick chopping motion. Put your arms down to break the fall, but keep your eye on the ball until well after the contact.**

leg vertical and your back parallel to the ground. Essentially it is a way of converting a ball which is at about head height but behind you. These are usually crosses and often moving at speed.

The foot used will almost certainly be the same one, no matter where the ball was played from. The advantages of two-footedness here are relatively small, while as a learned technique most players find it comes naturally to their better foot and develop the skill accordingly.

It is not, however, as complex as it seems. Once you have learned how to 'land', it is simply a question of patient practice for anyone who is agile and has good co-ordination, and will suddenly click after the basics have been tried. It should no longer be considered the province of a few privileged players; this kind of skilled improvisation must be seen as normal in opponents' goalmouths if defences are not going to continue to dominate the modern game.

◀ **This overhead from Dennis Tueart proved the deciding strike in Manchester City's 2-1 League Cup final win over Newcastle at Wembley in February 1976. The cross came from Willie Donachie on the left, a long ball looking for Tommy Booth at the far post. It found him, and Booth beat his man to nod the ball towards but slightly behind Tueart. Most players would have gone for a controlling touch and a turn or a lay-off, but the alert Tueart saw his chance and launched himself into a scissor-kick to send the ball inside the post.**

▼ *Practice makes perfect. Tueart's technique was so good that the ball bounced before going in; the problem with the overhead is usually getting 'under' the ball and skying it but the England man, his ankle cocked, makes exactly the right contact to keep the ball down and away from Mike Mahoney. Note also his hand already preparing to break the fall, with the fingers spread wide for maximum cover.*

HEADING THE BALL

Basic technique

Heading is unique to association football —no other sport uses the head to propel the ball. While some may claim that the game is at its best played on the ground, there is no doubt that heading is an integral and vital part of football, one with a peculiarly strong tradition in Britain and which, if anything, is growing rather than waning in importance. It is no longer simply a question of the centre-half clearing and the centre-forward trying to score; every outfield player should now be capable of doing both as well as using the various forms of headed pass.

The idea nevertheless still causes fear and doubt among many young players, who are convinced they will get hurt. This, plus the fact that it is such a special area of technique, means that more than any other aspect of the game it must be approached carefully in logical stages and mastered gradually. By following the basic principles (which apply whether you are defending or attacking) any youngster will develop touch, control and confidence with their heading. Using a light plastic ball to begin with will help.

The first principle is to use the correct contact surface. That is the flat frontal part of your forehead just below the hairline and above the gap between your eyes, where the skull is surprisingly tough. Remember too that a ball will indent up to two inches on impact if met correctly. The younger a boy learns where the ball should

◀ *Model technique for the power header from Bobby McDonald of Manchester City. All the basic elements of heading described above are there: firm contact with the forehead, eyes fixed firmly on the ball (even after impact), neck muscles flexed to support the head, and an obviously positive attitude to attack the ball. Notice how he has 'thrown' his head through his arms to get more power and distance as he pumps this early ball back into the opponents' danger area—a ploy reflecting the fact that heading for distance isn't always about clearance out of defensive positions.*

▶ Learning to head the ball with power must be a gradual process, and the younger you start the better. It's fine to start with a plastic ball, too, until you've mastered the correct position on the head. If you're on your own, throw a ball in the air and head it towards a wall, then move on to throwing it against the wall and heading the rebound. Keep one foot a little in front of the other, lean back as the ball approaches, tense your neck muscles and then thrust your head forward to make contact. You must hit the ball, not let it hit you. Later you can adjust this practice to heading the ball on the run, starting with a simple extension of the exercise just described, as shown here. Take off with a long last stride and push your 'free' leg forwards and upwards; arch your back and then 'punch' your head through your arms to attack the ball.

be struck the better; three or four years old is not too young with a gentle throw using a light ball.

The second rule is to keep your eyes open and on the ball. This may sound obvious enough—unlike the shot the ball is coming right at your eyes—but with heading there is a natural temptation to close your eyes just before you connect. It is a big cause—perhaps the main one—of mistimed headers, and thus of those headaches that can result.

Third, flex your neck muscles so that they are locked and thus support your head in taking the strain on impact. Heading is a passing and 'shooting' skill, the most obviously one-touch area of technique, and you need to tense the muscles to propel the ball rather than relax them to receive it.

The fourth guideline is to be positive. Attack and dominate the ball, hitting it rather than letting it hit you, and striking through it (like any striking action aimed at producing power) rather than at it. This is of course in part a question of attitude based on adopting the three principles already outlined.

Finally, practise patiently and often to improve your timing and your judgment. Begin if necessary with the simplest of ideas, such as gentle throws from a friend and runs at a ball suspended at an appropriate height below a crossbar. By starting with the basics and working carefully at building up your skill and technique you will soon find you are able to meet the ball with the optimum power every time, treating the header with the same amount of confidence as you do a shot with your foot.

Heading from defensive positions is usually a matter of 'power heading', getting distance, height and often width on the clearance. Whatever the source of the high ball—crosses, set pieces and long punts from the keeper are the main ones—your priority in defence is safety. If you can find a team-mate in space with the header that is a real bonus, but your first concern is to stop the opposition regaining possession in the danger area. A very general rule on crosses is to send the ball back the way it came, but on some it may be wiser to knock it out to the other flank or, in special cases, to put it away for a corner. If the point of contact is more than a few yards from the goal-line you can probably get a run at it, and this will obviously help with generating power, as well as overcoming the inertia to aid in your jumping.

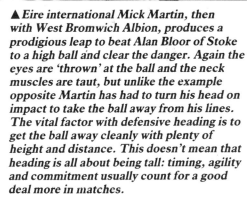

▲ *Eire international Mick Martin, then with West Bromwich Albion, produces a prodigious leap to beat Alan Bloor of Stoke to a high ball and clear the danger. Again the eyes are 'thrown' at the ball and the neck muscles are taut, but unlike the example opposite Martin has had to turn his head on impact to take the ball away from his lines. The vital factor with defensive heading is to get the ball away cleanly with plenty of height and distance. This doesn't mean that heading is all about being tall: timing, agility and commitment usually count for a good deal more in matches.*

◀This 'pig in the middle' practice can be played anywhere, and it obviously helps if one of the trio is a goalkeeper. The important thing is to build up the power stage by stage. Later you can introduce attackers to compete for the ball and make the exercise more competitive; this element seems to worry some youngsters as much as getting hurt by actually heading the ball.

◀◀Once the basic technique is mastered you can use various ways to improve your footwork and general heading. A simple example is improvised head tennis played over a goal or suitably high net. For power heading you can set one or two marks each side as targets for the ball to cross, perhaps worth so many points. If your partner falls short you literally have a 'head start'.

The headed pass

Between a quarter and a third of all goals come directly from headers, a statistic that automatically makes heading a vital feature of attacking play. Since opponents are trying to stop these scores, it is also a crucial aspect of defensive play.

But there is a third area of heading, one which is becoming increasingly important and sophisticated as coaches and players search for new ways of retaining possession, of creating and exploiting space, of opening up tight-marking, well-organised defences. This is the headed pass. With time and space 'shrinking' on the ground, this new battle for supremacy in the air has spread to every part of the pitch and is now fierce in midfield, where each side looks to players as targets to find teammates with first-time passes.

While this chapter concentrates on the two main aspects of this area of technique, often called target heading, it is worth recording a number of other broad forms of headed pass.

First, there is the power header. In defensive positions the priority on a high clearance has to be safety, and therefore you are usually concerned with areas rather than players as you go for height and distance to clear the danger. But finding a team-mate in space would of course make that clearance even more effective and set up the chance of a quick break against a side who still have people up in forward positions. Midfielders and forwards with deeper roles (especially wingers) should always be looking to make themselves available in space and pick up these balls inside their own half.

PETERS

Then there is the simple 'ground' pass, one which reflects a basic maxim of heading: do not jump to head the ball if you can make as good a contact by staying on your feet. This ball, as demonstrated by Ray Wilkins below, is the one that falls nicely for the head- or chest-high lay-off to a team-mate in space, anywhere in the right-angle between just behind square to almost straight in front, when you need to take quick advantage of the situation. It is usually played off a ball falling steeply, and a neat example came in the FA Cup final replay between Manchester City and Spurs at Wembley in 1981, to set up the City equaliser. It came when Tommy Hutchison, who had scored with headers for both sides in the first game, found himself under a high clearance about 25 yards out and to the right of the Tottenham goal; aware that Steve Mackenzie was in space square to his left, Hutchison crouched on impact to steer the ball carefully towards Mackenzie, who hit a screaming volley into the roof of the net with what was one of the best struck shots of the season.

Finally, and by far the most important and frequent, there are the headed passes near goal—the ball nodded back or down or across from beyond the far post to a player in a more likely scoring position, and the glancing header at the near post to a team-mate coming in behind or positioned at the far post. Since the techniques involved here are essentially the same as those used in the two forms of target heading, they are covered in the following sections on knocking down and flicking on the ball.

While target heading divides into these two broad types, the circumstances in

THE 'STANDING' PASS
The pass played with your feet on the ground appears the easiest of all headers, but as with all headers it is a first-time ball, a one-touch that has to be right. In the example shown here, taken during England's 2-0 win over Spain in the friendly at Barcelona in March 1980, Ray Wilkins is concentrating fiercely on getting the correct balance and contact to steer the ball to a team-mate. This pass is very useful for directing the falling head- or chest-high ball quickly to a better placed colleague or someone on a run. There is also a 'lower' stooping version, which some players (and more particularly ones on the short side) find an economical alternative to the high volleyed pass; it needs a little more time than the volley, but is ideal for the slower ball which comes at you at waist level and you want to put away over a few yards to a team-mate in space.

REEVES

RYAN

◄An example of each main type of target heading combined to set up the chance of a strike by John Ryan for Norwich City against Derby County in the First Division game at Carrow Road in September 1978. It came from a free-kick taken by right-back Kevin Bond inside the centre-circle, and his well-hit ball was directed at Martin Peters on the edge of the Derby area. Peters, facing the kick, got up well to beat his old England colleague Roy McFarland to the ball and direct it on to Kevin Reeves further inside the box. Finding the ball 'behind' him, with little chance of a strike at goal let alone a run at the ball, Reeves rode a strong challenge from left-back Steve Buckley to play the role of target man and knock the ball down firmly into the path of John Ryan, who was moving in quickly from midfield. Ryan, a midfielder with a taste for goals and a fine sense of timing (he was also the club's regular penalty taker) took the ball in his stride, cracking it low past John Middleton from well outside the area. A good example, incidentally, of a midfield player taking up a sensible position and then being confident enough to have a shot when the ball came to him. There can be few better models for heading than Peters, who throughout his long career showed how timing can pay—both in terms of runs and in terms of touch. Reeves' pass illustrates the point that the ball played back can sometimes be a better bet than the one played forward. At set pieces like this one defenders will be trying to get and stay goalside (note how every Norwich player is tightly marked up front) and it is the space in front of them, behind the forwards, that can be the area to exploit. The move shows how the headed pass is a very variable and adaptable area of play—if you have the solid technique.

►The knock-down to a colleague is an increasingly important aspect of the front man's play. In midfield positions the idea is to beat the defender to the ball and knock it 'into the hole' at an angle for a supporting player. The angle is important because it creates another angle for the receiver and therefore increases the chances of a break forward. The actual technique employed will depend on the nature of the high pass, the pressure on the front player and the options open to him—that is, where the ball can be safely played. The basic rules are to get there first, as always, and to concentrate on direction not power. With the faster, flatter type of pass it might well be a matter of taking a little pace off the ball and guiding it down for the man up in support. After making his pass, of course, the heading player should be looking to go forward and support the man on the ball. Nearer the opponents' area the target player can look to get wider in order to drag defenders out of position and play the ball down laterally for players coming through to exploit the gaps.

which a player will use them are much the same. Normally a forward, the target player will have his back to his opponents' goal, be trying to lose his marker and probably moving towards the ball as it is played up to him. Which type of headed pass he chooses (he may also take the ball down, lay it off with his feet or do a number of other things if it is below head height) will depend on the sort of pass he receives and where it is possible to direct his header to find an unmarked team-mate. This is an important area of technique for the front man: for every ball to his chest he will probably get half-a-dozen to his head.

The initial concern here, as with any aspect of competitive heading, is to get to the ball first, to get yourself between the ball and the defender. The advantage is with you: if the defender is going to win the ball he either has to get round in front of you or just hope you are going to miss it. This is partly why the short, 'flatter' ball is often more effective than the long hanging pass, which gives the defender time to move into a position to really compete for the ball.

Knocking the ball down or back entails playing a head pass towards your own goal-line, either to the feet of a team-mate but more often into space for someone on a supporting run. The precise technique employed will depend on the angle and power of the pass you

receive and, perhaps more important, on the movement of colleagues off the ball as you shape to go for the ball. Decide where you are to put that pass before you head the ball, not just before contact. If you take your eye off it you will almost certainly mistime it.

Aim to get up and well over the ball to steer it down. Though your neck needs to be taut, as with all forms of heading, you are looking for direction and control here, not power. If the pass is fairly hard and flat, and the pass you want to make is only 10 or 15 yards, then the problem is actually how to control the pace of the ball as you look to direct it down. In that situation you might find yourself leaning back as you land—though you should still hit the ball rather than let it hit you.

Creating an angle will not only help you with the technique; it will also disguise your intention a little. If you knock the ball back straight it all gets a little predictable as well as 'flat'.

The knock-back can be used anywhere in the opponents' half—or even just inside your own half. The nearer you are to your opponents' goal the more profitable it can be to go wide—for the front player to pull his men away from the middle and then knock the ball back at an angle to unmarked players in scoring positions out from goal.

This all reaches its logical conclusion with the genuine far-post return, the ball

headed back square across the goal or nodded back well out from goal, often from a set piece. It can be played simply because you are near the goal-line and there is little chance with a header at goal (an example is Tommy Booth's effort featured on page 106), or you may choose it even when there is a chance but there is a team-mate in a far better scoring position. This book has two illustrations—Tony Woodcock on page 155 and Dave Watson below—of players picking out colleagues rather than having a legitimate crack at goal themselves with a header. Other forwards and midfield players should always be looking to take up good positions when a cross goes to a team-mate at the far post, whether it is the knock-down or the 20-yard ball headed back to the edge of the area. Graeme Souness and Glenn Hoddle, both the owners of an array of fine shots, are two players who follow this rule.

Unlike the headed passes played elsewhere, which normally involve a run to the ball, the far-post knock-back is often made from a static position. The jump has to be straight up (sometimes even a little backward) without the benefit of forward movement; so you should learn to overcome that inertia by moving your feet and bending your knees in readiness for the leap, literally keeping on your toes. Otherwise much of the potential height can be lost in just 'getting started'.

The second broad area of target head-

KEEGAN

WATSON

BROOKING

◄The first two goals of England's quest for the 1980 European Championship, scored in a throbbing 4-3 win over Denmark in Copenhagen in September 1978, both came by way of Kevin Keegan headers from Trevor Brooking free-kicks. But while number one was a direct result of this famous combination (see page 185) the second was scored via the services of centre-half Dave Watson. Up in the danger area as usual for the set piece, Watson rose above several Danish defenders out from the far post to make good solid contact with Brooking's outswinger from the left. He had taken only a couple of small steps but timed his jump perfectly to make it look effortless. Most players in this position and with that cross would have gone for the directed header at goal—Watson has scored many a goal from such situations—but the Manchester City stopper instead opted for a carefully placed ball nodded down into space behind three Danes at the near post. Keegan, already moving forward for the possible rebound off a header at goal, read the pass quickly and moved fast, stealing in to dive full length and steer the ball home. Birger Jensen, who correctly had been in the middle of the goal for the strike by Watson, could do nothing to stop England going two up. Another fine example of the creative aspect of far-post knock-downs is featured with the Nottingham Forest goal against Liverpool on page 155.

ing, the flick-on, involves rather more skill and precision than the knock-back. Because the angles are so much greater, with the ball played in the opposite direction to the way you are facing, actual contact is far more exact with a small margin of error. In terms of sheer touch, it is the most demanding of all the heading techniques.

The flick-on is a 'young' footballing skill, a department of the game now increasingly exploited to set people free in space behind tight-marking defenders. The basic concept is simple: to play high balls towards a front player while teammates, often strong-running midfielders with a knack of timing their runs into good positions, look for the headed pass into space beyond and behind that player and his marker. This usually means that the heading player has come 'off his man', moving towards his own goal as he aims for the ball and, hopefully, drawing the defender with him and out of position as he competes for the ball.

The flick is thus very much a team move as well as a difficult technique, the header being the catalyst in a ploy that relies on a neatly weighted pass and a well-timed run by the receiving player. Players in good teams seem to develop almost a telepathic understanding for this type of move, and there are times when the flick can be made into space on the assumption that a player will be making that run, rather like the cross to the near post. It is important to remember that the supporting player should be on his way well before the ball reaches the target man. When the understanding is there and the link pays off it can be one of the deadliest passing skills in the game.

Technically the flick-on falls into two broad categories: the directed header and the glancing header. It must be emphasised, however, that it is an extremely flexible skill, and the variety of possible passes is almost endless given the variable nature of the three main factors involved —the trajectory and pace of the pass, the position of the front player and his marker, and the angle and speed of the run. All this makes it perhaps the most creative and interpretive area of heading, and if you master it you have a host of extra options in the air.

The directed header is used most often when the ball is a little 'low' and/or when the position (or intended position) of the receiving player creates a significant angle. Say you are about 35 yards from your opponents' goal in a central position; a high ball is played towards you from near the halfway line by the touchline, and before you go for it you spot a team-mate on a run a few yards off into the inside-right position. The angle you need to find the space in front of him will require more

▲ *Swindon Town striker Andy Rowland hooks home a low volley to score his side's second goal in the Division 3 promotion clash with Watford at the City Ground in April 1979.*

▼The move that created the goal began in the 78th minute when winger Ian Miller picked up a pass well inside the visitor's half. Jockeyed by Keith Pritchett and with cover behind from Roger Joslyn, Miller turned infield and played a simple pass to John Trollope, who had moved up in support. The veteran full-back (he was, incidentally, playing the 749th of his all-time record 770 League appearances for Swindon) had in his younger days been known for overdoing the overlap and sending in far from perfect crosses, but this time experience and age made their mark and, after a quick look up, he played a nicely flighted ball towards the head of Bryan Hamilton inside the area. Then a currrent Northern Ireland international midfielder with over 40 caps, Hamilton belied his lack of inches and slight build to head the ball backwards; it was too high to control and he knew that kind of flick can cause panic in defences. In the event it fell to Andy Rowland, who took full advantage.

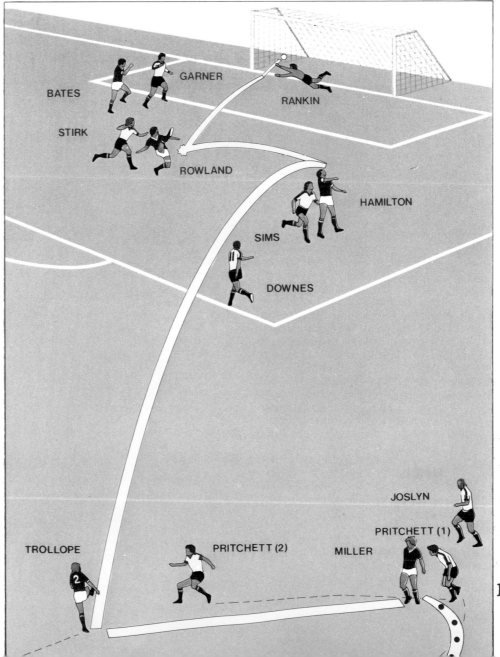

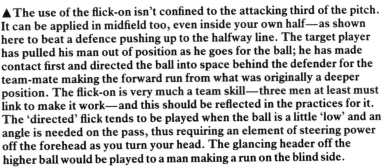

▲ The use of the flick-on isn't confined to the attacking third of the pitch. It can be applied in midfield too, even inside your own half—as shown here to beat a defence pushing up to the halfway line. The target player has pulled his man out of position as he goes for the ball; he has made contact first and directed the ball into space behind the defender for the team-mate making the forward run from what was originally a deeper position. The flick-on is very much a team skill—three men at least must link to make it work—and this should be reflected in the practices for it. The 'directed' flick tends to be played when the ball is a little 'low' and an angle is needed on the pass, thus requiring an element of steering power off the forehead as you turn your head. The glancing header off the higher ball would be played to a man making a run on the blind side.

► Just as the knock-back has its application in the danger area, principally with the ball nodded down or across from the far post, so the flick-on is used as the basis for the near-post header. This has been worked on hard by clubs over the last few years, especially with the early ball (see page 119) and with corners. For this there are two main approaches: the static one, relying on a tall player standing near the goal-line and flicking it on with a glancing or back header, often the merest of touches to beat his marker; and the mobile one, where a player makes a run to meet the corner, either across the edge of the six-yard area or, more often for the corner as opposed to the ball in open play, coming away from the near post itself. Kevin Keegan did just that against Northern Ireland in England's 4-0 European Championship win at Wembley in February 1979, to a low, hard inswinging corner from Trevor Brooking. Though his marker Jimmy Nicholl went with him, Keegan had stolen just enough space with his quick, late run. He fell forward as he flicked the ball on the 'inside' with his forehead, and it curled into the space his run had created behind him. Bob Latchford read the pass well to move in ahead of Pat Rice and steer the ball past the falling Pat Jennings. This goal is seen from a different angle on page 182.

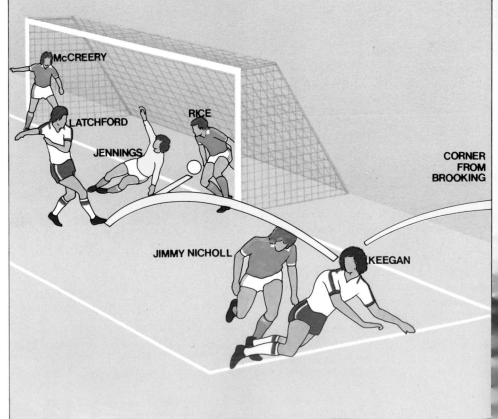

McCREERY

LATCHFORD

RICE

JENNINGS

JIMMY NICHOLL

KEEGAN

CORNER
FROM
BROOKING

◄ *The forehead should always be the contact surface for the headed pass. Here Paul Mariner turns his head in an attempt to direct a high ball into the path of Alan Brazil during the UEFA Cup quarter-final with St Etienne at Portman Road in March 1981. While Mariner has attacked the ball, the challenge of French international defender Patrick Battiston lacks both technique and commitment. It could be because Ipswich, 4-1 up from their trip to France, were on their way to a 7-2 aggregate win. Mariner scored three of those goals—and set up a couple more with his headed passes. By pulling defenders wide front players can often direct headers into the resulting space.*

▼ A ring of players round the 'target man' can form the framework for a range of routines and games for all types of headed pass, including the angled flick-on (A), the back header (B) and the basic knock-down (C), provided you tailor the practice to suit your level of skill and experience. At its simplest, the heading player would knock the ball back to the server, who would then slip it to the next player in the circle, or the receiver could select his own direction on the pass. At the other end of the scale there are the pressure training exercises where all the passers have a ball and a coach nominates both the server and the receiver for the headed pass, calling out instructions to test the ability of the target player to turn and respond quickly as well as make the pass. Whatever the level of skill, two points are worth bearing in mind. First, such passes are played to you when you are marked, often very tight, so the practice should have a defender shadowing the target player when the basic idea has been grasped. This is a good thing for youngsters, many of whom are a little worried about competing in the air for the ball. Second, don't try for the headed pass if it's not on; that's simply cultivating a bad habit. If the pass is poor use a different contact surface, still finding the nominated receiver if possible or simply controlling the ball and passing with the second touch if not. A good 'caller' could help here by nominating a suitable player.

than a deft touch. The pass by Paul Mariner on the left illustrates the point as he steers the ball carefully to his colleague. Anything with a very wide angle is a glancing header; anything less than a right-angle is really a knock-back.

The basics are the same, of course. You still have to judge the flight of the ball, time your run and jump well for the deflection. But the touch, far less emphatic, must be near perfect for the glancing header to pay off.

Improvisation is the name of the game here. There are the 'skimmers', high fast balls just helped on with the merest of contacts; there are the back-headers, a handy ploy anywhere (see the goal on page 178) but particularly effective at the near post on set pieces, where it sends the ball on for a third player to score, and works even against the most prepared of defences; there are more angled flicks into the danger area; and as Andy King has already demonstrated (see page 85) there are even glancing headers you can play to yourself.

These deflections rely on virtually perfect timing and touch to be successful, and so a great deal of practice is needed to attain that level of control. Every time you try it in matches will in some way be different from the last one, so practices for the flick-on should concentrate on those two aspects—timing the run and the jump and acquiring the quality of touch. The idea featured on the right is a good starting point for target heading in general, and for the basic contacts required for the flicks, but it should be made as mobile as possible to reflect the precise and collective nature of the move. Thus the supporting players should break on the 'flanks' for the flick-on, and the front player should be marked by a defender. The running is important not just to provide a mobile target for the header; it also helps to get players thinking about runs off those kind of high passes. The flick-on is an under-used skill because not enough players make intelligent runs at the right time in the right place.

Heading at goal

With so many goals coming from headers —the proportion can be as high as 40% inside the six-yard area—learning to head well in attacking positions is obviously a vital aspect of a player's football development. This should not be confined to forwards; since a fair number of headed goals come from free-kicks and corners, it is important that all outfield players, and especially the taller defenders, get plenty of practice in this area.

The attacking header is a part of the game where invention and improvisation are often more relevant than pure technique. The basics have to be right, of course, but heading for goal will almost always involve a slight variation each time, simply because there are so many factors involved in one movement and because, unlike heading out of defence, there is not a wide margin to play with. The header at the 'other end' has to go through a gap 24′ by 8′ and must beat a goalkeeper with special privileges and probably one or two defenders on the way. You cannot, then, afford to sacrifice accuracy in the quest for power.

The factors that make the attacking header an area of such 'adjustable' technique include the height and direction of the cross, your position in relation to the ball and the goal, the movement of defenders, the positioning of the keeper and even the ground conditions. Only by gradually building up the standard of your practice sessions and then applying what you have learned in matches can you acquire a proper feel for the type of reactions and skills necessary. Once you are confident enough about your heading ability, you can concentrate on developing the positional sense and timing needed to meet the ball on the run, using the ideas outlined on page 79 for the cross.

In addition to the four principles of heading skill covered under basic technique—correct contact surface, eyes on the ball, flexing of neck muscles, attacking the ball—there are a couple of special guidelines which can help with heading for goal. The fundamental one, almost a truism, is to make sure you get to the ball first. This also applies in defence, of course, but in attacking positions you are nearly always having to lose your marker, too, and that makes timing the run that much more difficult. If you do not get in ahead of your man there is little chance of keeping the ball down for a strike at goal or even of causing any real trouble in the opponents' danger area.

Players who are outstanding in the air can give the impression they are 'hanging' when they are about to head the ball, but it is an illusion created by perfect timing. They are at the peak of their jump at precisely the right moment while their

▲ *Bernd Cullmann looks on as John Wark exploits the ample space given him by the Cologne defence to head Ipswich into a 1-0 lead during the first leg of their UEFA Cup semi-final in April 1979. This goal, one of 14 the midfielder amassed in Ipswich's campaign to equal the European record held by José Altafini of AC Milan in 1963, proved the only one of the game and a crucial score. At 5′ 10½″ Wark is yet another fine example of the fact that it's not height that counts in heading for goal. Most of the great headers of a ball in the past three decades—men like Sandor Kocsis (Hungary), Uwe Seeler (West Germany), Pelé (Brazil), Denis Law (Scotland), Roberto Bettega (Italy)—are well under six feet tall. One of the best Britain has ever produced, equally adept in the air in defence or attack, was Wark's own team-mate Kevin Beattie. When it comes to the attacking header it's other factors that count: anticipation and judgment to pick up the flight early and time the run; agility to get up well and direct awkward balls goalwards; aggression and commitment to compete for the ball whatever the odds and make that solid contact.*

challengers are still on the way up or already on the way down. This aerial advantage enables them to make maximum use of their upper body and neck for power. There is a great temptation for youngsters and less experienced players to move in too early for the cross, especially on the far post, a tendency to rush in for fear of missing the action, and this must be carefully watched in practice.

Another tip is to concentrate on the ball and nothing else once you are going for it. Check on the positions and likely movements of defenders before you make your move, not during it, and have a firm idea of where you want that ball to go. Once you take your eye off it your chances of

making good contact are drastically reduced. Being aware of the position of other players and movement is a matter of cultivating the knack of seeing peripherally; this is discussed in more detail on page 135.

The two main areas where the power header figures in attack are the mid-goal and the far post. The precise nature of the contact will be determined by the factors already mentioned, and in terms of actual technique two of those are most important: the angle of the cross in relation to your position and the goal, and the height of the cross. The simplest example at the far post is when your run is on the line to the intended target, probably the 'back'

▼ *Oscar Fabbiani of Tampa Bay Rowdies fails to capitalise on his well-timed approach with this header against Vancouver Whitecaps during the 1979 Soccer Bowl at Meadowlands, directing it too near keeper Phil Parkes. The picture nevertheless illustrates the basic point about meeting the cross played behind the defence: Fabbiani had the ball in his sights and going forward, was able to get above the retreating defenders. Born in Argentina but a naturalised Chilean, he set the NASL alight with his scoring performances in his first season there, and despite a slump in the play-offs (only one goal) still finished one point ahead of 1978 leader Giorgio Chinaglia in the combined goals and assists totals with 58 points from 26 games.*

◄After a 3-0 European Championship win in Bulgaria and a respectable goalless draw in Sweden, England were looking forward to rounding off their 1979 summer tour with a result against Austria in Vienna. But in a pulsating game, those hopes were finally dashed by a headed goal from Bruno Pezzey. The talented centre-back had already demonstrated his ability with well-timed runs and powerful headers at set pieces, giving his side the lead following a corner (see page 181). Now, in the 70th minute, after England had pulled back from 3-1 down to 3-3, he did it again, this time from a free-kick. From about 30 yards out, Robert Sara put over a ball to the far side of the England area, but Dave Watson was somehow still in conversation with the referee, leaving Phil Thompson and Phil Neal marking three Austrians. As the kick came over two of them moved away, putting the two England men in two minds. Meanwhile Pezzey, running in about 15 yards, rose to meet the ball with what was a 'free' header, making perfect contact to direct it down and past the diving Ray Clemence, who had replaced Peter Shilton in goal for the second half.

▲A neat 'double header' secured Northern Ireland's win over Bulgaria in Sofia in November 1979—a result that gave the province their first away victory in over four years and took them, after three games, to the top of their European Championship group. The clinching goal came just eight minutes from time, at a point where the Irish were far more concerned with preserving their slender lead than adding to it. Indeed as Martin O'Neill took the corner they had only three men inside the area, and unless the cross was a bit special the Bulgarians should have had little trouble. So it seemed when the ball came over to the near post area but outside the six-yard box. Centre-half Chris Nicholl made ground very quickly from his position on the near post (where, one suspects, the corner was intended to go) and though moving away from goal he got up well to beat a defender and turn his head to direct the ball goalward. New cap Billy Caskey also reacted quicker than the defenders; from his position beyond the far post he nipped in behind Gotchev (7) to deflect the ball past goalkeeper Goranov with a firm header. Heading at goal is as much about anticipation and improvisation than actual technique or power, getting there first.

post. This is usually favourite because it means the keeper has to change direction twice—once to follow the ball across and again to follow the header—but if the height of the ball or position of the keeper suggest otherwise then aim for the 'front' post, which will be the nearest.

Another problem area is whether or not to head down. While it is true that keepers take longer to dive down than across or across and upwards, it is also true that the 'straight' header is the quickest route to goal—and that a defender on the line cannot stop a perfectly placed header into the corner without giving away a penalty. Circumstances will often dictate the choice, but in either case it is important to get well over the ball to keep it down unless you are very close to goal.

It is rare that you will be allowed a free 'frontal' header at goal, with a good angle and no markers to compete with. Usually there will be defenders in the way and the angles can be testing. So the practices for the attacking header, though beginning with the basic timing of the run and the actual contact, should try as soon as the

touch is good enough to reflect the competitive nature of the skill. The basic idea is to adapt the routines set out on page 76 for crossing the ball.

Finally, always bear in mind that heading is a skill involving and needing the whole body. Footwork, leg power for jumping, arms for balance, the trunk for that arching power—all are part of the same co-ordinated technique.

THE NEAR-POST HEADER

While coaches and defenders are now more aware of the danger at the near post, there is still little they can do if a forward gets there first to a ball with pace and finds the right sort of contact. This is particularly effective with the early ball curled in behind the defenders. It is a pass aimed at the space out from the near post rather than at a player—the so-called 'dead space' between the back markers and the goal-line or goalkeeper.

It is a dangerous ball even if the player does not make contact on the near post: the retreating defenders will be dealing with a fast-moving ball and facing their

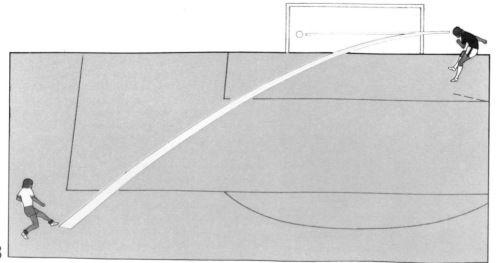

◀Although practice for the attacking header can be a little dull without a squad of players, it is worth working hard at it to get the timing and build up your power and confidence. Start with simple passes, throws if necessary—until that confidence is there—and then move on to longer passes, at first using an adaptation of the idea shown on page 121. Remember the three main points: give yourself plenty of room for the run, pick up the flight early, and attack the ball. Don't concentrate on getting a long or high jump—that will come naturally as a result of attacking the ball and making contact at the highest possible point. If you can, always add a defender and a keeper to make the practice more realistic as well as more testing: heading for goal is all about competing for the ball.

own goal, while the keeper may have an awkward decision—to come for a ball that could be moving away from him or to readjust his position on the line. There is the fair chance, too, that another forward can be coming in on the far post for a shot or a diving header. A difficult ball for defenders to cope with, then, but also a difficult one to get just right.

Though the basic theory can be traced to the Hungarian team of the 1950s and the Brazilians who followed them as the world's best, it was at an English club that the ploy was worked out and then perfected in the air, with West Ham manager Ron Greenwood applying the traditional British heading skills to the continental idea of the cross played in to the near post rather than the far post. Its two greatest exponents were Martin Peters and Geoff Hurst, and while Peters was himself a great judge of a run (particularly on the blind side) and a fine header of a ball, it was his crosses and Hurst's headers that caught the eye.

The first example for England came in their third game together for their country, in the 1966 World Cup quarter-final with Argentina (see over) but there were others, notably a goal against Belgium in Brussels in February 1970, when Peters' curling cross came from the other side, the right, and Hurst, this time under severe pressure from Jeck, put far more power into a header that flew inside the far post. Peters reckons it the best near-post header he has ever seen; Hurst says the 1966 classic, a delicate glancing flick off the top of his forehead, was 'a super goal —one that Martin and me had practised a million times'.

▲ *East Germany's keeper Hans-Ulrich Grapenthin finds himself facing the wrong way and misses his one-handed punch as Andrzej Buncol steals in to beat him to the near-post cross and score with his header, steering it well away from the defender on the line. This brave, well-executed strike gave Poland a 1-0 win over their neighbours in the tight three-team World Cup qualifying group at Chorzow in May 1981 to set his country on the road to Spain.*

▼ The near-post header is an 'area' of heading rather than a technique, but there are basically two types of contact involved. When you meet the ball 'inside' the near post, the best placement is usually just inside that post (A), especially off the flatter, faster cross. The important thing is to get there ahead of your marker, but to arrive at precisely the right moment to make solid directed contact. The exact form of contact will depend on the height and angle of the cross: it may be necessary to jump to get the control or perhaps stoop into a more crouched position. Either way, you should attack the ball and direct it firmly rather than let it hit you. If the ball does brush off your forehead, there's a chance of it still finding the target if you've aimed for the near post. When you meet the ball outside the line of the near post on an angled run, or when you have come away from the goal and your marker to get to the ball (B) and he is still goalside of you, the best placement is usually the far post with a glancing header, especially with the flighted cross. These are merely guidelines, however; the variety of heading techniques employed on the near post is almost endless. A four-man practice with a defender and goalkeeper is ideal.

▼ *The groping fingers of Argentina's Antonio Roma fail to stop Geoff Hurst's glancing header looping past him to squeeze inside the far post and give England the only goal of the controversial World Cup quarter-final at Wembley in 1966. The nicely flighted cross, met by Hurst about six yards out from the near post on an angled run, was supplied by clubmate Martin Peters (far left).*

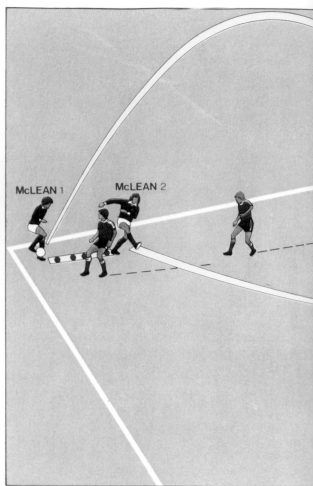

This linking aspect is central to the near-post cross. The pass is made into a space, not to a player, and it takes a special type of thinking to make it work. As Geoff Hurst explains: 'It's not easy for a player to appreciate that he can safely put the ball in short when his team-mates look as though they're waiting for it to be hit to the far side of the goal. It's vital to understand and trust each other. Martin had no doubts because he knew I'd make an effort to get there. The crucial thing for me was that I moved late. If I went too early then the man marking me would have a chance to adjust. The timing had to be just right. Stealing half a yard on him was enough to get a touch.'

The near-post cross can be a problem area to grasp and master because of these apparent contradictions. It relies on close co-operation and understanding between players, yet the cross is played into space not to people. The receiver must get there first, yet he must arrive 'late'; that is he must beat his marker to the ball but time his run so that he meets the ball at speed —any check will rob the move of momentum. It is thus easy to see why it is such a testing, precise area of skill.

The huge potential rewards, however, make the hard and patient practice required well worth the effort. This involves working on the timing of the runs; both long and short, as well as getting the right sort of contact. You can start by running at an angle onto passes thrown by a friend and trying to steer or deflect them to specific parts of the netted goal, moving on to kicked crosses as soon as possible, including those played from deeper positions—the 'early ball'. Because the near-post header is all about beating the defender and getting to the ball first you should introduce a marking player as soon as your level of skill permits.

If that level is sufficiently high throughout the team, then move on to a group routine. First, set up a full-back, a winger, a front player and a goalkeeper, playing across the pitch. The keeper throws the ball to the right-back on the 'halfway line' near the 'touchline'. He turns and plays the ball down the line to the winger, who takes it on towards the 'goal-line'. A few yards short the winger turns and lays it back for the supporting full-back to hit first time to the near-post, where the front player should have made his run. Defenders can be brought in to this activity, but with such a difficult skill they can easily dominate if 'activated' too soon, so it's as well to introduce 'passive' defenders to begin with. The practice can easily be expanded to involve the whole team or squad, with six or seven attackers playing four or five defenders in one full-size goal, using the wingers to get in near-post crosses.

Though the early near-post cross is the killer ball, the ball from the goal-line (either the set piece or in open play) is still a dangerous one when linked to an angled run and a good header. The goal with which Horst Hrubesch wrapped up the 1980 European Championship for West Germany (see pages 149 and 183) was quite simply a direct strike at the near-post from a corner-kick, with the goalmouth packed with Belgian defenders.

We have obviously concentrated in this section on the header at the near-post, and this is by far the most common way of converting chances in that part of the danger area. But the move can be completed by a shot too, and a superb example of the early ball bringing a volleyed goal (by West Ham) is illustrated under the chapter on the swerving pass on page 71.

THE DIVING HEADER

Only the overhead kick can match or beat the diving header as a spectacular strike at goal. And, like that skill, it is a dramatic but not ostentatious way of converting half-chances into scores, a way of reaching balls when no other approach could produce a realistic contact. Its use is not confined to attack, of course; defenders in tight situations will use it to clear the low cross or loose ball when, again, it is the only reliable form of contact in the circumstances.

◄Rangers wrote another proud chapter in their long European history in November 1978 against the Dutch champions PSV Eindhoven. Having beaten Juventus in the first round of the European Cup the Scottish treble holders could only manage a scoreless draw in the first leg of the second round, and the prospects looked bleak as they travelled to Holland to play a side who had won both the Dutch League and the UEFA Cup the previous May. They looked even worse when Lubse put the hosts ahead, but in the 147th minute of the tie Rangers scored their first goal, a near-post beauty that paved the way for a great fightback. It stemmed from a long and fairly hopeful ball from Tom Forsyth out on the left, which fell to Krijgh on the edge of the near box. With nobody near him, the full-back bungled his half-hearted clearance and then, under pressure from Alex MacDonald, he skied his second attempt—straight to the feet of Tommy McLean just inside the area. The little winger trapped the ball neatly, feinted to move out wide and then turned inside, totally selling World Cup defender Erny Brandts, before hitting an early curling cross low to the corner of the six-yard area, out from the near post. MacDonald had made ground well to beat the unfortunate Krijgh to the ball and his diving header gave Van Engelen no chance. A very Scottish goal—tricky ball skills and a brave header—to severely punish a defensive error and set Rangers up for a 3-2 win that was PSV's first home defeat in 23 years of European competition.

▼Before practising the diving header you should have mastered the basic contact involved. Don't get too ambitious at first: start perhaps with short straight throws that you can head back to the server over soft ground, or perhaps on matting if you're indoors. Always concentrate on heading the ball, though, and not on your landing—you'll instinctively push your hands out for protection and bending your arms will break your fall. The next stage is to learn to 'take off', a movement many players find surprisingly difficult. Technique is relatively unimportant here; just get your body off the ground and going forward. Finally, move on to the simple two- or four-man exercises shown below, with throws to begin with if necessary. Now you can start to work on timing your short runs and the knack of 'throwing' your eyes and head at the ball, aiming to put the ball away in the most suitable part of the net. But, as in matches, only dive when it's on: the skill is tailored for a specific type of situation and you could get hurt in practice as well as in matches.

Non-technical qualities—commitment, bravery and self-assurance—are probably more important for the diving header than the actual technique. The skill is rarely performed badly; rather it is not performed at all as players lacking a little in courage are unwilling to recognise the situations that may call for quick and bold measures. At the same time there is something almost instinctive about it, and the players who do go in among the flying boots (Joe Jordan, whose brave headers have helped Scotland to the World Cup finals on three occasions, and Brian Kidd are notable recent examples in Britain) do it often and do it well. It at first seems remarkable, too, that they so rarely get badly hurt; perhaps in that sense fortune does favour the brave.

Like any header, you have to attack the ball. The diving header is not a technique for half measures. If the contact is good, the chances of success are very high: the element of surprise and the natural pace of the ball give goalkeepers little chance.

While there are certain pointers that can help with the diving header, and guidelines for sensible practice are given with the diagram on the previous page, it is essentially an instant, impulsive, improvised skill. In this book there are no less than seven 'action replays' where the goal was scored with one: John Robertson (page 47), Kevin Keegan (112), Alex Mac-Donald (121), Frank Stapleton (144), Brian Talbot (160), Trevor Francis (162) and of course Roberto Bettega (see below). All were different propositions—two were scored at the near post, four at the far post and one in mid-goal, and the marking, type of pass and angles involved varied considerably. But they all had one thing in common; there was almost certainly no way any of them could have been scored by any other means. The diving header, overpraised but underused at most levels of the game, is a very necessary football skill.

◀ *Roy McFarland turns to see Italy's Roberto Bettega make it 2-0 in the World Cup at Rome in November 1976, thus securing a win that gave England an uphill task to qualify. Franco Causio, who made the telling pass 35 yards from goal, is now also unmarked in a scoring position.*

▼ The move showed not only the traditional Italian virtues of pace and flair but also an unexpected degree of versatility. The key figure was Romeo Benetti, better known as a midfield destroyer than a creative runner, and he played a wall pass with Causio—a nonchalant flick with the inside of his 'back' foot to sell Emlyn Hughes—and then took the return on towards the England line and, despite pressure from Dave Clement, sent over a left-foot cross. Bettega had begun his run outside the box and no-one picked him up as he came in behind the unsuspecting McFarland, checking at the last moment to twist and reach the low centre. When Benetti played the first pass eight England outfield men were behind the ball.

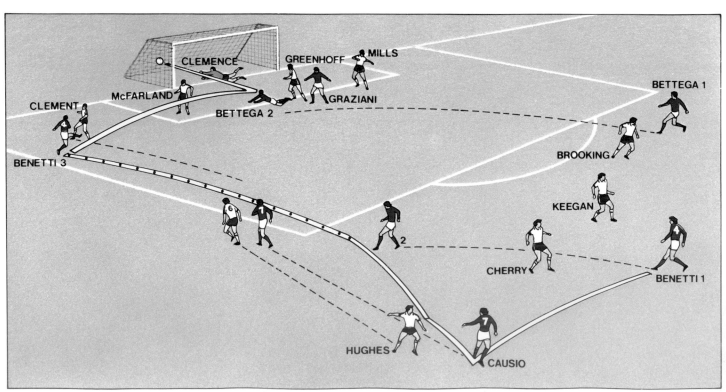

WINNING THE BALL

Basic technique

Possession is everything in football. No team can play without the ball, and good teams are not going to 'give it away' very often. Tackling is the most obvious way of trying to regain that possession.

While the emphasis in defence on organisation and denying space has undermined its role, and while the emphasis in attack on teamwork and interpassing has made it less common, tackling remains a crucial and irreplaceable part of defensive play. Not only does a good tackle stop an attack; it can also, by winning the ball, set up attacks against a side at that moment

▼ *While the ultimate objective with tackling is to regain possession, the first concern is to win the challenge and get the ball away from your opponent in order to break up the attack. This fine example is from Jan Pot of Fort Lauderdale Strikers, timing his contact perfectly to knock the ball away from Cosmos midfielder Julio Cesar Romero. From the upright position of his upper body it's fairly clear that he was always in command of this confrontation. Were a Cosmos player to pick up the loose ball, the tackle has still allowed the Strikers time to cover by diverting the attack.*

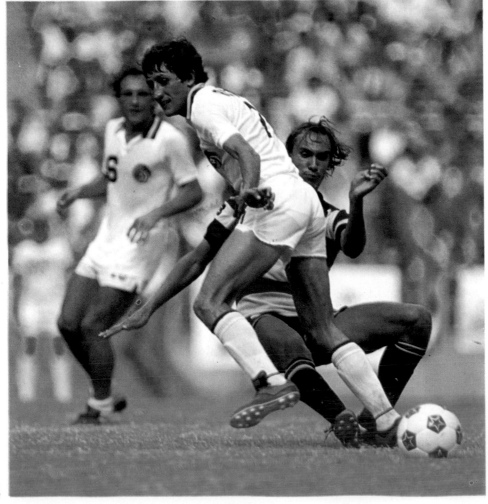

vulnerable to the quick counter. There are times, too, when only a tackle will save the day—and there are occasions when a poor tackle will cost your team a match.

Before looking at the techniques of tackling, it is worth recording some general points about the art and the tactics of this often neglected part of football skill.

First, every member of the team should know how to tackle; it is not a defender's skill, any more than shooting is a forward's skill. When you lose possession every player, irrespective of position, becomes a defender and must aim to regain that possession. Usually forwards are expected merely to close down their opponents, restricting their movement and options rather than putting in a tackle, but a ball-winning challenge in an upfield position (when there is little to lose) can leave the defence highly vulnerable.

Second, where and when you tackle is as important as how you tackle. If you are exposed and left alone to face an attacker in a dangerous position, there is usually more profit in delaying and backing off, in denying him space and trying to jockey him away from the danger zone, than in

diving in and risking all. Commit yourself only if you have cover or there really is no choice. Ideally of course the tackle should be as the player receives the ball, while he is concentrating on controlling it. If he has settled on the ball, the approach must be more cautious. Fools rush in to tackles then, with a good chance of being beaten and thus putting team-mates under pressure. You must hold off, trying to provoke him into a definite move, perhaps an error when he allows the ball to get that little bit too far from him—and then pounce. You should try and manoeuvre your opponent into a position where you can decide the timing of the tackle, where his chances of avoiding the tackle are small as possible and where, if the tackle does fail, the mistake is least costly. You should thus make the tackle when you are as sure as you can be in the circumstances that you will win the day.

Third, when you do tackle make it count. Half-hearted challenges not only increase the chances of failure; they also increase the chances of your getting hurt. Aggression and determination are essential ingredients of the good tackle and are far more important than size or strength, as the number of fine tacklers of short stature and limited weight—Nobby Stiles, Billy Bremner, Steve Perryman, and so on—would indicate. Indeed in the case of the block tackle height can be a positive disadvantage.

Finally, do not relax with the ball when you do win it. There is a great temptation to 'sit' on the ball for a second after you come away from a good challenge, but quite apart from the chance of being tackled by the dispossessed player you will also waste the chance of a quick-counter attack against opponents who have pushed forward. So move away quickly, playing the ball forward if possible to capitalise on the tangible as well as the psychological victory you have won. Be quick into the tackle, quick out of the tackle—and quick after the tackle.

The most basic of all the tackling techniques is the block tackle, and this divides into two main types. The front block tackle is described in detail opposite; the side block tackle applies the same principles but the approach is made from the side of (or just behind) the opponent. Here you try and get as close as possible before committing yourself, then swivel on the non-tackling foot to bring yourself round into the block tackle position. The most common fault is to try this when you are behind the ball; you are unable to pivot into the block position and are therefore unable to transfer your bodyweight forward into the tackle. If you have to make the challenge from a position behind the ball, the best course of action would be a recovery tackle.

▲ The front block tackle. The first rule is never to tackle 'out of range': close down your opponent, staying composed and balanced, and wait for the moment when you can put your whole weight behind the challenge. Play the ball just as your opponent tries to play it, placing your standing foot beside the ball, and drive through to make contact with the inside of that foot—the largest and safest possible stopping surface. Keep the ankle firm and the foot at right angles or, even better to prevent the ball rolling over it, in a slightly cocked position. On contact transfer the full weight of your body onto the tackling leg; keep your head down, shoulders forward, with your knee well over the ball. Both knees should be slightly bent to absorb the impact and to lower the centre of gravity. Contact must be made forcefully through the middle of the ball; too high and you'll go 'over the top', too low and the ball will squirt up, possibly not in your favour. Maintain firm pressure as you follow through with a determined challenge to come away with the ball. Though this technique is highly modified in matches, the errors are still the same. The first is going in too early, stretching with your opponent out of reach and often better balanced. Not getting over the ball is another fault: the tackler leans back or to the side, with the result that not enough force goes through the line of the tackle. Tall players tend to lean forward but then not move their lower body in the direction of the challenge—block tackling is a skill using the forward movement of the whole body. It is also about commitment: a half-hearted challenge will almost certainly fail.

◄ The technique illustrated above is very much a model one; the large number of variable factors involved in a tackle, plus the tendency of players to be strongly one-sided in challenging for the ball, means it is a flexible, adaptable skill. A good tackler is one who wins the ball consistently. This leads to highly individualistic styles, such as the scooping action of Ipswich skipper Mick Mills, seen about to demonstrate it to Paul Power of Manchester City.

The recovery tackle

With the spotlight on support play, the short-passing game and attacking in depth, the block tackle has lost a little of its lustre and importance in recent years. The recovery tackle, however, played when chasing or intercepting an opponent from a position behind or square of him, has hardly decreased in value and still enjoys two classic uses.

One is for the defender (usually a full-back) on the attacker (often a winger) who is moving down the flank at speed towards the goal-line, having already beaten that defender or at least got nearer the opponents' goal-line, whether by a pass or a run. The other is for the opponent who breaks clear near the middle with a direct route to goal or with perhaps only thin cover, when only a tackle can prevent a one-to-one on the keeper and a possible score. Again, he could have beaten defenders with the ball or been put clear with a through pass.

It is a far more dramatic skill, in terms of speed, technique and context, than the block tackle. While for the tackle on the touchlines there will still be some cover and the attacker has to get 'across' you for

a direct threat on goal (preventing the cross is thus usually the main problem), the break down the middle can be desperate: no cover, the attacker goalside of you and 'only the keeper to beat'. If you miss the tackle he is away with you out of the action, or he gains a free-kick in a dangerous position or even a penalty. The timing must be near perfect, and you can still look a poor judge if he just manages to get

that crucial touch in as your foot homes in to make contact with the ball.

In whatever circumstances the technique is used, it is not intended to literally 'win the ball'. It is designed for winning the challenge, stopping the attack by getting the ball away to a colleague or, near touch, for the relative safety of a throw-in or even corner. If the ball can be secured with luck or a hooking action of the foot or a combination of the two then that is a bonus—but it is increasing the risk unnecessarily to try.

The basic problem, assuming you can catch your opponent, is to time your chal-

▶ *The recovery tackle isn't necessarily about lunging legs. Here Bayern Munich defender Klaus Augenthaler, aware of the skill and speed of his opponent, Klaus Allofs of Fortuna Düsseldorf, goes for an 'optimum' challenge. Not wishing to risk a mistimed tackle in that position—with the chance of letting Allofs get in a dangerous cross or give away a penalty—he comes across at an angle and just does enough to get a well-timed contact on the ball, steering it to safety. Rigid distinctions between front and side block tackles, between sliding and standing recovery tackles, are usually pointless and misleading; the essence of tackling is to succeed at all costs, and that means legally dispossessing your opponent. The exact method, as long as it works, is relatively unimportant. It is also an area of the game where psychological factors play a big role. A good tackler, either by reputation or by a couple of strong, ball-winning challenges early on in the match, will enjoy an immediate advantage; his opponent will think twice about taking him on, start to look for the tackle rather than concentrate on the ball, and is more likely to choose an easy and therefore probably less dangerous alternative course of action. Any player, defender or forward, feels more confident and 'complete' if he knows he can tackle well with a variety of techniques, and of course the sight of a well-timed tackle (especially by a forward covering back) will lift the spirits of a side—and lower those of the opposition—whether it wins the ball or simply delays the attack.*

◄The recovery tackle. In fact with this tight angle the tackler doesn't leave himself enough room to work the sweeping action required, and the attacker may cut across his intended path and head for goal. Start gently with the practice, preferably on soft ground and even without an opponent, just to get a feel for the timing and action of the technique. Then move on to timing your tackle on a friend dribbling at jogging pace, building up the speed gradually until he is moving past you in earnest and you are turning as he goes past to catch him and get in your tackle. If you play it for real neither of you will get hurt.

lenge to make firm contact at precisely the right moment when both of you and the ball are moving at speed. This means trying to get as far 'back', as square as possible to your intended victim. This will help with vision and increase the chances of solid contact; if you have the 'time', veer slightly away from your man in the last few yards before you make the tackle. Of course, if the attacker has a real 'head start' on you or if he is very quick, you will be happy just to get a touch to 'nick' the ball away. Good players are always looking to ride tackles (see page 58) so the timing must be precise.

The exact technique and style used will be determined by a variety of factors, most notably the angle of your approach.

Basically you want to place your non-tackling foot as close to your opponent as possible. If you are using the 'far' leg (as above) you go to ground with your weight supported by that leg as your tackling foot comes sliding through to make contact. If the motion is a sweep rather than a push, it well may take the ball out even if the opponent gets a touch as you challenge.

Like any tackle, this is a technique involving the whole body and relying on a rhythmic and co-ordinated movement rather than just 'sticking a leg out'. The approach and the tackle itself should be forceful, with a strong follow-through. The body contact must come from the momentum of the successful tackle, not from a foul that takes the man's legs.

▼ With fast players like Mickey Thomas, pictured here in his Manchester United days, you don't always have a chance to make an angle for the tackle and you're forced to just go for that vital touch. In this case Alan Ainscow lunges with his 'near leg' to make contact and steer the ball to Archie Gemmill with his out-turned foot, doing well to time his dive and make contact when the ball is 'between touches' by Thomas. The third member of Birmingham City's retreating midfield, Alan Curbishley, looks on. Even good players tend to be very 'one-footed' with their tackling, using their stronger side no matter what the position. Had Ainscow been coming in from Thomas' right, he almost certainly would have used the same leg with the classic recovery technique shown above.

Closing down

When a team loses the ball every member of it becomes a defender, with the ultimate aim of regaining possession to launch an attack. The most productive way to do this is through tackling, but as we have seen the risks involved limit this approach to certain circumstances. More often regaining possession is a question of making it difficult for opponents to retain it. This means putting pressure on them by denying them space in which to make positive moves.

In football, of course, space is time; and in a match, time is the friend of the defenders, enabling them to get organised and cover. Closing down opponents gives your side that time—it is a mechanism for delay. No defence likes to turn and play facing their own goal; they want the ball and their opponents in front of them, in view, and if the midfielders are closing down people well away from goal then they will enjoy that advantage.

But it is more than just a holding operation. At some stage the pattern will change. The player on the ball, unable to settle and with his options restricted, will be frustrated into an error of control or forced to make a risky pass if he wants to make progress forward—and then your team can regain possession. Taken to an extreme, it has been the key to many a giant-killing act in cup competitions, where the less talented side, fit and full of fight, have harried and pressured their more illustrious opponents, getting tight as they receive a pass, not allowing skilled players to dwell on the ball, preventing them playing their usual game, and looking for the one mistake that could decide the match. Denying space means denying expression—in other words, not permitting players the time and opportunity to play creatively.

This philosophy begins with the forwards. Indeed you could say it starts with a front player closing down a defender as he receives a throw from the keeper. Even here this sort of pressure can pay off, with a supporting midfield player making it four-on-four and forcing the man on the ball to play it back, risk a hasty pass or put in a long hopeful ball upfield. The harrying of defenders can also produce a more indirect benefit: indecision is likely to spread through a side as the tactic unsettles the defence, while your midfielders and defenders will derive a boost to their confidence from seeing their forwards involved in that way.

Closing down opponents is nevertheless of prime importance in the middle and defensive thirds of the field. The basic theory is that the player nearest the man receiving the ball does the job; often, of course, this will be the defender who has been assigned to mark that man. The key to 'getting tight' is to do it as the ball arrives; if you move in after he has control he can easily knock it past you. But the greatest danger in closing down is committing yourself at the wrong time. If you are beaten with a simple feint and 'left for dead', the ploy has been turned around—instead of the man on the ball being under pressure he could be moving forward in plenty of space against a side that is now one player short in cover. While the art of closing down is denying space, far better to stand off and keep player and ball in view than rush in and 'sell yourself'. This is why, despite being a non-ball skill, it is vital to practise. When you have the basic

BLOCKING THE TURN
A defender who allows an opponent facing his own goal to turn with the ball gives him the chance to move the ball forward and thus put himself out of the game, so where possible he should block that turn without selling himself. But there are two common mistakes: getting too close to your man and going in too hard. The ideal position is about three or four feet away—far enough to see player and ball, close enough to make an effective challenge. React to the movement of the ball, not your opponent, who may try to dummy you. Be patient: he is the one with the problem. The time to tackle is when your opponent is half-turned, when his is least balanced.

idea and are involved in competitive games, look to follow your man if he passes under pressure—he may well be after the return ball.

It is far more difficult to close down a player in the middle of the pitch than near the touchline, simply because he has more options. It is thus even more important in such situations to stay balanced and alert, ready to move quickly in any direction, and watching the ball carefully but aware of what is happening around you (team-mates should help here with calling advice and instructions).

The positioning of colleagues is important, too. Covering for players closing down opponents means operating on a 'dog leg' basis in order that the supporting defender can see both the challenging player and the ball and cover any forward movement. In general the nearer the play is to goal the tighter the cover can and should be, but exact positioning may depend on the speed of the players.

While closing down is an individual technique, it is often employed within a general plan. That is, teams decide before a game on their lines of confrontation—where on the pitch they will apply the brake to the opposition. In Britain it tends to be well forward and 'immediate', a big factor in making the game faster and more physical, but in countries where the natural instincts are towards ball skills, and where the climate would not permit such activity, the line is nearer the defended goal and the move late. In Italy, for example, they tend to leave most of the midfield alone and close down nearer the edge of the defensive 'third' of the pitch, blocking the routes to goal. With little space to exploit behind the defence (especially with the sweeper), the opposition become frustrated and push people forward to help—leaving themselves vulnerable to the quick counter-attack when they lose possession. These collective applications of denying space are covered in more depth under the section on defensive team play.

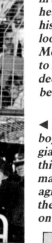

▲ *Trying to close down a player moving at speed near the middle of the pitch presents real problems, as Boca Juniors defender Mouzo discovers in confronting Noyos of Talleres in an Argentinian National League game. He has avoided a head-on approach and 'showed' Noyos to his left (possibly his best side) but the forward, ball on outside of left foot, looks to be about to swerve to his left (possibly his best). Mouzo may well be too committed and may not even be able to record a desperate tackle. In the danger area this sort of decision may be unavoidable, but further out the defender is better off to slow up rather than challenge his opponent.*

◄ *Barcelona's veteran Asensi shuts down Real Madrid's new boy Laurie Cunningham in the clash of the Spanish League's giants at the Bernabeu in September 1979. The visitors have this situation well in hand: as Cunningham struggles to master a difficult pass on the touchline, Asensi moves in agressively before he can control the ball. The position of the covering player, Zuviria, enables Asensi to get an angle on Cunningham and pin him to the line.*

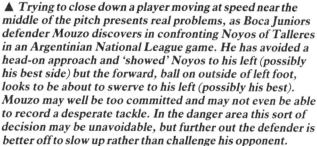

◄◄To get the knack of the timing involved—closing down is all about 'getting tight' as the ball is passed to the receiver, not after he has controlled it—practise by following in passes over 15 or 20 yards. Try to move within a stride or two of your partner to shut him down, cutting out his chances of moving or passing forward.

◄A three-man routine will illustrate the other major aspect of closing down: the importance of getting tight without selling yourself. The defender closes down the receiver at an angle so that the space in front of him is shut off. The man without the ball is thus dictating play and putting pressure on the man with the ball—one of the arts in defending well.

Jockeying

▲ The player required to jockey most often is the full-back, simply because of the limited space in which he usually operates. Here Wales left-back Joey Jones demonstrates all the virtues of the technique as he stalks winger Arthur Graham in the 3–0 win over Scotland at Cardiff in May 1979. He is just a yard away—close enough to get in a tackle or nick the ball away if the chance presents itself but far enough away to monitor and react to any movement; he is at an angle to the forward, not committed in any direction and poised to move anywhere quickly; he is watching the ball not the man; and he is blocking the direct route to goal. He has thus undermined his opponent's possession. While fans often want full-backs to 'get stuck in', Jones' patient attitude is the correct one.

▲ This sequence from the 1981 FA Charity Shield game illustrates both the value and problems of cover when jockeying an opponent. Knowing that Ossie Ardiles is moving back at speed to help out, Spurs right-back Steve Perryman can afford to seal the outside route; if he were on his own he would probably try to push Aston Villa winger Tony Morley down the line, but by keeping well past his man he tempts him successfully inside. With Ardiles there, the immediate threat has been thwarted on the edge of the danger area. But now it's taking two players to mark one. If Ardiles were further infield he could still perform this function but also look to pick up other attackers; in this position he is now of less value and Morley has options.

Jockeying is a 'directional' form of closing down. Rather than merely holding up your opponent to delay the attack, you are trying to steer him the way you want him to go, nearly always to a less dangerous position away from goal into decreasing space. As the term implies, you are 'sitting' on him, you are in the saddle. Jockeying is not just a case of covering his changes of direction; it is a positive technique that seeks to seize the initiative from the man on the ball. It is a 'shadow' skill, one which rarely gains the appreciation or earns the applause handed out for the well-timed tackle, but a crucial function of defensive play.

The key to jockeying well is positioning, getting yourself at an angle to block off the direct route to goal and put the man on the ball in two minds—whether to go on the inside or the outside. The stance is important. If you face him 'flat on' you are open to feints and dummies, so keep one foot in front of the other and your body at an angle to your man. Stay fairly crouched, keeping balanced with your knees slightly bent so that you can move quickly in any direction.

The jockeying process can obviously be a real cat-and-mouse affair. This applies even more if the adversaries know each other's strengths and weaknesses from previous encounters. Defenders will try to push opponents onto the side they prefer for the possible challenge, while a smart attacker will be aware of the advantages of going on the marker's weaker side. In the case of the full-back, the stronger side is nearly always the one nearest the touchline, thus reinforcing his intention to push the attacker wide. No matter what the standard of play, these basic strengths and weaknesses play an important role in all aspects of tackling and closing down.

'NICKING' THE BALL

The aim of closing down and jockeying an opponent with the ball is to hold him up, denying him space in which to move and express himself and to stop him advancing to more threatening positions. The onus is then on him to find a way out. At some stage he will have to glance up to check on the options, or perhaps lose total control of the ball for a fraction of a second—long enough for you to get that vital contact. Sometimes it can be a full tackle, but often it's just a touch, getting a foot in to 'nick' the ball away into touch or a colleague. You don't always look for it—nicking the ball is simply an instant reaction to the chance of dispossessing opponents—and you try not to do it when it might send the ball straight to another opponent. Another situation in which it can happen is when you are covering back for the break. As you come across you may sense the chance to nip and take the ball 'off his toe' to push it to a team-mate (as above). This mini-skill is something of a knack, but like any technique it deserves practice. In the exercise shown here, player B tries to nick the ball in the centre-circle as his friends take turns to dribble towards the centre spot.

Trying to deny space is not always a simple matter of one player pitting his wits against another. It can also be a case of two-against-one. If the odds favour the attacker, the ground rule for the defender is to try and jockey the man with the ball but not move in close, in an attempt to hold up the move (and reduce the angle of the pass) until a team-mate can cover the second opponent. If the odds favour the defenders, then they should position themselves so that one is free to commit himself to a challenge for the ball while the other covers. As in most closing down situations, the timing will depend on where exactly the confrontation occurs.

◀Jockeying an opponent with the ball 25 or 30 yards from goal is a matter of keeping him away from the danger area, giving your defence time to cover while manoeuvring him into a position where, ideally, you can get in a good tackle or nick the ball away to safety. If the winger doesn't take you on or lay off a ball to a team-mate in support, there are two ways he can go. Nearly always you should be looking to jockey him towards the touchline (B), away from goal and with diminishing space in which to work, continuing to close him down but not committing yourself to a challenge unless a good chance presents itself or he tries to beat you. This will reduce his options and give another defender (4) time to cover, thus denying the man on the ball the use of the space behind you. If your opponent does come inside (C)—and you may even pull him that way if you have a covering player there or if it is his weak side—then you stay goalside of him. He has more options here but the play is in front of the defence, there is plenty of cover and the man in possession is marked tight.

131

TACTICS

The nature of team play

The secret of a side's success in football is to harness the talents of its individual members to a team pattern that best suits them. It is a valid cliché in the game that the stronger teams are greater as a unit than the sum of their individual skills. As the young footballer grows older he must therefore become more aware that he is involved in a team sport and appreciate the needs of his team-mates.

In the preceding sections the emphasis has been on learning techniques and sharpening skills, and this is of course of paramount importance. Young players can be restricted if the demands of team play are imposed on them too early. In the formative years it is crucial for players to be able to control the ball, to kick the ball correctly, to pass the ball accurately, to be confident of heading technique, to tackle well and so on.

Once the basics have been mastered team coaching becomes more straightforward. We believe that this should not be imposed too quickly or heavily on youngsters, that 11-year-olds worrying about the shape of playing 4-4-2 or trying to grasp the principles of marking are being given wrong priorities. But football is a team game, and the earlier any player starts to 'think collectively', to see the application of those basic skills in an overall framework, the better he will be.

The joy of a successful side, of course, is that it can cater for all types of talents. However delightful the abilities of a Glenn Hoddle or a Trevor Francis, no team can be a consistent winner with 11 of similar attributes and style. Team play revolves around blending different types, and this chemistry is its fascination.

The role of the coach is to put the talents at his disposal to their best collective use. The most famous team in England's history is the one which won the World Cup under Alf Ramsey in 1966. Ramsey has been criticised for setting a trend without wingers, as many top clubs copied his method. Yet many critics forget that England's first three games included a winger as Ramsey shuffled his pack and looked for his most effective blend. Manchester United's John Connelly played against Uruguay, Terry Paine of Southampton was tried next against Mexico, and then came France and an opportunity for Liverpool's Ian Callaghan to establish himself. None of the three convinced the England manager they were the right man.

That World Cup winning side was full of marvellous 'team' players who gave consistent and solid support to the world-class abilities of Gordon Banks in goal, Bobby Moore in the centre of the defence and Bobby Charlton, the orchestrator in midfield.

George Cohen from Fulham was a buccaneering full-back, a fitness fanatic rather than a stylist. But the England defence knew that George was so quick that very few wingers would be able to run

▼Few football fans would dispute Pelé's position as the finest player of his generation. Allied to his great physical abilities—strength, agility, balance, speed and massive ball skills—there was another quality that brought the game some unforgettable moments. It was more than imagination: it was a joyful quest for the impossible. The 1970 World Cup in Mexico was littered with such gems, but one stands out above all. It did not involve control nor produce a goal; it was simply unrivalled for sheer audacity and invention. It came in the semi-final against Brazil's bitter rivals Uruguay in Guadalajara. Clodoaldo hit a low diagonal ball from the left, and Pelé raced towards it from the 'inside-right' position. But Ladislao Mazurkiewicz, one of the finest of all South American goalkeepers, had seen the danger early and was coming out fast to clear; even though he would be outside his area, he looked the favourite to get there first. Pelé's quick solution was stunning in its simplicity; he swivelled his hips a couple of times and moved to the left just before the ball reached the keeper. Mazurkiewicz turned to follow the man—and the ball went right across him. When he recovered and looked round Pelé had done a right-angled turn and was after the ball, having beaten the keeper without a touch. But the angle proved too much, and as Ubinas moved swiftly to cover the near post Pelé's screwed shot drifted a couple of feet past the far upright. This intuitive skill can't be coached, of course, but every player can be more inventive if his basic techniques are sound and his confidence therefore high.

▶One of the factors behind Liverpool's long run of success has been their all-round scoring ability, their knack of getting midfield men quickly forward into dangerous positions and making it pay with good finishing, often following moves involving several players and passes. At Derby in February 1979 Ray Kennedy chose an even faster route—interception. The prey was a cross hit low and hard by Terry McDermott out on the right, aimed for Kenny Dalglish. A master of the late run, Kennedy came in not on the blind side of Dalglish and his marker but in front of them, taking the ball a foot off the ground in his stride to split the County defence. His momentum took him on and his coolness in front of goal (he was a striker in the Arsenal 'double' side) did the rest for a very special opportunist goal.

KENNEDY
3

McKELLAR

◀Brazil's Oscar calmly blocks a full-blooded shot from Karl-Heinz Rummenigge of West Germany during his side's 2–1 win over the European Champions in May 1981. This kind of composure is the result of supreme confidence in ability as well as more tactical qualities like positioning. Oscar hasn't just 'stuck a foot out' and hoped; despite the speed of the ball he is well balanced with his foot at the correct angle, while an ambitious lunge would just lead to a dangerous deflection. Interception is a generally underrated aspect of technique and of tactics. It is often the most emphatic way of regaining possession, more particularly on a pass where it means succeeding against the odds (one against two) and temporarily putting two defending opponents out of the game. If the intercepting player is moving forward then the advantage is even greater, with the opposition pushing up. Interception in defence is not usually down to luck; it's most often the result of sensible positioning and an appreciation of passing angles. Interception in attack is all about timing runs and, as illustrated above, it doesn't have to be from the opposition.

past him and get behind the England defence. By contrast left-back Ray Wilson was an artist who could dispossess an opponent like a pickpocket lifting a victim's wallet. Wilson's tackles were so well timed that in his long League career he was never booked for a foul.

Jack Charlton, 'the giraffe', was another lacking in classical style, but he was superbly effective in a defensive unit. He too won his place because of Ramsey's quest for blend. Bobby Moore was an England certainty, but he still had weaknesses that needed to be covered. Moore was never outstanding in the air, nor particularly gifted in natural speed. Charlton's long legs could eat up the ground, and his height stifled many an aerial attack on the England goal. 'Big Jack', gangly and ungainly, was a vital cog

in the England defensive machine.

In the midfield Nobby Stiles became a symbol of England's success. Famous for the 'fangs' that showed when he removed his false front teeth to play, he provided the bite for England to win the ball and thus give Bobby Charlton, not the strongest tackler himself, the chance to exert his influence on the game. The commitment of Stiles very nearly led to a FIFA ban after one horrendously mistimed challenge that seriously injured the Frenchman Jacques Simon. Ramsey stood by his man, recognising the contribution Stiles made to England's pattern of play.

Also in midfield the energy of Alan Ball, then only 21, compensated for the absence of a natural winger. Ball's running down the right flank undermined West Ger-

many during extra time in the 1966 World Cup final, and it was from his chase and cross that Geoff Hurst turned to score and re-establish England's lead at 3–2. It is also often forgotten that when Hurst broke clear to create the final act of drama with his third goal and England's fourth, the tireless Ball was alongside him and would have had a goal as a reward for his endeavour if, as Ball was politely suggesting at the time, Hurst had drawn the goalkeeper and slipped him a simple pass.

In Martin Peters Ramsey spotted a clever reader of the game and subtle passer of the ball who was on the same wavelength as his West Ham colleagues Moore and Hurst. Moreover in a side that did not always find goals easy to come by, Peters was always likely to arrive unmarked in scoring positions. But for a

KENNEDY

McFARLAND

McDERMOTT

MORELAND

DALGLISH

▼Learning how to get into the right positions to view the play and receive passes 'sideways on' will make a huge difference to any player's game. The broken blue line shows the range of effective vision the receiver has for a ball played to him by a defender when he faces that defender square-on; he is 'blinkered', with only his own defence in view. The solid red line shows the range of vision the receiver has if he plays sideways on; he can still see the defender but he can now also view a far bigger area of the pitch upfield. He can thus have potential targets and passes in view before he takes the ball. While this approach to the game is obviously of greatest value to the midfielder, it benefits all positions—even for a full-back taking a throw from his keeper.

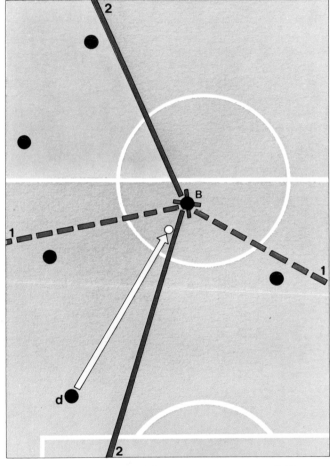

◄ *Trevor Brooking, one of the greatest exponents of side-on play, uses the approach to dummy Sammy Lee with a bouncing pass in the 1981 League Cup final replay at Villa Park. The method has far more benefits than improving vision and all that implies—more awareness of movement upfield, more accurate and penetrative first-time passes. For one thing, as we see here, it is helpful in discovering the exact position of your marker and therefore increases the chances of 'turning' him, especially if you've dummied to move towards the ball and then let it run—a skill in which Brooking has no peer. You are better positioned, too, to take the ball in a different direction as it reaches you. And you are able to ride and withstand tackles more easily because you form a moving and not static barrier with your body as you turn. The positioning must be good, of course, and it takes practice both to get the hang of the idea and to learn how to position yourself so that the ball is not too far away or comes right 'at your side'. Once learned, it becomes a habit.*

135

▼ In this fragment from a 1979 NASL game between Los Angeles Aztecs and Washington Diplomats, Johan Cruyff demonstrates two aspects of 'awareness' and shows how control and vision (the ability to see the play one move ahead and be able to do something about it) are linked. It starts when he rises in the centre-circle to take an awkward Washington clearance on the chest . . .

▼ Having trapped the ball, Cruyff readjusts his stance as he glances up, unhurried, to see what's 'on' in terms of a pass for his second touch. His manager at Aztecs (as well as with Ajax, Barcelona and Holland), Rinus Michels, reckons Cruyff the quickest 'reader' of a situation he's ever known. It is all made practicable, however, by that excellent killing first touch . . .

contentious free-kick that led to an equaliser by West Germany and extra time, the honour of scoring the winning goal in the final would have belonged to Peters, who had given England that 2–1 advantage with a coolly taken volley.

Ramsey's two front players underlined the team aspect of football. Roger Hunt, who played in every game in the competition, and Geoff Hurst, who took his chance with both hands after an unfortunate injury to Jimmy Greaves, covered

miles in England's cause. Hunt popped up with critical goals against Mexico and France, and though his unselfish graft went unappreciated by certain sections of the public and the media his industry was essential to England's hard-working style.

England therefore became champions of the football world not with the 11 most gifted players in the country at that time, but with a blend of attributes and skills that made the unit function.

This is a prime example of the principle

that should apply to all levels of the game. As a player be aware of the strengths and contributions of those around you. For example, if you are a skilful player on the ball don't go off on self-indulgent solo runs until you have learned what part of the pitch is most effective for them.

Basic command of the techniques of controlling the ball will help you become a better team player. When you watch any top professional in action you will notice that he is constantly looking up when he is

HEAD DOWN

HEAD UP

◀One of the finest 'habits' any player can acquire is 'getting his head up'. It's why good players always seem to know where they are going and what to do with the ball. It's a quality that distinguishes the good player from the ordinary; it means the man on the ball has control, confidence, and time. Not looking up is a common fault in youngsters, usually because lack of confidence in basic abilities makes them concentrate on actual control. The answer is simply to practise—and the younger you start the better, since the habit is not so easy to cultivate once you're older and 'set in your ways'. The knack is not to change your dribbling technique by pushing the ball further ahead to gain time to look up; that way you'll just lose possession. It is to work on glancing up between touches to see what's going on around you, but keeping your eye on the ball when making contact. It will come, like automatically looking in your rear-view mirror when driving a car. 'Head up' is a simple but essential aspect of ball skill, a prerequisite of good passing.

▶An exemplary case of 'head up' from Forest's Trevor Francis during the World Club Championship match with Nacional at Tokyo in 1981. His change of direction has wrong-footed Juan Blanco, but even as he starts to move off at speed, not yet clear of the late tackle, the England man is looking up to check on the position and movement of players. It is a hallmark of the good player, no matter what his position.

In the fraction of a second it takes for the ball to drop to thigh height Cruyff makes his choice and acts on it—a volleyed pass with the inside of his foot to a team-mate on his right, just beating the lunging of Paul Cannell. The Dutchman knew his man was there well before he had taken the ball because he was aware of what was opening around him and could see the option in advance . . .

▼*Away it goes for a swerving pass. Looking around you when you're not in possession, and looking up when you are, are two of the best 'habits' you can acquire in football. By being aware of the movement of people when you don't have the ball you'll have more and better options when you receive it. Becoming a player-watcher and not a ball-watcher is a major advance in anyone's game.*

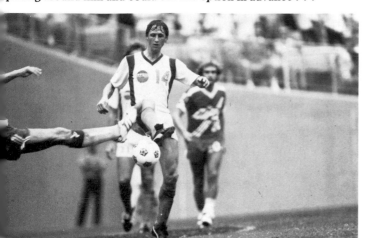 

in possession. If you can cultivate a touch on the ball that brings quick control you will be able to respond to what is happening around you. If the head stays down your abilities become 'blinkered', and there is less possibility of producing an end product.

A good player will still be involved in the team's play when he is 'off the ball'. Such is the nature of the game that most of a match is spent with others in possession. Here every youngster must learn to con-

tribute. Sensible calling—and the key word is sensible—will ease the task of the man on the ball. If you switched off the crowd noise at every top match, you would here constant conversation, designed to encourage, warn and advise.

Goalkeepers, particularly, are well placed to advise their team-mates. The game takes place in front of them, and well-judged calls can tell a colleague if he has time to control the ball, if there is a team-mate well placed to accept a pass or

if danger is threatening and he should work for safety. Conversely if a player is caught in possession he can legitimately complain when he has received no call to warn him of an opponent's arrival. In the same vein, a player jumping for a header focuses his whole attention on the ball. Others around him are better placed to advise the direction the header should take, so again a correct call will help the player and the team.

One common type of calling is to tell a

team-mate that you want the ball played in your direction. To young players it is a temptation to do this all the time through sheer enthusiasm, to want to be brought into the game. But through experience you must develop the knowledge of when you can reasonably receive the ball and when you are too tightly marked. Nothing is more frustrating for your side than if you regularly ask for the ball in circumstances where you will probably lose it.

It is worth reiterating the key rule of team play—make the best of your resources. Look at what types of players your team has rather than automatically copying the patterns exhibited by the top clubs. If Liverpool have just won another trophy with a four-man midfield, it simply means that the Liverpool playing staff are best suited to adopt that method. It does not automatically have a spin-off for every school first team or Sunday morning side.

Once your team's style is decided there are plenty of ways to sharpen it so that your system stands a greater chance of succeeding. Just playing matches together breeds understanding and confidence. You are learning how to bring out the best in your team-mates. If your centre-forward is not particularly quick, then you will appreciate more that he wants the ball to his feet, and not struck over the opposing back four where he has to chase after it. If you have a wide player who hasn't yet developed his strength to cross the ball to the far post, the team should be concentrating their forces around the near post, where there is a greater chance that the ball will arrive.

The more time you can spend together as a team the greater the feeling of collective play. One simple routine that builds confidence can easily be worked on a training night, providing that all the team are keen enough to be available. It is called shadow play, and on the whole pitch the chosen 11 play against just three or four opponents. Those defenders move about to make challenges sufficient to force the full side to keep the ball moving, but that movement must be to the pattern of play. Undisciplined chasing around ruins the point of the exercise. This type of repetition, properly co-ordinated, breeds the habits that are the difference between good teams and ordinary ones.

The same principle applies at set pieces or set plays. Watch any weekend's televising of top games and you will always find a regular proportion of goals coming from corners, free-kicks and even throws. Much of the scouting done at the highest level involves making a team aware of the ploys used by the opposition in such situations. Yet goals are still regularly conceded even though defenders are aware of the possibilities.

A well-rehearsed move from guaranteed possession of a dead ball will always be an advantage. The clever teams at all levels will capitalise on that. If your team wins a corner and you are not sure what is supposed to happen then you are wasting a chance of scoring a goal. Again the details must be worked to suit the players on your side; there is little point looping high corners into the opposition goalmouth if you are a relatively short side, while if your team is blessed with a player with a powerful shot it makes sense to have a variety of free-kicks designed to create a shooting position for him.

At free-kicks close to the opposing goal the principle is to work the ball past the defensive wall, but there are a host of alternatives. You can go over, to the side of or even through the line of defenders. Whichever plan suits your team, the key

once again is practice. There is nothing so demoralising as wasting the potential of a good position when a free-kick ploy breaks down through a lack of understanding between team-mates.

Often neglected, but just as important, is the possession earned when a throw-in is in your favour. If you are fortunate to have a long throw specialist in your side, practice again will create possibilities not just for goalscoring situations but also to relieve pressure with a long throw, from near your own corner-flag, down the touchline.

It is also vital that you do not discard possession: a simple cross-over routine by two receivers will usually create enough space for an accurate throw to be delivered. Because it is rarely a dramatic phase of the game leading directly to an attack on goal the throw-in is often forsaken. But as an indirect route forward it is essential; routines when the ball is out of play should form part of a team's collective understanding.

Similarly young goalkeepers often have problems with their goal-kicks. Physical strength to propel the ball to the halfway line comes only in the maturing process. Badly struck goal-kicks only lead to more pressure on the defending goal, so again a team should be aware of the difficulties. One solution is for a number of outfield players to offer possibilities for short goal-kicks so that the goalkeeper can eventually clear his lines with a kick from his hands. He will then get more distance.

In recent years discipline and organisation have often been blamed for stifling individuality in the game. The contrary is more accurate. Proper attention to detail in terms of planning the way you play as a unit will create more situations in which the individual can flourish.

▶ **Whatever the technical and tactical differences between two sides, the key factor can be psychological rather than physical. And one vital aspect of the game is mental preparation—as the Italians found out in their opening match of the 1978 World Cup finals in Argentina. After nearly two years of build-up, and after weeks of intense pressure and publicity, they were a goal down in just 31 seconds. They seemed to 'freeze' at Mar del Plata as the French, alert and mobile, launched their first genuine attack of the game from a throw by keeper Jean-Paul Betrand-Demanes. He rolled the ball into the path of Nantes team-mate Maxime Bossis, who hit it in his stride up to winger Didier Six. Closely marked by Claudio Gentile, Six knocked it inside to Jean-Marc Guillou, who in turn pushed it on first time to Michel Platini as he was closed down. Platini struck a long ball into the run of Six, who had stolen a yard on Gentile with his turn and he knocked the ball forward and headed for the line, sending in a sweeping cross . . .**

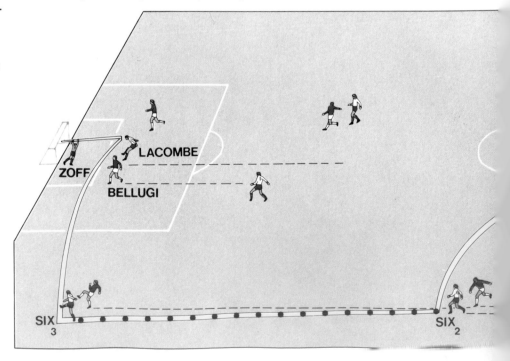

▶ *Alan Ball is the personification of the will to win in football—he even gets a big kick out of beating Willie Johnston in a training sprint as Vancouver prepare for the 1979 Soccer Bowl against Tampa Bay Rowdies. Ball set up both goals for Trevor Whymark in that game to help Whitecaps to the title and take the award for the most valuable player of the play-offs. Despite gaining the highest honour in the sport (a World Cup winner's medal) at just over 21, and despite more than his fair share of disappointments and set-backs since, Ball has always been pushing himself on, striving to get better. Early in 1982, approaching 37 and with over 700 League appearances behind him, he was an essential part of Southampton's challenge for their first championship. Character and a player's approach are almost as important as natural ability in football—an array of 'wasted' talents testify to that, while many less endowed players make the grade. Hard work and dedication is the name of the game, no matter how good you are. You have to want to improve and you have to motivate yourself: the basic drives are there long before the chances of fame or financial reward. Irrespective of age, players who want to get on will have enough pride to make sure they're fit.*

THE EVOLUTION OF TEAM PLAY

As a team game football has changed dramatically from its chaotic origins to today's sophisticated patterns. Its roots were in the street battles of rival villages where no holds were barred as two opposing mobs tried to force the ball into an area marked as a goal.

An offside law when the game became more formalised dictated the style around the 1860s. Any player ahead of the ball was offside, similar to today's rugby regulations. Consequently the game became a series of individual breaks, a contest of dribbling skills. Few details were paid to

defending and at least seven outfield players on each side would chase the ball around the pitch looking to attack when their side was in possession.

The passing game that we know today was formed in Scotland. Queen's Park, the great amateur club of that era, first recognised the rather obvious value of being able to kick the ball over a distance so that it travelled quicker than any player dribbling it. The tactic was a response to a change in the offside regulations. An attacker was onside if he had three opponents between his position and the defending goal. Queen's Park produced a

formation that involved two full-backs, two half-backs and six forwards, and through their influence Scotland held sway in the early internationals against England. Gradually their tactics spread south with the growth of professionalism that attracted skilful Scotsmen to earn a living in the new Football League, which began its life in 1888. The first championship was won by Preston North End without losing a match, and with a strong Scottish contingent in their line-up they also lifted the FA Cup without conceding a goal—the first 'double'. It is generally attributed to Preston that they slightly

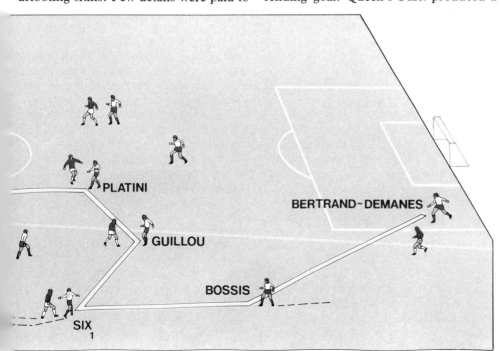

PLATINI
GUILLOU
BERTRAND-DEMANES
BOSSIS
SIX
1

Bernard Lacombe came in unseen behind the ball-watching Mauro Bellugi to head powerfully past Dino Zoff, who seemed fixed to his line. The move was neatly constructed—built from the back, four first-time passes, good running off the ball, a well-placed cross and a crisp finish—but the Italians certainly made their contribution, with everyone concerned making uncharacteristic mistakes: Gentile too tight on Six and then being beaten for speed, Bellugi 'losing' Lacombe, Zoff spectating at a ball he should have plucked comfortably out of the air. The skills Italian defences are renowned for were hardly in evidence. There was an aura of sluggishness about them. While the French thought and acted faster, the Italians seemed asleep, the result of nervousness more than any over-confidence. It's unlikely that such a goal would be conceded by them well into a game, when they had 'settled down'. As it was the Italians came back to win 2–1—and then went on to beat Hungary and eventual champions Argentina.

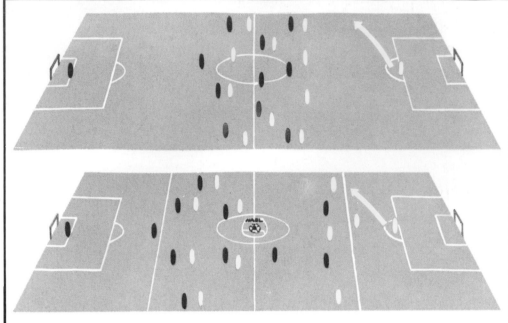

NASL: THE 35-YARD OFFSIDE RULE   The 'blue line', introduced in 1973, is drawn 35 yards from goal and players can only be offside between it and the goal. The intention was to take the edge away from defenders (helped by narrow US pitches) and stifle the offside trap, getting rid of the cramped 'middle third' as teams push up and thus make for more open football. In fact a gap tends to develop between back players and forwards: the results are a decrease in support play, especially from full-backs, a scarcity of through balls, congestion around the 35-yard line, and an unrealistic burden on midfield players.

altered the team formation in to what became the classic style. A goalkeeper had in front of him a right and left full-back; right-half, centre-half and left-half; and a five-man forward line: outside-right, inside-right, centre-forward, inside-left and outside-left.

The key player in this style of line-up was the centre-half, who was expected to control the play rather like the governing central midfield player of today. The centre-half at the turn of the century was expected to attack as much as defend.

Once again, though, a change in the offside law altered the tactical thinking of the game. In the early 1920s Bill McCracken, an Irish international full-back well ahead of his time in terms of tactical thinking, refined an offside trap that continually frustrated visitors to his club, Newcastle United. McCracken and his fellow full-back cleverly timed a move forward that regularly ensnared forwards trying to cope with the old offside rule. As more teams copied the play, goalscoring in the League began to fall—and so did the game's spectator appeal.

The law was changed in 1925 to the one still in operation today; the number of defenders needed to allow an attacker onside was reduced from three to two. Goalscoring rose immediately to the point where Everton's Dixie Dean established a First Division and Football League record that could stand for all-time: 60 in his 39 games during the 1927–28 season.

Naturally the change provoked a tactical rethink. As centre-forwards totted up the goals, the response was to restrict the role of the centre-half to pure defence. Arsenal, under the influence of manager Herbert Chapman and his perceptive forward Charlie Buchan, pioneered the strategy, and Herbie Roberts became the best known of a new breed of 'stopper' centre-halves. The midfield creativity was now thrust on to the shoulders of the wing-halves and the inside-forwards. Arsenal entered an era of success, their model was copied—and another spell of stereotyped football began.

It was from abroad that the rigidity of the British system was dramatically exposed. In 1953 Hungary arrived at Wembley as Olympic champions and with an impressively long unbeaten record. The prevailing opinion at the time was that 'continentals' had good skill but could not shoot. The 'Mighty Magyars' overturned that belief with a 6–3 demolition job of England's unbeaten record against sides from outside the British Isles. Above all, however, it was a tactical victory. Nandor Hidegkuti, wearing number nine, played in midfield and was given so much room that he still scored a hat-trick. Harry Johnston, England's centre-half, did not know whether to follow him or stay back and cover.

The evolution had begun, but England were slow to learn the lesson. Brazil won the 1958 World Cup with a formation that included a back line of four defenders (including two centre-backs) two midfield players and two central strikers alongside two orthodox wingers; 4–2–4 in turn overtaxed the two midfield men, and a third and later a fourth would be added as 4–3–3 and then 4–4–2 grew in fashion.

Parallel to this change in emphasis Italian football entered a more cynical phase, the era of *catenaccio* from which it has yet to completely emerge. Whereas the more conventional methods of play required defenders to mark zonally, the Italian gospel was of a rigid man-for-man style with markers following prescribed opponents all over the pitch. Behind them a sweeper was free to plug the gaps that opened up. It was stiflingly effective in the climate of the Italian First Division, and the Milan clubs, AC and Internazionale, also influenced the European Cup until counter-active methods were successful.

The game happily entered a more adventurous age with the advent of a supremely talented generation of Dutch players whose splendid technique, with Johan Cruyff at the helm, brought thrilling spectacle on both the European and world stages.

The decline in attendances throughout the professional game in the late 1970s nevertheless brought a further reminder that entertainment is a top priority in the game. Yet in a commercial world winning remained the most crucial commodity. In football the margin between success and failure remains narrow, and the tactical innovator continues to look for the new approach that will bridge that gap.

DEFENSIVE PLAY

Principles of defensive play

The ultimate aim of a team that has lost the ball must be to regain possession and launch an attack, but before that there is a more urgent consideration: to prevent the opposition scoring by defending your goal. This entails decreasing the time, space and alternatives available to the attacking players.

While this requires a high level of co-ordination to be effective, good defensive play as a team is based on the good defensive techniques and tactical appreciation of the individuals in it. And this means every person in that team, not merely the back players, since just as all players automatically become attackers when possession is gained, so all players become defenders when possession is lost.*

It is thus important to summarise the essential points of individual defensive technique covered in the section on 'winning the ball' to serve as the foundations of collective defence. Keep goalside of your opponent, that is between him and the goal you are defending; go for your challenge only in an emergency or when you are sure of success, but otherwise contain your opponent, exercising restraint and patience; restrict the space he can use in front of you and deny him use of the space behind you; jockey him away from the danger area; if you do go for the challenge, be decisive; be hard and competitive but not reckless; and when you have gained possession, through whatever means, think positive.

This last point is an important aspect of defensive play, one to bear in mind from the earliest stages. Try not to allow your protective instincts and abilities, however valuable, blunt attacking potential when the chance arises. By pushing up you can support midfield players and leave 'lazy' forwards stranded. A good defence dictates play whenever it can, and does not simply respond to the initiatives of the opposition.

The basic role of defence, however, remains preventative. This function rests on two basic principles—delay and depth, or holding up the progress of the opposition and providing cover at all times.

When a side loses possession its first concern is to minimise the forward movement of the opposition. The attack must be deflected or held up long enough for players who have pushed forward to recover their defensive positions, for as many people as possible to get into positions 'behind the ball'.

If you are goalside of the ball this means retreating when the defence is outnumbered, trying to buy time for team-mates to recover while still denying the attackers space behind you. This is done by zigzag-

▲ *Full-back Phil Neal leaps and twists athletically to clear a goalbound header from Manchester United striker Joe Jordan (centre) to safety and keep Liverpool's hopes temporarily alive in the FA Cup semi-final replay at Goodison Park in April 1979. Defensive play, whether marking or covering, is all about positioning, and Neal's header here, made in the perfect covering position, owes far more to tactical awareness, experience and a knowledge of his colleagues' strengths and weaknesses than it does to luck. In open play too full-backs are expected to 'fill in' behind their centre-backs and even the goalkeeper when those players have been pulled out of position by an attacker on a run or by a good cross—just as midfielders should cover for him if he is on an overlapping run upfield and the move breaks down. To defend well as a team you have to be able to defend well as individuals—and that means an appreciation of tactical and positional play as well as solid technique. Defenders are constantly having to decide when to cover and when to mark.*

142

ging on a line towards your own goal, positioning yourself in such a way as to keep both opponents and the ball in view. This 'retreat' should be slow enough to allow colleagues to recover, but still fast enough to maintain space between yourself and your opponents. Obviously there comes a point, near the ege of the area, where you should retreat no more and you can no longer maintain that gap; but by then other players should have covered and the space between you is governed by the goalkeeper.

If you are on the wrong side of the ball it means recovering when the defence is outnumbered, taking the shortest route to the danger area and then reassessing the situation: to challenge the man with the ball,

▼ *A scene from the FA Charity Shield game at Wembley in August 1981 between Football League champions Aston Villa and FA Cup holders Tottenham Hotspur, a fixture that ended in a 2-2 draw. The most striking point as a Spurs player takes the ball forward (just out of picture) is that no less than 75% of the outfield players—eight defenders and seven attackers—are at this moment crammed into an area comprising less than a sixth of the whole pitch. There is a gap of 40 yards or more between Villa's rearmost defender, Ken McNaught, and the goal-line. If a long ball was now played into that space, Mark Falco and possibly Steve Archibald would be caught offside; the linesman, in fact, is very much in line for such a decision. Villa certainly have plenty of men back and they are all picking up opponents. The back four are marking the three Spurs front players and Ricardo Villa, their most attacking midfielder, while Andy Blair and Gordon Cowans are policing Glenn Hoddle and Ossie Ardiles. Des Bremner, the third Villa midfield player, is also moving back into a covering position. Note the run down the Spurs right of full-back Steve Perryman (arrowed), and the fact that Villa left-winger Tony Morley, aware of his defensive responsibilities, is getting across to mark him. If Morley hadn't covered the move, then either Blair or Colin Gibson would have been put in the difficult position of having to try and defend against two men, with a fair chance of Spurs finally getting a man free. Morley, indeed, is the only player who is not actually looking towards the man with the ball. Most teams in Britain use a zonal marking system without a sweeper, though one of the two centre-backs may play a little deeper than the other.*

▲ The hard-line professional approach to defensive play is that the majority of goals are conceded because at some stage in the attack a defender has not performed his role properly. Only a small proportion of scores are seen to be inevitable, the result of the unstoppable brilliance of opponents. This is usually put down to one of three causes (or a combination of them): lack of pressure on the man with ball, lack of support for the challenging player, or failure to track the man with the ball. Whether the Italian should be praised or the West German blamed for allowing this chance on goal in the World Cup game at Buenos Aires in 1978 was rendered academic by a superb piece of quick and intelligent covering by centre-back Manny Kaltz, who got across to stick out a heel and preserve the goalless deadlock after Roberto Bettega, following a delightful one-two with Paolo Rossi, had beaten the challenges of Holzenbein (17), Rüssmann (4), Zimmermann and finally the spreading figure of Maier, who had come out to narrow the angle. The alert Zimmermann recovered to head the ball clear—as Bettega held his head in disbelief.

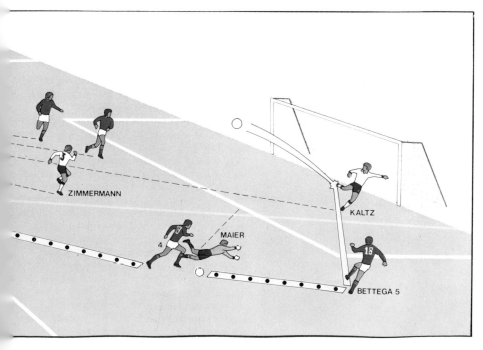

143

cover the challenging player, mark another attacker or occupy important space goalside of the ball. It is vital not to recover too far, to go past a sensible covering position valuable in a possible counter-attack.

Having retreated and recovered to a position of relative safety, the defenders can pressurise the man on the ball, getting goalside of him to deny him space and stop the ball moving forward, using as a flexible unit all the individual defensive techniques of restrained aggression. The aim of the delaying tactic is to keep the ball in front of the defence and deny the attacking side the chance of playing into the space behind it.

This whole process, executed at speed, is a 'team skill', not a job just for the back players. Front runners can put pressure on the opposing centre-backs and full-backs, while deeper forwards and midfielders should harry and close down in the middle of the pitch, threatening lines of intended passes and forcing the ball

across the field rather than forward. A team that falls back sensibly in front of the attacking side not only gains time, allowing rear defenders to adopt covering positions against forwards looking for space and through balls; it also has a very real chance of frustrating the opposition into error and regaining possession.

If a side has retreated and recovered well then it has cover. In football's numbers game, this is the antidote to support play in attack, and just as you are always looking for two-against-one situations going forward, so you look to prevent them in defence and create your own; instead of supporting the man on the ball by making yourself available or creating space, you are supporting the man who is challenging the man on the ball by covering him and closing down space. In building up their attack the opposition are looking to find the extra man, and good cover prevents there ever being one; if one defender is beaten another is there to cut out the danger. Cover means having numeri-

cally superiority deployed correctly between the ball and your goal.

A square defensive line, one without cover, is extremely vulnerable to the through ball, since a pass that takes out one man beats them all. They are covering neither each other nor the space behind. Defences must thus be 'stepped' to provide cover. As so often in tactics, midfield players hold the key to the superiority in numbers required; they fall back to protect the danger area and give the depth in defence.

An important aspect of cover is balance, the notion of a 'self-righting' unit which can provide cover at all times, no matter how mobile the opposition are or where the threat may come from. Players must beware of being pulled out of position, either forward or towards the flanks especially when tracking opponents on diagonal runs, but aware of the need to 'fill in' when team-mates are forced to move away to thwart real danger. Thus the sweeper covers for all the backs, the

◄ One of the gravest crimes in defensive play, both as an individual and as a unit, is 'ball-watching', and it's a common fault even at the highest levels. The basic error is to see only the play around the ball and to be unaware of the movement of opponents well away from the ball—particularly into dangerous space on the blind side. This means that it is at its most glaring and dramatic with high crosses, which can go over the heads of stranded defenders. There are several examples in the action replays featured in this book, but this move also illustrates another aspect of the danger—that of actually being drawn towards the ball. The attack produced the third goal in Arsenal's 5-0 trouncing of North London neighbours Spurs in December 1978, and began with a Liam Brady tackle on Ossie Ardiles near the edge of the Gunners' area. The ball ran to Graham Rix, who beat right-back Terry Naylor on the inside before pushing a pass past striker Colin Lee into the path of Brady, whose clever run had taken him free of any marking and into space near the halfway line. With Naylor hopelessly out of position centre-half John Lacy came out to try and close Brady down, but the Irishman jinked his way into the Spurs area. He continued towards the bye-line while Lacy, with Lee and Naylor still recovering, tried to block the cross. He couldn't, and over went a looping centre to the far post, where Frank Stapleton dived in undetected on the blind side of the ball-watching John Gorman to head powerfully home. An attack of three players against six had produced a simple goal because one forward hadn't been picked up by the defence. Ball-watching is something that must be worked on in training; defenders should learn to take quick looks around them, to check on the movements of opponents, without losing sight of the play round the ball, developing an awareness of their wider responsibilities.

winger or midfield on that side should watch for the space left by the overlapping full-back, full-backs should look to move quickly behind the centre-backs and keeper, particularly on outswinging crosses—and the tireless midfielders should always be alert to fill in wherever they sense the space for opposing players to exploit. Defending is a team affair.

The most important decision a defender has to make is when to cover a player marking an opponent and when to mark a player themselves—that is, whether to mark a man or a space—and back four players must make these decisions often and quickly. Sometimes they are looking to do both, seeking a point that enables them to get tight on their opponent if he receives the ball at his feet while still providing cover for colleagues. This is one of the great arts of defensive play.

Marking is all about positioning yourself most effectively in relation to your opponent and the goal. If you are doing it well you must be goalside of your man and be able to see both him and the ball without having to turn. You should be near enough to your opponent that if the ball is played to him you can intercept, tackle or shut him down; but too close and you may forfeit the possibility of interception. Should the ball be played into space behind you, you must be in a position to beat your immediate opponent to it. The precise positioning will depend on a variety of factors. You may back off an extra yard, perhaps, if you know your opponent is very fast. Generally speaking, the closer he is to goal the tighter you will try to get—though at the same time the greater the need for restraint.

Finally, three points that may help with defensive teamwork. First, defending will always be more difficult if your team has been 'stretched', easier if it can remain 'compact'. This can be better achieved if forwards and midfielders work hard to close down the opposition in their own half and get back behind the ball, and by the same token if rear players move up when the ball is pushed forwards, thus leaving their front runners stranded and gaining a temporary numerical advantage as the basis for a team attack.

Second, defences operate better if there is mutual understanding. There should be plenty of calling to inform, warn, help and advise colleagues, particularly about what is happening on their blind side; there should be a 'boss' in defence to decide when to push up and how far; there should be an agreed area in which the keeper is king. All this can be worked on and built up in training; partly it will be an automatic result of playing and practising together, but it still needs plenty of careful attention from the defenders concerned as well as the coach.

Third, there are the important psychological aspects of defensive play. In addition to their technical and tactical qualities, defenders must display certain mental attributes, not the least of which are concentration and self-discipline. Knowledge, skill and understanding are of little value if they are not applied with concentration, and quick decisions and judgements have to be made in rapidly changing situations.

Defences seem particularly vulnerable to relaxing after their concentration has been broken by a set piece, when they are very tired, when their side has just scored and, even more ironic perhaps, when their team-mates have good possession. It is easier to get things right when you are under pressure—that is what defensive systems (and defenders too) are designed for—but when your team has a lot of attacking ball you can get caught napping on the break either by getting cold and 'spectating' or because you have drifted upfield – to help your team-mates score.

▶ *Defending is a team affair, and every player must think and act like a defender when his side loses possession. Forwards and midfield players should always make it difficult for the opposition to use that possession by helping to deny them time, space and options, closing them down while looking for the chance to regain the ball wherever possible. In this example, taken from the 1981 Charity Shield game, we see two of the finest creative midfielders in England battling away for Tottenham. As Aston Villa left-back Colin Gibson moves into the Spurs half (1) both players try to cover the break but Ossie Ardiles senses not only the chance of a good challenge but also of steering the ball to Glenn Hoddle. The Argentinian times his tackle neatly to make contact when the ball is outside the playing distance of his opponent (2). He wins the ball (3) and at the same time guides it to his waiting colleague; and Hoddle, after a controlling touch, sends a swerving pass in to the space on the left of the Villa defence left by Gibson (4). One of the Villa centre-backs will be pulled out of position as he comes across to close the receiver down. Even when they don't win the ball midfielders can perform a vital role in defensive play by covering back, closing down opponents, gaining time for defenders to recover their positions.*

Systems of marking

ZONAL MARKING

▲ In a zonal system each defender patrols a strip of the pitch and picks up any attacker who enters that area. When the opponent moves into the next zone he is 'handed on' or 'passed on' to the next defender. Thus in this stylised model situation the full-back confronts the winger on the ball and forces him across the pitch. At the edge of the zone he is passed on to the next defender, the right centre-back, while the full-back peels off either to pick up any player on a run into his own zone (as here) or if his zone is free then towards the next one to help cover his team-mate. This system obviously requires a good deal of mutual confidence and understanding among defenders, and this has to be achieved gradually in practice and matches. Apart from mastering the actual system it means learning how colleagues play— the way they jockey their man, their positional sense, the aspects that need covering. This is a loose system, and players must know when to break out of their zone. Its inherent weakness lies in the confusion resulting from forwards massing in one area, or hovering on the 'borders' of areas, or moving quickly in and out of areas; its strength lies in the support it can provide, and in its very flexibility. It is a guide rather than a system and can be used in conjunction with a certain degree of specific marking, like a centre-back on a striker.

▼ In a strict man-for-man system the winger would be tracked by his designated marker, the full-back, if necessary right across to the left-back position, while the other defenders concentrate on marking their designated opponents. This approach, more rigid than the zonal method, which can be easily dropped, relies in theory on every player doing his job perfectly and never being beaten, so to guard against the natural frailties of a one-to-one basis the system usually employs a sweeper as insurance covering behind the three markers. While it requires sound defensive technique and adaptability (markers can find themselves playing almost anywhere on the pitch), man-for-man in a sense surrenders a basic positive rule of defensive play: that wherever possible you dictate. The positioning of defenders is determined almost entirely by the movement of opponents. It is unrealistic, however, to expect each man to mark his opposite number for 90 minutes, and a good defender will find time to move into forward positions and support the attack, covered by the sweeper. The key to beating man-for-man marking lies in 'escape', looking for ways of stealing a yard or two by neat turns, little one-twos and 'checking out': sprinting to go for the imaginary through ball and then moving back for the pass, or vice versa and going for the through ball.

It is generally accepted that four players provide ample width 'at the back', and almost every defensive tactical formation at nearly every level deploys four men as out and out defenders. There are, however, two basic ways of operating those players—with zonal marking, as used by most British teams, and with the more mobile man-for-man marking, the predominant approach on the continent, which usually has a 'sweeper'.

A good deal of unnecessary effort has been spent on discussing and writing about the relative merits of marking systems and, especially when it comes to the coaching of younger players, it is important to rationalise this aspect of defence.

First, these systems are rarely rigid regimes. Rather they are frameworks within which to function as a unit, models for defensive organisation that must be flexible enough to adapt to unpredictable and changing circumstances. Many British teams, for example, will employ a zonal approach as a basis but each player will pick up the nearest opponent and, as well as watching him, try to block the space he is hoping to use.

Second, players and coaches should not get bogged down with jargon and complicated concepts. Marking systems should help rather than hinder the understanding of the theory and practice of defending, acting as a medium for the application of individual technique and tactical skill.

Third, like all sensible thinking about the tactical side of the game, any system must be geared to the talent available to implement it; there is little point in playing a sweeper if none of the team have the qualifications for the role, or trying man-for-man marking if the players are not yet very good at it.

Fourth, the back four are not the only defenders in the side. All the players in a side without the ball are defenders, and any system should be treated as an integral part of team tactics, not seen as an isolated entity in which midfielders and forwards take no part. In any system, the support-

MAN-FOR-MAN MARKING

THE ROLE OF SWEEPER

Because of the obvious weaknesses of the man-for-man system—if a defender is beaten the goal is immediately threatened and it too easily confines backs to a purely defensive function—one of the back four drops back to cover the other three, each of whom are responsible for marking an opposition forward, to 'sweep' behind the back line. This original concept of the sweeper has undergone many changes, and the term, like those of 'libero' or free-back, are used somewhat loosely to describe any player who has a wider covering role in defence. This can even include the ball-winning midfielder deployed in front of the back four, detecting danger before it reaches them, cutting out passes, harassing opponents, preventing diagonal runs and plugging any gaps; in short, the ball-winning function frequently employed in Britain, where the genuine sweeper, patrolling behind the back line, is a rarity because of the predominantly zonal systems of marking. Wherever he plays he must be a good reader of the game, anticipating moves, positioning himself to cover colleagues, making timely interceptions. While the older variety of sweeper relied more on his physical qualities in defence, the new breed tends to present a different image: they are tactical perceptive, capable of seeing and playing good long early balls, sensing when to come forward in support undetected by opponents.

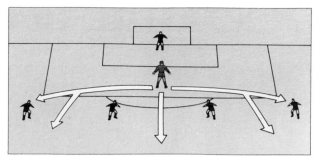

▲ The negative image of the sweeper reached its zenith with the Inter-Milan sides of the mid-1960s, which normally used a defender patrolling behind a full complement of four men. Rather than move forward and initiate and support attacks like the later type of 'libero', the sweeper slotted in for whichever member of the back four was playing further forward. Playing man-for-man against three forwards and still having two more men is great defence but it cripples a team's attack.

---

ing and covering role of the midfield players is of vital importance.

Last, there are times when the system simply does not matter. When an opponent is unmarked in important space near goal, with or without the ball, it is immaterial who picks him up as long as it is done and the danger of conceding a goal averted. Mark the man, seal the gap, cover the break, fill the space—and sort out the details later. As a basic rule, the nearer the player is to your goal the more marking space and marking men become the same thing.

At the highest levels of the game, where teams know a good deal about each other through television and dossiers, the methods usually combine certain elements of both systems: playing man-to-man just on the twin strikers, using a shadow marker on one star player, employing a ball-winning 'sweeper' just in front of the back four and so on. The approach may depend on the strengths of the opponents, the players available, or whether the game is home or away. It is also up to players, and particularly experienced captains and centre-backs, to adjust

their defensive tactics and systems of marking during a game if required. Even at humbler levels looking for strict distinctions between systems can be unrewarding and misleading. The essentials remain the same whatever the method: get goalside of the opponent, allow him less space the nearer he is to the goal and watch for movement into space well away from the ball.

Players can sometimes be detailed to mark a particularly dangerous opponent throughout a match, minimising his contact with the ball, restricting his time, space and options when he does receive the ball and, as the saying goes, trying to 'mark him out of the game'. It may be a ball-winning midfielder or an especially mobile or tenacious back-four player. This 'shadow marking' can be a real talent in itself, as men like Nobby Stiles, Berti Vogts and Romeo Benetti have proved in top club and international fixtures, but all too often it results in great players being kicked out of the game rather than being beaten by positioning and technique.

▼ *A sequence illustrating how systems and players must bow to pressure and adapt to the continually changing patterns of play on the pitch. As we pick it up a loose ball is up for grabs in the opening game of the 1978 World Cup finals in Argentina between the holders, West Germany, and Poland. Three people are converging on it: Wlodek Lubanski and Andrzej Szarmach (17) of Poland and Rüdiger Abramczik of Germany. Lubanski wins the day and, temporarily free of the policing of his marker Berti Vogts (background, with armband) he presses forward. Centre-back Rolf Rüssmann moves across to cover Lubanski's run into space while Abramczik, a midfielder, continues his run by switching his attentions to Szarmach who, having turned, will head for the space vacated by Rüssmann, possibly looking for a cross from Lubanski. While this is simply reacting to circumstances, crossovers can be coded and practised in training. Diagonal runs (particularly ones punctuated by checks, turns, and changes of direction) can be difficult for defences of any type to monitor, and switching can be devastating against man-for-man or zonal marking if executed with disguise and at speed. Like the defences they are seeking to break down, however, they need a good deal of practice and mutual understanding to work in matches.*

Defending at corners

With goals becoming increasingly hard to come by in open play teams at all levels of the game have paid more attention to assaults at set pieces, and this has led to growing pressure on defences at corners. Now they must try to combat tall players on the goal-line, flicks at the near-post, short corners to change the angle of the cross, hard low balls to the edge of the area and so on. Like any situation where a team is under pressure, it needs organisation and practice in training.

Defence at corners reflects three basic principles: concentration (of numbers), marking and cover. The first priority is simply to get enough people back. This normally means all the midfield plus one or two forwards, but it often pays to leave at least one front runner upfield, around the halfway line, for the quick break. All players in attacking positions should be marked, and there should be plenty of cover for the goalkeeper in the form of defenders on or near each post.

The keeper is the key figure at corners, simply because of his huge legal advantage, and his positioning and reactions are crucial. The traditional thinking is to stay just inside the far post, but with the 'rise' of the near-post area and the development of three-touch corners the best position is now probably around halfway and slightly infield. He must remain alert and mobile, watching the ball but not allowing himself to get locked in. He should be able and prepared to come for any high ball played into the back two-thirds of the goal area and preferably well out from it. If he cannot get a clean catch, he should always be in a position to use the punch. Calling is vital here to let everyone know where they stand; and it should be a positive call, not a defender issuing instructions by hopefully yelling 'keeper's ball'.

▲ *The modern preoccupation with guarding the near post at corners can sometimes make life difficult for players behind. Here Kettering Town keeper Lane and left-back Lee have to peer over or round the cluster of opponents marking Stafford Rangers striker Alf Wood in the 1979 FA Challenge Trophy at Wembley. These defenders, none of whom are glancing around to check on the movements of other attackers into dangerous positions, would probably be better off spreading themselves round the area, guarding space and picking up other players, leaving two men and the keeper to handle the actual goal.*

▼ *Numbers are no guarantee of protection at corners unless you make good contact with the ball. Seattle Sounders can count themselves lucky in this case that a fine leap by attacking full-back Bob Smith didn't come off for Cosmos in the 1977 Soccer Bowl. Mike England, usually so dominant in the air, has failed to get direction on his header and simply helps it on to the far post area, while goalie Tony Chursky is caught in no-man's-land.*

Most teams deploy a defender on or by each post, traditionally but not necessarily the two full-backs. Though it is a rather protective instinct to literally grab the post, these players can guard and seal off far more space if they are slightly infield; this applies particularly at the far post, where the defender has marginally more time to react.

Defending on the near post at corners has become something of an art. The man there cuts out the curling inswinger and the hard low drive to the near-post area —both difficult balls for keepers—as well as marking space in front of him and looking out for angled runs. Many teams play another man near the edge of the six-yard box to guard against the near-post flick-on. His biggest problem (and he is not alone here when it comes to corners) is whether to obey the golden rule of marking and stay goalside, thus giving his opponent the chance of that crucial contact, or to move in front of his man. Experience will tell you which positions are best in these areas, but if in doubt then stay behind your man and attack the ball if you can make it first.

No defensive system or organisation, however well planned and rehearsed, can be rigidly enforced at corners. It helps if certain players have automatic responsibilities—one man to each post, the centre-backs to mark the two strikers, the centre-forward to pick up their defender coming forward, the player looking for the near-post flick and so on—but this can only operate within a framework. Players must be able to react to particular situations as they arise, thinking in flexible terms about guarding important areas and marking dangerous players. If the defenders are spread around, there will always be someone going for the ball.

◄ **The goal that enabled West Germany to regain the European Championship, scored in the 1980 final against Belgium in Rome, holds some classic lessons about defending at corners. For one thing it was converted by the attacker most likely to succeed in that situation—the big centre-forward Horst Hrubesch, or 'the monster' as he is known in the Bundesliga. He took his position on the edge of the area and then dummied his marker, Millecamps, to gain enough room to make the run pay off; as Rummenigge's corner came in to the near post Hrubesch met it perfectly at the end of his diagonal run to steer it home. It's difficult to mark any player running at speed, however, and a bigger query is why, with so many defenders around that area, Belgium failed to clear. The answer is that nobody attacked the ball. Near-post balls aren't easy for keepers, and Pfaff if anything was impeded by his own players; with two minutes left, Belgium blew the chance of their first major title through lack of positive action at a simple corner—despite plenty of players back.**

149

Defending at free-kicks

Marking wide ball

To attack sideways ball

To attack ball

To mark behind wall

Line up on post with left foot

Keep right foot still and bring left round

◄ Free-kicks around the edge of the area are pressure situations, and that means teams should get everybody behind the ball, with players not in the wall taking up their specific defensive duties. One player attacks the ball played short to get a shot past the wall; another closes down the man taking the longer pass which improves the angle; a third watches for the ball played wide to an overlapping player, who could then shoot or cross; one man should guard the space behind the wall against the chipped pass. With a four-man wall that still leaves two players: one to mark the crucial far post area and the other as a rover, picking up any opponents near goal. To line up the wall the anchorman places himself level with the near post and then turns so that his body is mostly outside it. This is the basic approach: top teams, of course, will need extra cover against the more exaggerated swerving shot on that side (see page 94). The keeper must always be in charge.

▼ *Peru use a seven-man wall to reduce the target for Andrzej Szarmach at a 20-yard free-kick during the World Cup game at Mendoza in 1978. Kazimierz Deyna is still organising his players as the kicker starts his run. Poland have put a player on each end of the wall, and they will 'peel off' as the ball is struck to unsight the keeper as it bends through the resulting space. Such ploys were first worked by the Brazilians, the classic one being Jairzinho taking up a position in the line and then moving away to leave a gap for the rifling drives of Rivelino. Putting seven men in the wall means only three men are available to mark a possible total of nine opponents, and is valid only in central positions well within striking range. When a free-kick is given against a side in a shooting position, that team must be organised with their wall, knowing who sets it up, where it will be, how many players are in it—and when it breaks. The 'loose' defenders should also be aware of their specific responsibilities in such situations.*

Apart from a penalty, which is a very special case, a side is at its most vulnerable from set pieces when it concedes a direct free-kick within shooting range of their goal. The opposition can deploy large numbers of attacking players in pre-planned positions; they have the option of going straight for goal or for the two- or three-man move; and they have the privilege of being able to play the ball with the nearest defender no closer than nine metres away.

These benefits were fully exploited as soon as footballers developed the technique to shoot powerfully and accurately from 20 to 25 yards, and to deny them that advantage defenders then placed themselves in a 'wall' to protect as much as possible of their goal from direct threat. This in turn led to the evolution of both the sophisticated individual skills to beat the wall (chips and swerving shots) and

well-drilled, often complicated ploys involving two, three or even more players. Today this whole area of tactics has become something of a mild obsession with some coaches and players—and a good percentage of goals are still scored from these positions, particularly on the continent and in South America.

The wall, though too often too big, is a necessary evil of defensive play. If it were not there the opposition would simply have a long-range penalty and would convert an unacceptable proportion of them. But it does put defences at a severe numerical disadvantage: the more players you put in the wall the more vulnerable you are to other ploys, since attackers can make runs and take up positions and not be marked. Six men in a wall, for example, can mean in theory four defenders coping with nine attackers; and even if two players stay back to cover the vague

possibility of a break, it is still four marking six. Since the wall, of whatever size, must be there, it must perform its function well and the 'loose' defenders must be on top form in order to compensate for the temporary imbalance.

The positioning of the wall for approximate positions on the pitch is worked out in training, and implemented in matches by the keeper and his 'foreman' in the line (less often by a player not in it, who will stand nearby for the kick), and covers the near side of the goal. The wall should be staffed by forwards and attacking midfielders, thus releasing backs and defensive midfielders for the specialist role of marking and covering. They will be far better equipped to check and cover any runs and moves by the attacking team, while it makes sense for the forwards and midfielders to get quickly forward when the wall breaks up. The exception may be the anchorman in the wall, who could well be a defender.

The role of the keeper is even more central than at corners. He must know, from experience in training, how many men he needs in the wall for a free-kick in any given position. The wall covers the possibility of a shot to the near side, while the keeper is responsible for the far side. This is not one of the easiest areas of the goalkeeper's craft, since for one thing it relies on a number of team-mates acting as a unit, and he must be seen always as the boss in such situations.

One of his problems is that however well placed the wall is it cannot stop the swerving shot, often a chip, into the near corner. Some keepers prefer to adopt a more central position against certain

▲ *West German defender Karl-Heinz Förster dives in to challenge Aki Lahtinen of Finland before he can get a shot in during the World Cup qualifying match at Lahti in May 1981. Förster's designated job at free-kicks in dangerous positions was to attack the ball touched to a second player for a shot from a better angle past the wall, and he has done it comprehensively. This is a role for a sharp, quick-tackling defender. Others will mark specific opponents or look for balls played into space nearer goal.*

▼ *The Brazilians are the world's greatest exponents of ploys at free-kicks and sides playing them must be well organised and alert to a host of direct and multi-touch strikes on goal. Here, in the friendly at Wembley in May 1981, the ball is chipped by Zico over Socrates on the end of the England wall and into the space behind it for Reinaldo to run onto. But left-back Kenny Sansom, neatly positioned to watch ball and opponent, spots the danger early and moves across to clear. The five man England line—comprising Rix, Withe, McDermott, Barnes and Wilkins—reflects the rule that the wall should be made up of forwards and midfielders, thus releasing the backs for the specialist role of defending, for marking players and guarding space. Everybody should be pulled back in such situations: a team's first concern is to prevent a score from a very dangerous position and, with players locked up in the wall, there's no room for leaving a player upfield for a possible counter.*

1 ▶ The specialist defenders not in the wall have to be alert and mobile at free-kicks around the area, where opponents can work various pre-planned moves. Most important, they shouldn't get caught 'ball-watching', and must constantly glance around for attackers making runs into dangerous positions. The basic rules are to keep goalside of the opponent, preferably a couple of yards off him, but that the nearer the kick is to the goal the tighter the marking. The three basic

2 passes to guard against are shown here: the one low to the feet, the one short in front of the man, and the cross to the space behind—a ball for which the attacker may well make a dummy run forward before checking back to try and gain room. It's vital to stay alert.

◀ *The theory that Brazil's skill and organisation at free-kicks lies in attack rather than defence gains some support in this example from the 1974 World Cup clash with Scotland at Frankfurt, which ended in a goalless draw. As Peter Lorimer takes his*

3 *free-kick from just outside the corner of the area (1) Brazil have eight players back to cover—three in the wall (one suspects a European side would have had more) and five in mobile positions to guard four attackers: Rivelino watching Willie Morgan, Paulo Cesar (C) taking Billy Bremner, though he is in front rather than goalside of his man, with Mario Marinho and Nelinho guarding the runs of Jim Holton and Joe Jordan. The fifth defender, centre-back Luis Pereira, is in a good position to cover moves by Bremner or runs to the far post. As the cross comes over (2) the two big men move for the ball, tracked by their markers, Jordan having dummied to go away from goal to steal a yard on Nelinho. It worked well, and by the next 'frame' (3) he has raced in to make contact with his marker*

4 *hopelessly out of touch. Cesar, turning to follow the ball, has 'lost' Bremner, who hurries in for the possible knock down from his Leeds colleague. Pereira too has been caught ball-watching as Jordan came in behind him. Unfortunately for Scotland Jordan could direct his header neither to goal nor to his captain and it was scooped up by goalkeeper Leao. It's unlikely he would have found space so easily in the Football League, where defenders are more aware of the far-post ball, stay well goalside of attackers, and are far more aggressive and competitive in the air. The basic lesson here is that excellent positioning at free-kicks means little if you don't use it and attack the ball; Pereira's lack of awareness could well have lost Brazil the match.*

players to guard against this; there is then the chance to go both ways but the ball is seen 'late', not from the moment it is kicked. Another problem for him may be players in or at the end of the wall, peeling off or moving away at the last possible moment after the ball is struck—through the place they had been occupying. This can be niggling for defenders, but it is important to retain discipline.

Organisation and planning are even more important for defending against free-kicks than for taking them; any player, after all, can have a shot at goal with a chance of success, but defending sides must be disciplined under pressure. To save time and avoid confusion, everyone must know who is in the wall and the mobile defenders must know what specific tasks they have. Unless teams understand what is going on and how they are to cope in such situations, they must expect to concede goals. All this should be worked out in pre-season training when, even without a coach, it is possible to create a framework for set-piece defence and a job for every player within it. The players in the wall can then be taken with the keeper as a unit and team-mates encouraged to score direct.

The indirect free-kick is shooting range in also a great danger, though defences at least know for sure that two players have to touch the ball. The same principles apply, however, and the fact that so many direct free-kicks at this distance are now converted by choice into two-man moves suggests the distinction, as far as defence is concerned, is increasingly irrelevant.

SUPPORT PLAY

The supporting run

Support is the key to successful teamwork in football, whether in defence or attack. In defence, as we have seen, it means covering, supporting the player who is challenging or containing the man on the ball; in attack it means supporting the man on the ball, making yourself 'available' in space for a pass, either to relieve the pressure on him or to create a two-against-one situation.

Every player who receives a ball needs support because it gives him options. If at least one team-mate is not running into the right place at the right a pass cannot be made and possession will eventually be lost. And in football possession is everything; you cannot win without the ball.

Support play is also the means of capitalising on that possession. Most teams play three recognised 'forwards', sometimes only two, and most teams field a line of four 'backs'. Apart from relatively rare instances of individual brilliance (often aided by 'hidden' support play off the ball), the only way to redress the imbalance and break down the defence in open play is to create and exploit space in the attacking third of the field. This can only be done by teamwork based on support and movement.

While front players must drop back to forage for the ball and to draw defenders, and while they must make wide runs in advance of the ball to create space both for themselves and others, the greatest burden of providing support falls on the shoulders of the midfield players. They have to provide support in defence, of course—covering, guarding space, falling back to pick up short passes from the back four and initiate attacks; they have to

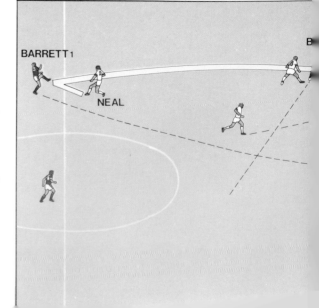

▲ Colin Barrett caps his 40-yard run with a fierce volley past Liverpool captain Emlyn Hughes to make it 2–0 to Nottingham Forest in the first leg of the European Cup clash at the City Ground in September 1978. In only the second instance of two Football League clubs being in the same competition (the first was the two Manchester sides in 1968) they had been drawn together in the first round—and this goal gave Forest a decent lead to defend at Anfield. They changed tactics drastically to get a goalless draw there, and (as Liverpool regained the League) went on to succeed Liverpool as European champions.

▶ Left-back Barrett began the 87th-minute move as well as finishing it when he blocked a Phil Neal pass near the halfway line and the ball rebounded into space for Garry Birtles to pick up and take on. Phil Thompson recovered from an upfield position to challenge but Birtles rode the England defender's tackle well and gathered the loose ball to head for the bye-line. From there he played a nicely flighted cross to the far-post area—and the head of Tony Woodcock, who had taken up the classic position. Though he wasn't moving in at speed Woodcock could have been excused for aiming at goal, but with Alan Kennedy close and Ray Clemence well positioned on the line, he chose to knock it down to the player in support . . .

LOSING YOUR MARKER

Support play in attack is as much about front players making intelligent and telling runs to help players on the ball behind them as it is about midfielders making themselves available to forwards under pressure from tight-marking defenders or putting in long runs from deep positions. To find that vital space (if only for a more 'comfortable' lay-off) you have to lose your marker—and there are several ways of gaining that extra yard on your man to receive the ball. Even with the simplest form of target play, moving away from goal towards the player on the ball, a little dummy can do the trick. This important skill, called 'checking out', involves feinting to sprint away from the ball as though looking for the through pass and then doubling back sharply for the one played short. For the run into space behind your marker the move works the other way; you go towards the passer, as though looking for the ball played to your feet and, as your marker starts to follow, you check and turn sharply to accelerate away towards goal for the through pass. Though these are the two basic approaches, improvisation is the name of the game; any number of devices can be used to fool him, provided the initial movement is convincing and there is sufficient change of pace as well as direction. One is the 'lateral check' (top right), where you dummy to pass your man on one side and then move sharply across him to take the ball on the other side. A variation on this theme (centre) is to duck out of his field of view and then move across him; this can be even more effective if done behind the bemused defender. A third ploy is to lean slightly into your marker, forcing him back on his heels, before moving off fast as the ball is played forward (right).

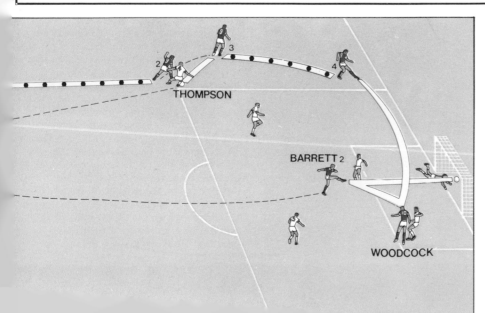

That player wasn't another forward or even a midfielder: it was Barrett, who had kept going to cover almost the whole length of the Liverpool half and move into an unmarked position only seven or eight yards from goal. The fine run wasn't wasted as he kept his head to bury his volley in the visitors' net—and with it their realistic chances of a European Cup hat-trick. At 1–0 up and with three minutes to go Barrett could have been forgiven for holding back and guarding against another Liverpool attack; but in an era of defensive domination it is this kind of adventurous support that's needed if attacking sides are to win the numbers game against well-organised units. It also emphasises the point that the attacking role of the full-back is by no means confined to the overlapping run; they can provide penetration as well as width going forward.

155

support each other in midfield, support backs breaking out or overlapping, and support forwards in attack. It is obvious that to always be helping out at the back, to keep making yourself available and, perhaps most of all, to keep putting in long supporting runs (many of which will be fruitless) the midfielder needs to be extremely fit. In short, good support requires stamina.

As in defence, support play in attack means providing depth. This can involve supporting in front or behind the player on the ball. There is an inherent risk in non-forwards supporting in front of the ball, greatest when defenders move up-field—they must not leave team-mates outnumbered at the back—but penetration of the opposition defence is difficult without it.

At its simplest, this provision of depth entails taking up an unmarked position behind and at a distinct angle to the man on the ball, most urgently when he cannot either move forward or play the ball for-ward. The distance you are from your team-mate will depend on the space you have and on the location on the pitch, and can vary from five to 30 yards; the impor-tant thing is to give the man on the ball the option of the pass, allowing him a margin of error and yourself time in which to control the ball and make a play. Remem-ber, you are in a supporting position when

◄ Running off the ball means supporting the player in possession, either by creating space for a pass to yourself or by taking the attention of one or more defenders in order to create space for others. It can often entail long, meandering, possibly 'stop-start' runs which aid team-mates on the ball and help set up chances—but which are rarely seen or appreciated by ball-watching spectators. In this 'model' attack the player in possession (A) begins to move forward. The supporting player (B) runs at an angle to him (in front or behind—the end is the same) to draw one of the two defenders (Y) away from the ball. As the second defender tries to close A down, he changes the direction of his approach and B, looking to take up a fresh supporting position, responds with another diagonal run to make himself available for a pass or take one defender out of the game: good support play can provide both. When he sees a third attacker in support (C), B veers right, again with the intention of helping A and this time drawing his man away from any contact with C. As the persistent X is joined by another defender (Z), A slips a pass to the advancing C to create a clear chance on goal. This stylised move also raises the possibility of at least two crossover ploys to help gain valuable time on the defenders. Ideally two players should be making such runs, behind and in front of the man on the ball, while other attackers should look for wider supporting positions to draw defenders away from the middle.

you are available to receive the ball—and in a good team any player on the ball in attack should always have at least two such possibilities on hand. This simple premise is, for example, the very essence of Liverpool's sustained success, the art of 'working for each other'.

The notion of 'stepping' is just as important in attack as it is in defence, where it ensures cover. Supporting in a square position—except in certain circumstances, like standing off a colleague closed down on the touchline—weakens the potential of the attack, since penetration is difficult and there is always the risk of interception on the pass, especially on the long crossfield ball. It is relatively easy to contain a 'flat' and static attacking line, where the front runners fail to make diagonal runs and midfielders fail to fall into supporting positions behind.

Sometimes it is necessary to go back before you can go forward. The basis of the lay-off to the man in support, made when the front player cannot move forward, is 'give and go'; the front runner making the pass will be looking for space wide of or behind his marker, while the receiver in turn will be looking for a forward run (and another supporting position) after making his pass.

This movement off the ball is vital if attacks are to result in a team threatening the opponents' goal. Well-organised de-

▶ As Rodney Marsh controls an awkward ball while facing his own goal, trying to shield it from his opponent, Tampa Bay team-mate Oscar Fabbiani moves forward to support his Rowdies colleague in a square or advanced position in space. He thus gives Marsh the options of turning to his left and feeding the ball or going for the earlier angled pass. The receiving player should be aware of such movements and the alternatives they provide before the ball arrives. Marsh, having played the ball, should in turn be looking for space away from his marker to support Fabbiani.

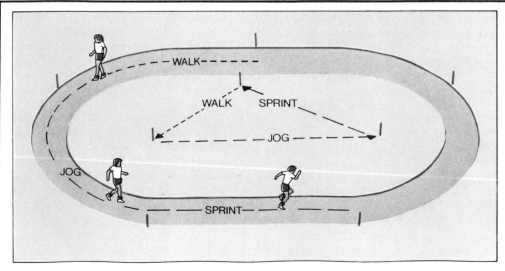

IMPROVING YOUR STAMINA
To provide for team-mates right through a game means being fit, and in particular having a high degree of stamina. You're not tearing around for 90 minutes, of course—you'll sprint, jog and walk during games, and the training should reflect this. An ideal set-up is an oval shape, divided into sections, but you can do it with a triangle of 20- or 30-yard sections. As on the 'track', make the sprinting leg shorter than the jogging one. By retaining the same routine you'll be able to gauge your improvement. Linked to longer training runs, this will build up your stamina—and that's bound to make you a better team player.

◀Fully aware of the pace and direction of Steve Heighway's beautifully weighted short through ball, Terry McDermott takes time out to glance up and check on the position of Borussia Moenchengladbach's Kneib at the end of his run. A second later he had beaten the keeper to give Liverpool the lead in the 1977 European Cup final at Rome.

▼That superb goal involved two supporting runs. The first came from Ian Callaghan, who having won the ball with a fine tackle just inside his own half and played it out to Steve Heighway on the right, then followed up to support him on the outside. This gave the Eire international something every player needs: options. He chose to move inside, putting Wohlers in two minds (close him down or cover Callaghan), and then drew two more defenders before slipping the ball between them for McDermott. Liverpool's newest recruit had given them another dimension with his long runs from deep positions into dangerous positions near goal. Very few, however, are so fruitful; McDermott will make several runs like that during a game, and many more over shorter distances, with no reward.

fences, based on solid technique and good tactical awareness, can only be broken down by mobile, interchanging attackers who are continually creating space to receive passes or committing defenders to false positions to create space for others.

One way of achieving this is with diagonal runs. Defenders prefer opponents to play 'up and down', making it easier for them to mark and to cover and, if necessary, to retreat. But when attackers move across them at an angle without the ball they have to decide when to move with the man, and if so then how far, and when to mark space. The result can be doubt, hesitation and confusion. Diagonal runs can be from the flank to central positions or from the centre towards the touchline, sometimes called inside-to-outside runs. These can drag defenders out of position, leaving space in the middle for supporting team-mates to move into, either from deeper central positions or with diagonal runs from further out on the flanks. Front runners must always be prepared to make these runs to create width and draw defenders (often without recognition, especially from 'ball-watching' fans) if they are to be good team players.

Diagonal runs can be devastating to defences if two players, one with and one without the ball, cross each other's paths at an angle. These 'crossovers', which must be carefully practised in training to work in matches, can both create and exploit space, and are particularly effective against a side marking man for man. As the two men cross, the player without the ball either collects it and carries on (the 'takeover'), thus switching the direction of attack, or he simply acts as a decoy for his team-mate to continue his progress with the ball. The element of doubt in the defenders' minds, however short-lived, is crucial: thus the two players must have a good understanding of when it is a takeover and when a 'dummy' version, the player in possession must be screening the ball from his opponent to heighten the chance of disguising the ploy, and the movement should accelerate rather than slow down as it is executed.

The other main methods of creating space with supporting runs are the overlap

BEATING THE OFFSIDE TRAP
The run made from behind the player with the ball into a position behind the opponents' back line as they push up is the ideal way of beating the offside trap, and perfectly illustrates how support play, by creating the extra man going forward, is the key to penetration in attack. Timing is vital and stems from an understanding of team-mates' play. The same principle is at work in both goals on these pages.

▲ The highest-scoring final in the history of the European Cup Winners Cup, between Barcelona and Fortuna Düsseldorf at Basel in 1979, was triggered off by a fine goal after just six minutes. Like the one by Terry McDermott featured opposite, it was made possible by a long and intelligent supporting run from a midfield player into space partly created by defenders being drawn to the man on the ball. In this case that man was Carlos Rexach, who received a ground pass from Albaladejo in the Spanish half and turned neatly. He found himself facing centre-half Kohnen, but he kept the ball on his favourite left foot and edged forward. Kohnen didn't look in control against the experienced Barcelona captain, and centre-back Zewe, aware that two other defenders were behind him with nobody to mark, came to help close him down as he moved well into the danger area. Then came the killer pass—a neat through ball into the huge space now being exploited by José Sanchez. The timing of the run—getting away from the marker (Schmitz) and being available at the right angle for the most destructive pass—was the crucial element. Again the finishing matched the move—Sanchez slotting the ball past the spreading figure of Daniel—showing that today's midfielders must not only take up good supporting positions near goal but also must be capable of putting away the chances when they arise. Barcelona went on to win 4–3 and it proved a special night for Rexach: the sole survivor from their previous final in the competition, on the same ground against Slovan Bratislava ten years before (they lost 3–2), he scored the vital third goal in extra time.

and the blind-side run, both of which, in their different ways, apply the criterion of creating and exploiting width in attack to break down a well-drilled defensive unit. These are covered in detail in the two subsequent chapters.

Just as midfield men are expected to support front players who are in possession, so those front runners must make intelligent runs when team-mates have the ball behind them. Even at top levels, forwards can be guilty of 'laying up' against defenders, rarely moving quickly or into telling positions. They, too, must provide support by giving the midfielders options, by 'showing themselves' and indicating to their colleagues where to play the ball.

The overlap

One way of trying to break down well-organised, 'concentrated' defences is to get width in attack, pulling defenders out of position in order to create and exploit space in the areas nearer goal. A good ball-player can sometimes do this on his own, drawing his marker and one or more covering defenders towards the flank, but more often it needs that vital extra man in support on the outside to make it work. This type of supporting run is usually called the overlap.

Because the majority of such runs occur near the touchlines, they have become mainly (though by no means exclusively) the province of the full-back. The overlap is the most regular and 'safest' way for a full-back to go forward and join the attack, and its growing importance as a weapon against crowded defences has led to the emergence of a new breed of player in that position. While still responsible for a host of defensive duties, today's top-level full-back is fast and adventurous, more tactically aware and more technically equipped for attack than his predecessors. He needs to know when and where to move up in support; he must think and play like a forward when he pushes up into the opponents' half; he should be adept not only at getting in crosses but also confident enough to cut inside and shoot at goal when the chance arises. Many, indeed, are 'converted' wingers.

As the name implies, the overlap involves giving support by moving from a position behind the player on the ball to a position well in front of him. Providing the space is there to be used, the time to apply it is when the player in possession no longer needs support from behind, and when (in the case of the ball being first played up to him) he has the time to turn and lay the ball forward. If there is no covering player behind the challenging defender, this automatically creates a two-against-one situation and gives the man on the ball options. He can use the team-mate on the outside or he can move infield. Much will depend on the reaction of the defender: if he moves across to cover the supporting player (or even if he is obviously in doubt about his course of action) then the better bet may be to take the ball on—towards a defence now put under a little more pressure by the decision about whether to cover the man making for the break near the line.

It is vital for the supporting player to get well in front of the man on the ball with an overlap. To be effective the run must take him past the defender as well as the attacker and if there is a specific covering player, then also past a point level with him. The move must seek to turn him as well as draw him across, destroying both his position in terms of his angle and distance from the challenging player and his normal line of retreat. It is of course two-against-two, but the advantage lies with the attackers because they have forced the defence to become unbalanced. In terms of cover, the overlapping player is now an extra man. If he now receives the ball, a third defender is forced to consider pulling away from a central position to cover. The player making the pass should, in turn, move into a supporting position in order to capitalise on the advantage gained, almost certainly helping out the player he has released.

To make these runs regularly, a player needs to be fit. Full-backs are expected to get back into defensive positions quickly if attacks break down—and then to be available for another sortie when their side regains possession.

▲ *Mick Martin (7), Paddy Mulligan and John Wile can only watch as Brian Talbot's brave header powers into the roof of the WBA net despite a despairing touch by keeper Tony Godden. The goal, engineered via a fine overlapping run by left-back Mick Mills, set Ipswich on the way to an FA Cup semi-final victory in 1978 and their first ever appearance at Wembley—but the clash of heads meant Talbot was substituted and Wile carried on courageously with a injury.*

▶ Timing was the key to Mills' fine run, and he sensed the moment was right when Paul Mariner, closed down on the edge of the Albion area, slipped the ball to Clive Woods. The winger put his foot on the ball, looked up to see what was on and then stroked the ball into his path. A first-time near-post cross and Talbot's commitment finished the move.

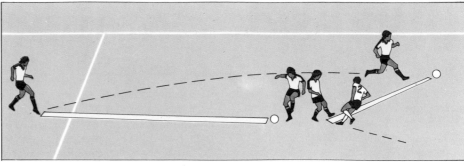

▲The 'classic' instance of the overlapping run entails the player who makes the pass moving well in front of the receiver to take the return, and most often involves the full-back playing the ball up to a midfielder or front man positioned near the touchline. The ideal situation in which to use it is when there's plenty of space available behind the 'target' player and when, possibly despite being marked by a defender, he has the time to turn (and if necessary to hold) before playing the ball forward at an angle. No matter how well players know each other's styles, calling is important here: a call of 'outside you' lets the receiver know the run is on and gives nothing away, since the defenders can see the move for themselves. This area of support play rarely owes anything to disguise; rather it rests simply on creating two-against-one by pushing an extra man in front of the ball. If the defender is tight or closes down the receiver quickly, he can play the ball back to the passer and peel off to look for the space behind the opponent near the touchline and the possible ball knocked forward. The end result may well be the same.

▼Much of support play is based on mobile triangles of passer, receiver and supporting player, and the overlap can provide another dimension to the pattern by creating more depth as well as width in attack. Player A, an attacking left-back or a left-sided midfield player, passes to winger B. By moving into space behind B's marker, A produces a range of new alternatives for the side in possession—either with a ball passed to him (by B, by supporting player C, or via a lay-off from player D), or by drawing at least one covering player out of the middle, thus improving the odds of a direct threat on goal by players C and D. The overlap should not be seen merely as a run to receive the ball; any movement into the opponents' third of the pitch by an extra man out wide will stretch their defence and therefore increase the chances of penetration. In the inevitable battles that occur between full-backs and their opponents, an early psychological advantage can be gained by putting in a couple of well-timed runs up the line to support team-mates.

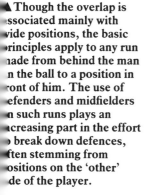

▲Though the overlap is associated mainly with wide positions, the basic principles apply to any run made from behind the man on the ball to a position in front of him. The use of defenders and midfielders in such runs plays an increasing part in the effort to break down defences, often stemming from positions on the 'other' side of the player.

WOODS

MILLS

Blind-side running

In attack, support play means taking up the position that enables the player in possession to make the most effective pass possible in the situation. Often the best runs 'off the ball' are those made on the blind side of defenders, out of their field of vision. Defenders are put under most pressure when movement takes place behind them, when they have to turn and face their own goal. The well-timed blind-side run, even if detected, always causes problems for covering players.

Some players have a natural flair for blind-side running, almost an instinct. Whereas the hard-working, bustling type of front runner cannot help advertising their movement off the ball, more sophisticated players are sometimes able to steal into dangerous positions from 'nowhere', to ghost in unseen with perfect timing to head or shoot for goal. These perceptive players, usually midfielders, have developed the knack of 'watching the ball-watchers'. They know defenders can all too easily concentrate on the play around the ball and neglect their broader duties, failing to take stock of the overall attack and to check on the movement of opponents well away from the ball—especially on their blind side—and they take full advantage whenever the opportunity presents itself.

The shrewd runner keeps the play in view but also looks for the chance to exploit space behind the defenders. Blind-side running near goal requires vision, good positional sense, subtlety of movement and perfect timing, and of course the ability to finish the job—there is little point in creating the chance if you cannot convert it.

Though it is a skill most immediately associated with use in scoring positions, and particularly with high crosses, the blind-side run is an all-round form of support play that can be applied in the simplest of situations in any area of the pitch. Players should always be looking to make runs behind attackers for the quick ball out of defence, for example, using diagonal runs from central positions towards the flanks. And a basic method for making forward progress in midfield is to lay a ball square and then move behind the opponent challenging the receiver to take

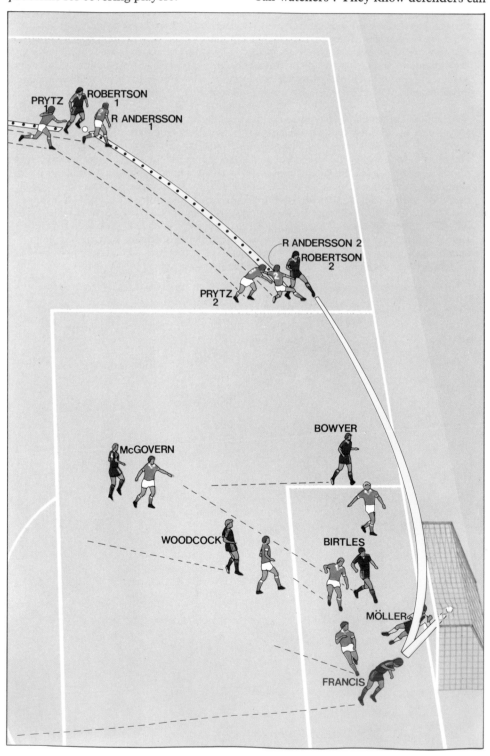

◄ **Possibly the most unattractive of all European Cup finals, the 1979 affair between Nottingham Forest and FF Malmö in Munich could boast one spectacular moment—when, on the stroke of half-time, Trevor Francis steered his diving header into the roof of the Swedes' net for the goal that would settle the match. With everyone expecting a half-time whistle, Ian Bowyer hit a long ball out to John Robertson on the left touchline. Robertson took it forward but was soon confronted by Andersson and then also by Prytz. They combined to keep him wide but when he got level with the area the Scot, with that deceptive change of pace, burst away at an angle towards the bye-line, beating a final challenge from Andersson to send a cross deep to the far post. The ball cut out keeper Möller and a gaggle of players—to be met by the head of Francis. Deployed deep and wide by Brian Clough, he had made a long late run to come in on the blind side of the ball-watching Malmö defenders, as though anticipating the cross from Robertson. Notice the position of Robertson now—standing outside the field of play.**

► *Francis had to hurl himself at the ball to make contact yet still angle it back and up to beat Möller at the near post. The header was perfect and the man bought for over £1 million three months before (and making his debut in Europe) had paid back a huge chunk of that fee by keeping the trophy in England. Apart from the marvellous timing of the blind-side run, the goal also shows that you must have the confidence and ability to finish the job if the ball arrives.*

the return pass. In one-to-one marking situations, too, the attacker must be constantly searching for the chance to slip out of his opponent's vision and get behind him, forcing him to turn.

Running in order to create space and provide options for the player on the ball is the essence of support play, and you must always be willing to run into positions that threaten most danger to your opponents' goal—even when the odds are against your receiving the ball. Those odds can be high on the blind-side run: while a good proportion of attacking runs behind the defence are made to make contact with crosses hit to specific areas, notably the far post, many are also made on the assumption that tailor-made passes can and will be supplied to exploit the chance. Often, however, the run will not be seen by the player on the ball or he may choose an alternative course of action—a simpler pass, a shot, another type of cross or a run at the defence. All players, and especially midfielders, have to be prepared to make such runs again and again in the knowledge that they may not be rewarded. They may not even be recognised: fans are even more guilty than bad defenders of watching only the play in the area around the ball.

◄The ideal situation in which to make a blind-side run is when play develops down the flank, because defenders will tend to watch the play around the ball—to look towards the touchline instead of glancing around to check on the movement of opponents away from the ball. The run behind the last covering player onto a cross can be devastating if he is 'found guilty' of ball-watching. If the defender does pull out wide to keep you in vision, that will widen the gap between himself and his team-mates and it may well be possible to dart in there on the blind side of the other defenders to meet a cross played in shorter. If you are making the extra man, the run is useful even if spotted by the last defender, since he then has the awkward choice of leaving his man to cover you or staying put and risking the chance of a goal if the ball is played to you in space.

THE REVERSE PASS

One very special way of switching the point of an attack is the reverse pass. This is where you carry the ball in one direction, shaping to continue moving that way or to play it that side, and then suddenly pivot or swivel to play it at angle the other way to a team-mate making a run on your 'blind side'. The idea is to draw the attention of at least a couple of defenders and pull them across, thus creating space for the supporting player. You know the man is there because either before or during your run you've had a quick glance around you—though some colleagues seem to develop a sixth sense for knowing each other's positions. The angle of the pass can vary: in the example below, for instance, the ball could be played behind the two central defenders to the player running in. The ploy can work well out wide, too, where a player cuts inside from the line and then puts a reverse pass into the path of a full-back on the overlap, and can be incisive when combined with a crossover, where the man on the ball retains possession and then turns to send the ball into the path of the player on the supporting run. Surprise is a crucial element.

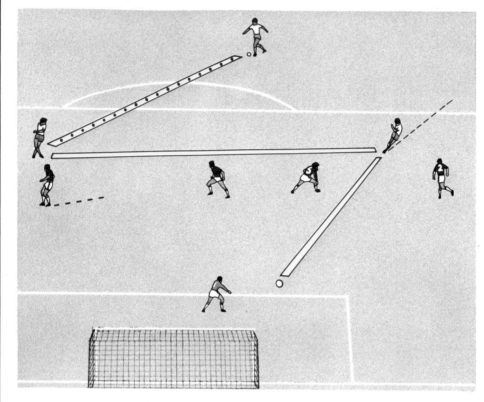

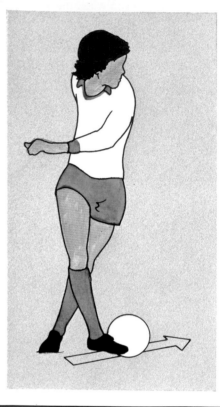

◄ An illustration of how the tendency of defenders to watch only the play around the ball leaves them vulnerable to the blind-side run of an attacker moving in behind them. It happens at the highest levels, as the Aston Villa players demonstrate here at Wembley in the 1981 Charity Shield game with Tottenham. The gravest offender is centre-back Allan Evans: with Ken McNaught (5) well placed goalside of Mark Falco (11), Evans is neither facing the cluster of Spurs players near the ball nor covering the movement of Tony Galvin (9) behind his back. Glenn Hoddle isn't slow to spot the chance of a strike on goal and sends over the chip for Galvin, who will be looking to get in front of the last defender, right-back Kenny Swain (out of picture). The blind-side run can be far more dangerous against a zonal defence than those marking man-for-man with a sweeper; they are less likely to 'lose' players and the sweeper can monitor any developments with an extra man coming in beyond his back line. A higher proportion of such runs in attacking positions will bear fruit if a side has perceptive players who can both see the possibility and respond to it—and Hoddle is a fine example. Crosses are the most plentiful source because the defenders' field of view excludes much of the play away from the ball

Dummying on the ball

There are situations in which one of the most penetrating ways of setting up a chance on goal is *not* to take the ball played to you, to ignore the pass and let it run to a player in support behind you. Such 'dummies' are usually worked best by players who have been in the same side for some time and enjoy a good knowledge and understanding of each other's play; the most productive combinations are the twin strikers. At the same time the dummy can be effective as a critical aspect of a play at a free-kick or even a throw-in, when team-mates have the advantage of actually knowing it could be played.

Dummying on the ball in open play, however, is largely a question of improvisation. It will only work if it is done convincingly, and while there are certain movements which can help achieve this, like 'dipping the shoulder' or moving first towards the ball, the actual technique matters little as long as the defender is deceived into following the man without the ball, even for a split second. The precise movement will depend on the nature of the 'pass', the relative positions of defenders and the supporting player, how tight the marker is, the location on the pitch and, perhaps above all, the build and personal 'style' of play of the man executing the move.

Assuming there is a player available in the right position, the pass still has to be of sufficient pace to beat the marker and reach its 'new' target. The skill itself needs to be performed at speed to make the movement effective and exploit the element of surprise.

The dummy is a very special kind of skill and is unlikely to come off more than once in the same game, because the marker will be wary in a similar position next time. And while it provides an extra option in attack, it is not a ploy to try in the defensive third of the field.

▼A well-executed and neatly disguised dummy can create a whole range of options for a threat on goal. The vital thing is the initial movement by A: it has to be convincing enough to draw X with him, to throw him sufficiently for the ball to 'beat' both players. In this instance, a pass infield (or perhaps a strong throw), a timely run by B would give him a number of options to put pressure on the defence: a direct thrust or shot at goal; a first-time return to A, who should be using the advantage he gained to take up a dangerous position near goal; a pass inside the full-back to C; or a ball behind the defence to D, thus continuing the switch in the direction of play. He also has the alternatives of playing the ball back to the passer, who may well have made himself available, or (if the run wasn't quite right or Y reacted quickly to the ploy) the simple lay-back to E. While such movement revolving round a dummy could be practised for a free-kick, in open play it is more likely to be an intuitive combination, with the others responding to the result.

The wall pass

Known as the 'double pass' in most of Europe and often called simply the 'one-two' in Britain, the wall pass is a fundamental aspect of support play. The concept is a very basic one. Any youngster who has played pick-up games in the street or in five-a-side games knows that one of the neatest ways to beat an opponent is to knock the ball against the wall or boards and go past to collect the rebound on the other side of him; on the pitch, the part of the wall is taken by another player.

The wall pass is a relatively comfortable way of playing the ball out of defence, where the team going forward will usually hold a numerical advantage, but it becomes increasingly difficult to apply the further upfield it is tried, since opponents can prevent it by retreating and conceding space. Though it is in theory at its most applicable in the opposition's danger zone, where the defenders can retreat no more without presenting the chance of a shot, there is a widespread reluctance to use it in the very area where it can be most productive, by setting up the possibility to score. Ironically this tends to be exaggerated at the highest levels of the game. Attackers feel that with knowledgable, numerous and well-organised defenders, the odds are stacked against them. Yet played to perfection it is virtually unstoppable, and the wall pass has been one of the trademarks of some great sides, where quick-thinking, fast-acting players were renowned for cutting paths through the opponents' lines near the edge of the area. The Holland team that reached the final of the 1974 World Cup, and the Argentinians who won the 1978 tournament, are two examples. The Dutch in particular, pioneers of 'total football', were adept at using their midfielders and adventurous defenders to come through on the break and play one-twos off forwards.

While simple in essence, the wall pass is not an easy move to execute. Unlike the real thing, the 'wall player' is relatively small, mobile and somewhat unpredictable. It relies on timing, control, pace and an element of disguise to be really effective. Essentially it is a skill governed by four basic guidelines, and in discussing them we can assume that the target player is marked and the move is played in a 'two-against-two' situation rather than the 'two-against one', which obviously does not require such precision.

The first area concerns the problem of

◄ **The simplest practices for learning to play the wall pass are small-sided games, either 'keep-ball' or competitive matches with marked goals, in a confined space: two-against-two or three-against three in the centre-circle or penalty area, for example. These force you to be accurate with the first pass and quick to move into space for the return, and teach you the control and speed necessary to perform the skill in tight situations. The wall pass is only a building block of support play, however, and shown here are some variations on the basic idea. Another is for the target player to turn with the ball across his man and play a reverse pass to the passer, who makes a run round the 'blind' side of all three players. Such moves must be first tried in training.**

when to release the ball. The one-two only works well if the first defender is committed before the ball is passed, but no defender likes players to run at him with the ball and he may well be retreating, trying to slow you down. While drawing your man, you must not allow him to dispossess you or deflect the pass. The ideal 'point of release' is just outside tackling range—if you pass too early he can readjust his position (falling back to block the return); pass too late and he may intercept.

Second, the initial pass should be played to the feet of the receiver. There are many instances where a closely marked player can lay off a high ball to a third player moving into space using a volley or a chest pass, and even in the wall pass itself the receiver may elect to chip or loop the return to the running player in certain circumstances; but the one-two is jeopardised from the start if the first pass is not 'on the deck'. The ploy relies on speed of movement and the accuracy of the first-time return, and the chances of a good second pass will almost certainly be lost if the ball bounces awkwardly or comes in at a difficult height to the receiver.

Third, it must be the man who plays the first ball who dictates where and how the return is made, not the wall player. The first player should be positive, leaving the receiver in doubt as to what is expected of him—a pass of the right weight into the right place at the right time. To get this

◄ *George Wood's attempt to smother the ball is in vain as Kevin Keegan beats him to Trevor Brooking's pass and slips it under his diving body to give England a 3–1 lead against Scotland at Wembley in May 1979. The goal virtually sealed the match and the Home International Championship.*

► That England goal captured all the main features of the wall pass: simple in concept, it needs pace and precision to execute and can be one of the most devastating moves in the game if played well. It was set up when Keegan, enjoying one of his finest internationals, picked up a pass inside the Scotland half and moved quickly forward. Brushing off a challenge from John Wark, he headed for the area and the confronting figure of Gordon McQueen. Brooking, attacking the defence without the ball, had made an intelligent supporting run to make himself available for the pass—and Keegan duly pushed the ball inside and accelerated for the return. Brooking turned slightly to get a good sideways stance and swept the ball forward. At first the pass looked a little strong; but Keegan's crucial change of pace and determination, helped by a moment of hesitancy on the part of Wood, gave the England captain a sliding touch. It's interesting to compare this one-two, where both players were moving forward at speed, with the one overleaf, where both players were facing their own goal. The wall pass is all about improvisation in attack.

▲ As well as being used to cover the variations of the triangular movement round a defender, the term wall pass also describes a one-two where the runner has no opponent to beat but where the marker has come in tight on the receiver. This ball is a useful one for full-backs to play up to midfielders or front runners out wide, when there is little space to use on the flank (in this case the left) and where the defender is closing down the first turn. As the ball is played up to him, the receiver plays it back at an angle to the passing player, who has moved infield to create an angle on the third pass; a sharp turn and a nicely weighted ball can see the forward peel off to run onto the ball in space. The game is full of these apparently simple passing movements, but they all need practice and understanding to work in matches.

across he must run hard at the space he intends to exploit, beginning that move in the same stride as he releases the ball. After playing with others, you soon develop the knack of judging when and where and how team-mates are likely to use the technique.

Within these essential guidelines there are some further pointers, all of which can help to make the wall pass more effective. First, and like all inter-passing movements, it stands a far higher chance of success if performed with a change of pace. It can be done at one speed, but that little burst into the space will steal extra yards on the first defender, giving you more space and time in which to work, and help to tell the receiver exactly what you want.

Another way of gaining vital time is to disguise the pass as much as possible, in an attempt to throw not only the first marker but also the covering player. This can be done by striking the ball with the instep, 'off the laces', but is more deceptive when playing the ball in your stride without a shaping motion and without changing the pattern of your run, using the front-foot pass technique described in detail on page 66.

The move will be made considerably easier, of course, if the receiving player is in the best position possible to play the ball. This does not just mean he should be at a good angle and have enough room to work his return; it also means his turning sideways on to improve his vision and awareness of what is happening around him. With at least four players involved, the situation can change in an instant, and he will be in a better position to react. If his marker has anticipated the one-two and moves round to try and nick the ball, for example, or to go across and try to cover both target player and runner, the receiver can more easily choose and execute an alternative if his stance is at an

angle rather than flat. He is then also better positioned to play the ball back to the runner with the foot that is farthest from the marker—and the one which, of course, allows him the maximum control on his pass.

The wall pass is not an isolated skill. It will be part of an attacking movement, and the receiving player should, like all players who have made a pass forward, be looking to get past his marker after playing the return and search for the best position possible in which to support the first player. It could well be that he could receive the ball a second time.

Finally, it is important to make two contrasting points about the wall pass. First, there is no point in trying to work the move if the correct framework for it does not exist—when the defender has not been drawn, when the initial pass is poor, when the first player has not moved quick-

ly enough for the first-time return and so on. If you try and find the running player at a difficult angle or with a ball played too high or too far behind you, you will at least be under pressure and could well lose possession. Far better to hold, shielding the ball until another option can be taken up, or simply lay the ball off to a supporting player. The ploy is not wasted: you have retained possession, the first player has made a run into forward space, and at least two defenders have been forced to change their positions.

At the other end of the scale, the wall pass must be seen as a platform for a whole range of moves. It is far from a one-dimensional skill. The relevant 'action replays' in this book (see pages 65, 69, 71, 104 and 122 as well as the previous page and below) recall the use of a variety of angles, contact surfaces and locations on the pitch, all based on the 'old one-two'.

▶ *Italy's Roberto Bettega wheels away in triumph after scoring what proved to be perhaps the best team goal of the 1978 World Cup finals, leaving a bemused Argentina defence in his wake—notably Tarantini, Galvan, Passarella and Fillol. One of the finest finishers in the game, he set up the chance himself with an audacious one-two with Paolo Rossi, despite having his back to his opponent. In their next game against West Germany the two players almost brought off another score from a wall pass, 'straighter' this time with the passer facing forward; Rossi, however, passed with the inside of his 'back' foot (see diagram on page 142). These two players alone are ample proof that when it comes to playing the one-two round the box, variety and invention are the keys to success.*

▶ **Bettega's breathtaking goal came in the 68th minute of the last group 1 game in Buenos Aires. Both teams were through, but the hosts had a point to prove. In the end it was the Italians who proved a point—and to the side who, with Kempes and Luque as the main exponents, were illustrating already in the tournament that little can stop the one-two if it's played with pace and precision. Italy's own remarkable version was made possible when Rossi, having battled to win a throw-in against Olguin, shaped to cross but then slipped the ball back to Antognoni, who neatly disguised his first-time pass up to Bettega. Though the Juventus star must take the credit for the 'flick and turn' manoeuvre (not to mention the actual score), the inventive parts played by the supporting cast were crucial. As Antognoni made the pass he could see Rossi's sensible run infield to make himself available . . .**

ROSSI 1

RO

ANTOGNONI

◀While the wall pass is an important weapon for any side in their attempts to penetrate the opposing defence and set up scoring chances, its more common if less dramatic use is as one of the basic tools of midfield and approach play. Much of the forward movement in central areas of the field rests on the principle of 'give and go', modest but productive support play revolving round a continually changing pattern of triangles—where the golden rule is to look for a fresh position forward after making the pass. It's a question of making the ball do the work, relying on teamwork and constant movement; it's far easier to take an opponent out of the game and make progress by laying the ball off and running by him to collect the return than by trying to take it past him. Here a midfielder receives a short ball from a defender, controls it, slips a pass to a supporting player with his second touch and then goes off for the first-time return on the wall pass. Further forward he may well be looking for another one-two, possibly to his left. This interpassing is vital to control the midfield.

BEATING THE OFFSIDE TRAP

Few areas of the game cause as much controversy as offside, and for every goal scored there must be half a dozen or more indirect free-kicks awarded for it. Apart from debate over the law itself (see page 173), there is the thorny issue of the offside trap—where a defence pushes up to leave forwards stranded as the ball is played to them. Outside the NASL, where the attacker cannot be offside on his team's side of a line 35 yards from the goal-line, this can mean pushing up as far as the halfway line. While rarer now in top-class football than in the 1960s and early 1970s—the pace of the game makes it too risky, and most sides prefer the insurance of a covering player—it is a sensible defensive tactic when employed in moderation and the right places, though certain clubs do still use it as their basic tactical ploy in away games against particular types of opposition; aimed at securing a goalless draw with the outside chance of a win with a quick counter-attack, it hardly makes for attractive play. The classic ways to beat a defence pushing up are the individual dribble, the various forms of through ball (see pages 170–3), and the wall pass. Played sharply and accurately, with that vital change of pace, it can be the answer to even the best organised of defensive units. The wider the angle the more forward the pass will be and therefore the more forward the run, so it's important for the 'wall player' to try and play sideways on.

When Bettega, policed by Argentina captain Passarella, flicked the ball to him with the outside of his foot, Rossi responded with a first-time pass using his right heel. Bettega ducked round Passarella and latched onto the return, steering it away from Galvan's covering run and then, just before a sweeping challenge came in from Tarantini, he rifled a fierce drive past Fillol into the corner. 'If you have to be beaten, perhaps it's better to be beaten by a great goal,' mourned Argentina team manager Cesar Menotti afterwards. But, like their predecessors in 1974 (when West Germany also lost their third game by 1–0), the hosts had lost a battle but went on to win the war. Italy, meanwhile, brilliant one moment and brittle the next, finished in fourth place, losing to Holland and Brazil.

169

The through ball

In general, defenders will be content if they can retreat to good covering positions and hold up the advance of their opponents, if the play is kept in front of them and the ball played square or back. They can afford to bide their time, waiting for the chance to regain possession by an interception or a challenge. Players who make easy passes to unmarked or loosely marked colleagues are often wasting time and giving the opposition valuable time to recover and readjust. Even the long cross-field pass, useful as a means of switching the point of attack, rarely deserves the applause it gets, which rewards skill and technique as much as tactical awareness. What is lacking is penetration: and the pass that is the most penetrative, eliminating defenders (or 'putting them out of the game') is the through ball.

The best pass in football is the one played between opponents to a team-mate running from an onside position into the space behind them. No defence likes to turn, to play the game facing their own goal, even for a break right on the touchline; the pressure on them is never greater than when a player has got in behind them and is moving towards the ball.

Like the wall pass, the through ball appears an obvious and reasonably simple way to break down crowded defences, particularly those who play square without a covering player. The intended receiver has an automatic advantage, simply because his opponent has to turn or partially turn to chase, and that can take valuable fractions of a second. Yet it is a rarity compared to the cross.

There are three basic reasons. First, with midfield players dropping back to assist, defences have become more dense and, if not playing the offside trap, also 'longer'. It is thus more difficult to 'see' the route for the shorter through pass, and there is more distance to clear and for the receiver to run for the more classic type of long through ball.

Second, defenders have become more tactically aware as well as faster as individuals, and defences have become increasingly reliable as organised units. This applies to a certain extent at all levels of the game. The defender is now more likely to read the situation well and intercept or jockey rather than challenge clumsily; less likely to be 'lost' or beaten by an attacker. With their well-drilled approach to covering, an 'as one man' use of the offside trap, and sensible goalside marking of opponents as the basic starting point, defences are not as vulnerable to the through ball as they once were.

▲ A short, square pass and then a penetrating run at the defence can be the perfect platform for beating a side that's pushing up and trying to catch players offside. In tight situations like this where the ground pass may be difficult the answer can be the chip, which clears the opponents but holds up for the receiver to run on to beat the recovering players to the ball.

Third, the through ball is very precise skill, allowing only a small margin of error. It is not a matter of 'kick and rush': the pass and the run must be synchronised almost to perfection if they are not to fall victims to interception or offside, and the space into which the ball can effectively be played is nearly always relatively small. These three factors have combined to put a premium not only on the positional sense, mobility and speed of the intended receiver; they have also forced ball players to concentrate on more subtle types of through ball.

The main effect has been to make the majority of through passes more diagonal, and the ability to swerve the ball can be a huge asset. Thus the classic through ball today is the one played in early from a wide position, between two defenders, curling round the back of the central defenders towards the path of the runner. This can work too from centre to flank positions, for the ball played 'inside the full-back' to a winger or full-back making a run down the line or cutting in.

It has meant, too, that the through ball now demands more sophisticated techni-

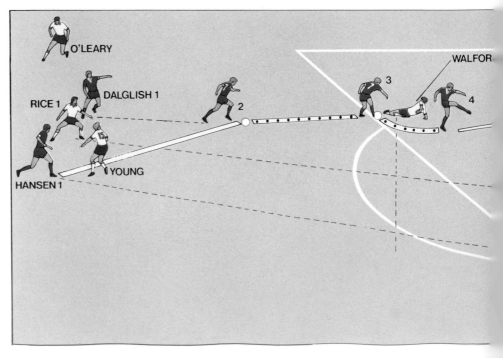

▲ The through ball is not a skill confined to passer and receiver. Forwards and midfield players must work hard to create the space necessary to play it or at least to cause distraction and hesitancy in opposing defenders. Here, in another ploy to beat the organised offside trap, two strikers have pulled away from their markers in an arc, hoping to draw them out of position, while a midfielder makes a break forward onto a diagonal pass. Like the move opposite, it's most effective played on the halfway line against a side pushing up.

ques and tactical awareness. The chip and the swerving pass are great weapons here; an element of disguise can steal vital fractions of seconds, so the use of the front foot should be cultivated; receivers must think far more about losing their markers and getting into potential positions with blind-side runs.

Another affect of improved defences has been to make the through ball (like many other moves and ploys) an open-play tactic concerning far more players than just passer and receiver. All the members of the team in potentially attack-

ing positions should always be looking for the chance to create the space in which the move can operate successfully. Front runners do this by movement off the ball, drawing their markers away from positions in which they could cover a possible break with a through pass. Inside-to-outside runs, dragging central defenders away from the middle by moving towards the touchline on a diagonal course, are one answer, while looping runs, at first away towards your own goal (see above) can distract defenders and cause indecision.

Midfielders and full-backs can help by

making overlapping runs down the flanks. As we have already mentioned, the ball played inside the full-back can exploit such support. This forces the defence to turn and retreat, and the cross can be played in to attackers moving forward—while the defenders face their own goal.

The type and exact nature of the through pass used in a given situation can be tempered by the pitch on which it is to be tried. On a wet, slippery surface, for example, the ball can easily skid and thus pick up speed as it lands, and the weight of the pass should be adjusted accordingly,

◄ In August 1979 Liverpool warmed up for yet another successful season—one in which they would retain the League Championship to record their fourth title in five years—with a ruthless performance against FA Cup holders Arsenal in the Charity Shield game at Wembley. They scored three fine goals, but the one that clinched the match was perhaps the most outstanding. For one thing it was started from a deep position by a central defender, when Alan Hansen showed both tactical awareness and solid technique to cut out a Graham Rix pass aimed at Alan Sunderland well inside his own half. With plenty of space in front of him and Arsenal stretched having pushed players forward, Hansen forged upfield and way past the halfway line as the depleted defence retreated and tried to hold him up. About 12 yards from the edge of the area Pat Rice and Willie Young held their ground—and Hansen, seeing Terry McDermott covered by Steve Walford to his right, slipped the ball between the two defenders to Kenny Dalglish, who had managed to lose David O'Leary and come up to support Hansen on the blind side of Rice. It was no 40-yard special, but it was a devastating through ball. Walford had no choice but to try and stop Dalglish, but his desperate sliding challenge played right into the Scot's hands; he turned sharply inside the centre-back, looked up to check on the positioning of Pat Jennings, and then picked his spot. **171**

SUPPORT PLAY

▼The ball played 'inside the full-back' to a team-mate on a diagonal run towards goal is one of the most effective of all through passes, and a splendid example came in the derby game between the two Manchester giants at Maine Road in February 1979. Always a special fixture for the clubs and their supporters, this clash was particularly important as both managers (Malcolm Allison and Dave Sexton) were under mounting pressure to stop the slide of a side bursting with famous names and expensive signings. City had recorded only one win in their 14 previous League games, a week before at Tottenham; United had lost their four previous League matches, three of them at home, conceding 13 goals. Over 46,000 fans braved the bitter February day to see the encounter, and it was United who stole all the glory. England man Steve Coppell was the key figure, scoring twice in a 3–0 victory that gave the visitors their best ever result at Maine Road. His second goal came when Sammy McIlroy won the ball from a Joe Corrigan punt, controlled it and passed up to Jimmy Greenhoff in space towards the right. One of the best touch players in Britain, Greenhoff killed the ball on the volley with his right foot and swivelled through nearly 180° to hook a left-foot pass past Dave Watson and well inside Paul Power for Steve Coppell. It was tremendous awareness as well as technique from Greenhoff: the pass, neatly placed between the two defenders, was hit 'blind' because Coppell was directly behind him when he recovered the ball. Forcing the defenders to turn on treacherous surface, it was the ideal ball for the conditions, and though Coppell had to adjust his run slightly, giving Power the chance to get very close to a successful challenge, he kept his footing and balance to beat Corrigan with a superbly struck topspin 'lob volley'.

while on a muddy ground it will tend to stick, so a chip may be more effective.

The actual shape and size of the field of play can also be factors. On a long narrow pitch it is possible to play the ball deeper and try to stretch the defence lengthways; on a wide pitch it can pay to concentrate more on the diagonal ball played in behind the defence. This is a consideration which applies at all levels of the game; a few extra yards of space can make a world of difference to a top player, while in the more modest amateur and schoolboy areas the size of pitches can vary a great deal from club to club.

The through ball, executed with pace and precision, can be the perfect way to break down a square defence, to get free in space with the ball without being caught

offside. As with all ploys that can beat the possible trap—whether that is applied as deliberate policy or merely a sensible tactical response from defenders—it relies on the front runners getting back on their side of the last covering opponent.

Because of the inevitable link between the through ball and offside, and because of the doubt and confusion which seem to surround the law, it is worth recording here the relevant parts of Law XI as determined by the International Board and published by FIFA: '(1) A player is in an offside position if he is nearer to his opponents' goal-line than the ball, unless (a) he is in his own half of the field of play, or (b) there are at least two of his opponents nearer their goal-line than he is. (2) A player shall only be declared offside and

penalised for being in an offside position if, at the moment the ball touches, or is played by, one of his team, he is, in the opinion of the referee (a) interfering with play or with an opponent, or (b) seeking to gain an advantage by being in that position. (3) A player shall not be declared offside by the referee (a) merely because of his being in an offside position, or (b) if he receives the ball, direct, from a goal-kick, corner-kick, a throw-in, or when it has last been dropped by the referee . . .'

The Board, wishing to clarify that the rule centres on the decision being made when the ball is passed, further stipulates that: '(1) Offside shall not be judged at the moment the player in question receives the ball, but at the moment when the ball is passed to him by one of his own side. A

player who is not in an offside position when one of his colleagues passes the ball to him or takes a free-kick, does not therefore become offside if he goes forward during the flight of the ball.'

Though at its most lethal played into positions near goal, the through ball is by no means just an attacking skill. There is unlikely to be the same type of space available in the defensive half of the field—except for the ball inside the opposing winger to the full-back moving up, perhaps—but then the through ball does not have to be a 30- or 40-yard special. A 10-yard ball between two opponents still puts them out of the game, and midfield players must always be looking for the chance to exploit such situations—and of course to follow up in support.

IMPROVING YOUR SPEED OFF THE MARK

Speed can be the factor that separates success and failure in football. You need speed to beat opponents when you have the ball, you need speed to beat opponents when you don't have the ball (to reach that through ball or collect that return on the wall pass), and you need speed to beat opponents to the ball, to 'get in first' for a shot on goal or to clear in defence. Rarely is speed the sustained kind, though of course that's necessary at times, and particularly for wingers whose very function relies on it; but more often the game demands the short sharp burst, either from a standing start or in the form of acceleration—that crucial 'change of pace'. Every player benefits from improving this area of his play: the goalkeeper dashing off his line to dive at a forward's feet, the defender making a last-ditch tackle, the midfielder turning sharply or nicking the ball from an opponent, the striker moving in quickly to snap up the half-chance. While some claim the game in Britain is 'too fast', they are right in that all too often team play is hurried and ill-conceived. Speed of individual thought and movement, anticipating and reacting fast, is a very different matter, a vital commodity that can distinguish the good player from the ordinary. Skill, on its own, is usually not enough, but skill allied to speed is priceless. We're not just talking about running: it covers starting and stopping, turning and twisting, changing direction as well as pace—all the movements that footballers use. The simple examples shown below can be a starting point for sharpening this part of your game.

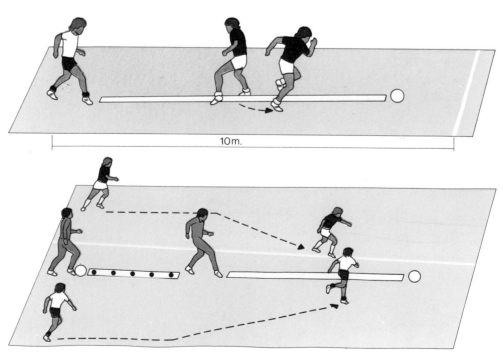

► While you can't increase speed as much in terms of proportion as you can strength and stamina, working at simple routines will sharpen your reactions and improve the suitability of your muscles and joints for obeying the commands they receive. You can start on your own, simply sprinting between markers placed five metres apart, but to make it more 'lifelike' you should use a ball: lob it into the air, sprint to touch the marker and then sprint back to control the ball before it bounces a second time. Keep the angle sharp because that's how it is in matches—all twists and turns and short, sharp bursts. Another way is to throw it straight up and turn round the marker and come back.

► This two-man exercise tests the speed to turn as well as the speed forward over those vital first five or six yards. All outfield players must be quick to react to balls played past or behind them, whether it is a striker giving chase to the through ball or the defender trying to beat him to it. As the ball goes through his legs the second player turns to chase.

► It's easy to make these exercises realistic and competitive with three players, particularly if one is a coach or a more senior player. He moves slowly forward with the ball and the two players jog each side of him; he then suddenly releases the ball with either foot for them to chase. If he tries to vary the practice by doing something different, like backheeling or turning to play the ball the other way, so much the better. Exercises should always aim to improve speed of thought as well as movement.

First-time play

Despite the array of individual skills with which players can entertain the public, few sights in football are as rewarding as the sweeping, penetrative move made up of a series of first-time passes. It is where teamwork, the essence of the game, reaches its height.

Just as every player should think defensively when their side loses possession, so every player should think positively when they regain it. The first-time ball is the extreme example of 'thinking positive'. And it is when two or more players all think positively and move and play accordingly (sometimes perhaps as many as seven or eight), that the best team moves occur. A fine example is the goal by France featured on page 194: end to end with seven men and eight touches.

In general, the more effective a team's tactis the fewer and quicker the passes and touches can be. Time is the defence's friend, enabling them to organise and cover, and quick one-touch moves can be devastating simply because it does not allow them that luxury. Ultimately it relies on penetration, one or more passes that cut open the defence.

Not all the movements involved need be forward, however. The first pass may be a little lay-off played back a few yards as the passer goes looking for a new position; the move may involve a simple square ball, as shown below; a ball inside the full-back may be followed by a first-time cross from the winger to the head of a forward running in.

To play a ball first time normally assumes that the passer has assessed the movement of others and the possibilities before he receives the ball. Subtle forms of one-touch play therefore require a certain level of vision and awareness. One-touch practice games will help to heighten this faculty, and to help players make decisions quickly.

Successful first-time play relies above all on movement, the ability of players to move and make contact with the ball in such a way that the defenders cannot cope. A defender's job is at its most difficult when both the ball and a number of players are both moving quickly.

◀ *Manchester United keeper Alex Stepney fails to reach Bobby Stokes' shot and Second Division Southampton take the lead in the 1976 FA Cup final. It proved the only goal of the game—but United and Tommy Docherty came back the following year to beat treble-chasing Liverpool.*

▼**The move that caused yet another upset at Wembley was classically simple, a lesson in one-touch football. Mike Channon, policed by Stewart Houston, played off a long clearance by keeper Ian Turner square to Jim McCalliog. The little Scot, totally aware of Stokes' potential run before he received the ball, hit a superb first-time pass between Martin Buchan and Brian Greenhoff. Stokes met the ball on the edge of the area, finding the only space Stepney couldn't cover with his first-time shot.**

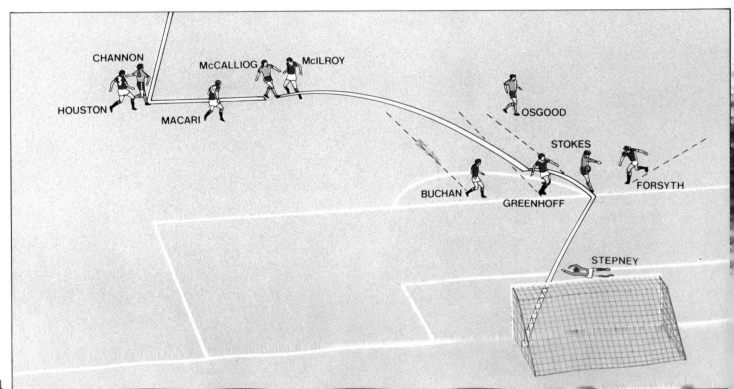

ATTACKING AT SET PIECES

Throw-in

Every team can expect to take anything between 20 and 60 throws during an average match, no matter what their standard of play or level of competition. This is up to ten times as many free-kicks near goal or corners they are likely to be awarded or win. Even adding goal-kicks, throws-in still account for more than 70% of all restarts in football.

Yet the throw-in remains a largely neglected aspect of tactical play, even at the professional level. Few teams give it much attention in training compared to the free-kicks and corners, and in the main it is a poorly performed set piece. Often this is the result of an almost casual attitude towards the throw. Most players and many coaches see it almost exclusively as a mechanism for getting the ball back into play, rather than as a platform for positive action. This is certainly the case in the middle third of the pitch, where both potential and danger to the goals seem distant from the touchline. Players lose concentration very easily at throws-in; they 'stop thinking'. Control, skill and discipline are somehow shelved when the ball goes out of play. They thus become vulnerable in defence and impotent in attack.

This sloppy approach is caused by a combination of four factors. The throw-in is a comparatively common restart, and familiarity breeds contempt; it lacks the

THE DEFENSIVE THIRD OF THE PITCH
Losing possession through lack of care and attention is the biggest crime at a throw-in, and nowhere is it likely to be punished more severely than in the defensive third of the pitch. Safety first is the golden rule, with throws taken from anywhere just behind a point level with the front edge of the penalty area being played to the keeper when it's on. If an opponent is trying to block that route, a defender can make a run into space to draw him off; if he doesn't follow, that player can become the target for a return ball and the thrower can then play it upfield. The alternatives are the ball played back to a defender near the goal-line—and then possibly back to the keeper—or the longer ball 'down the line'. If you are defending at a throw-in near your goal, then the basic approach is simply the application of good defensive play: marking tight near the ball and putting the receiver under pressure to make control and a pass more difficult, marking loosely and covering elsewhere, guarding important space, staying aware of movement well away from the ball (especially on your blind side), and above all keeping goalside of your opponents. Defenders are even more likely than the side in possession to lose concentration when the ball goes out of play and be slow to react, and are thus vulnerable to the quickly taken, well-placed throw. The antidote is quick, tight marking and covering as a result of being alert and well organised. It's important to spend a little time in training on defending as well as attacking with the throw-in.

THE MIDDLE THIRD OF THE PITCH: 1
Players of both the side in possession and the defending team all too easily see throws in the middle part of the pitch merely as a mechanism for getting the ball back into play and fail to think or respond in a positive way. A pass with the hands that far from goal seems to present little potential and no real danger. Yet every throw can and should be a springboard for attack. Keeping possession is the priority, but with teamwork and understanding developed in training this can be enhanced by striving to get someone going goalwards with the ball and into more penetrative positions. Basic switches are often enough if done well. In this example a midfielder switches with a winger as the two men pull their respective markers around to create enough space for the number six to receive the ball down the line and move forward. The same affect can be achieved with a wide-angled crossover ploy. The odds should favour the side taking the throw because they're initiating the moves—but will only work if the play has been practised in training. It also helps if the thrower disguises his choice until the last moment. Most opponents will be reluctant to follow the full-back if he pulls back to receive the ball—but all too often this move is followed by the hopeful long ball upfield.

immediate potential or danger and thus the drama of a free-kick near goal or a corner, when players, aware of the pressure, are psyched up to concentrate to the full; it is a somewhat 'loose' and scruffy set play, with plenty of latitude provided in the rules and the interpretation of them; and there are a multitude of options open to the thrower, encouraging players to feel that someone else will make themselves available, to convince themselves that they are too closely marked.

Except perhaps in the case of the long throw to the near post, the throw-in is of course bound to be the poor relation of the set-piece family. But in theory—and to an increasingly high proportion in practice, too—each throw-in presents the chance to start an attacking move with the advantage of pre-planned tactics.

No matter what is planned, however, the basic concern at throws is to retain possession. Your team may have worked hard to get the ball and it is a crime to throw it away through lack of concentration or simple control. There are obviously occasions in the attacking third of the field when possession has to be risked for the potential reward in terms of creating a chance on goal, but in general (and certainly in the defensive third) safety first is the name of the game.

There are several ways in which that possession can be immediately forfeited. The first is simply to throw the ball incorrectly, which results in a foul throw and a throw to the opposition. This is surprisingly common among youngsters, often because they do not look for the easy ball,

THE ATTACKING THIRD OF THE PITCH

The basic aim here should be to get the ball into the danger area as quickly and as positively as possible. Defenders are likely to lose concentration at a throw-in and are vulnerable to the quick throw. Thus the nearest man to the ball should take it and other players should be looking for good positions as soon as the ball goes out of play, not after it has been retrieved. You are looking for penetration and results here, and retaining possession is not the primary consideration it is in deeper positions. If the throw is taken from 30 yards or more from the goal-line, still try to play the ball forward: the pass that goes beyond a defender leaves him the wrong side of the ball and having to recover. Remember, too, that you can't be offside from a throw-in, so if the defence have pushed up a little far or have no cover, you can go for the throw played in behind them for a team-mate to run on to. Fairly simple movement can create the space necessary to get the cross in with a first or second touch from the receiver. The example above shows a switch between two forwards to make room for the retreating player to hook his centre to the far post. There are obviously many variations on a basic theme like this, and they are well worth working on in practice, incorporating the players who will receive the ball near goal. By using markers in these training sessions, the defenders in your team will also get valuable practice at coping with movement at throws. Sadly, this aspect of set-piece play is still neglected in comparison to free-kicks near goal and corners.

THE MIDDLE THIRD OF THE PITCH: 2

This variation of the move illustrated opposite aims to get the winger 'in'. He comes short for the ball and then checks sharply across his marker to move into space inside and the thrower tries to put the ball into the path of his new run. If it works well the midfield player (10) continues his run and becomes available on the overlap for the reverse pass and possible cross—or at worst pulls a defender out wide. Changing direction is a key factor in the kind of practised moves required to create space and make the most of throws. Another example is a forward running slightly away from goal towards the thrower, hoping to take the short ball and then suddenly turning at right-angles to go down the line for the longer throw into his path. One mistake a lot of youngsters make is to 'crowd' the thrower: this restricts the space available to the receiver (and the thrower if the ball is returned), and the only reason for being in close is to pull a defender in with you to create space behind—either for a sudden kickback by the receiver or for a third player moving up from a deeper position. The rule is to spread out and keep moving to make it difficult for the opposition to mark and cover. The thrower, if he doesn't get the return, should of course be looking to get back into the game quickly and positively.

177

and is a sad waste. The ball must be thrown, not dropped, using both hands to 'deliver the ball from behind and over' your head. You must face the field of play with some part of your body and both feet must be in contact with the ground on or behind the touchline. You can step onto the field of play only after you have released the ball.

Possession can also be lost if the throw puts unnecessary pressure on the receiver —another result of the casual attitude towards the throw-in. It is important to remember that the throw is simply a pass played with your hands instead of your foot, and the basic principles of good passing should apply. Thus the throw must make control as easy as possible for the receiver, played at the pace, angle and height that presents him with the least possible problems. It should be thrown to him, not at him. If it is low, it should be thrown directly to his feet, not at hip or waist height or bouncing up awkwardly off the ground; if it is to be a headed return, it should be low rather than high so that he can move in to nod it back.

Your team obviously has a far greater chance of retaining possession and beginning an attack if the receiver is unmarked. Team-mates should be trying to find space in which to receive and use the ball, and you should respond to their movement by delivering the ball to the right player at the right time. If there are two unmarked players available, throw to the one farther forward; if no player is 'free', play the ball to the team-mate who can most easily come off his marker and lay the ball off, most probably back to you, or send it 'down the line' to the man nearest touch.

▲ The longer throws in attacking positions don't always have to be played direct to the near-post area to be effective. The key to exploiting this talent, if a side is fortunate enough to have it, is to vary the tactics now and again, to keep the opposition guessing. Manchester United made the most of their resources in the First Division game at Villa Park in October 1978, and it brought a goal that squared the match after they had been trailing 2-0 down to a couple of John Gregory goals at half-time. The move came in the 71st minute after United had won a throw on the left, almost level with the edge of the Villa area. Sammy McIlroy, always the willing worker and aware that Ashley Grimes wouldn't go for the really big one to the near-post area, looked for a position about 20 yards away to get the flick into the danger zone. He received the pass, doing well to beat the tight marking and backhead the ball almost to the six-yard box. It was an excellent contact in the circumstances and the ball looped further than the square defenders expected. It was further than Lou Macari expected, too, and the ball sailed over his head as Jimmy Rimmer came off his line to collect. Always dangerous in crowded areas near goal and obviously in his best quick-thinking form (he had scored twice the previous Saturday against Middlesbrough) the little Scot staggered everyone by turning almost a half-circle and lunging at the ball to send an immaculate lob over the stranded Rimmer for a real opportunist equaliser. The throw-in in attacking positions is ultimately about getting the ball into the danger area; it doesn't always work the way it's planned but with a positive, alert and hard-working approach in such situations a team can reap unexpected benefits.

▶ *Even the best professional players are prone to losing concentration and lapsing into a casual attitude at throws. This example is taken from the Charity Shield game between Tottenham and Aston Villa at Wembley in August 1981, with a throw from Glenn Hoddle just inside the Villa half. Their players are fully aware of Hoddle's ability to get length on his throws, yet as he releases the ball to find Steve Archibald three of them are effectively marking only one player, Ossie Ardiles (7). While the positioning of winger Tony Morley (11) makes good sense in terms of covering back on Hoddle, that still leaves Gordon Cowans (10) and Ken McNaught (5)—a strange place for a centre-back, this—taking one man. Substitute Andy Blair appears unaware of Archibald's movement behind him, and will be hard-pressed to turn and get to the ball before the Spurs striker. Des Bremner (7) will in fact be the man who can better cover the pass. A team that thinks and acts positively at throws will always have a huge advantage over a side whose players lack interest and commitment, viewing it essentially as a mechanism for returning the ball into play.*

THE LONG THROW

Though by no means a new skill, the long throw became a fully-fledged tactic when it was married to the emerging use of the near-post header in the 1960s, exploiting players' ability to time their runs and get in flick-on headers to send the ball on to team-mates coming in behind them. It has other valuable uses—increasing the safety margin of the throw to the keeper, gaining distance down the line, the longer throw to a player with plenty of space in midfield—but its most dangerous application is in the attacking third of the field where, performed well by thrower, receiver and supporting players, it can be almost as profitable as a corner. This is very much a team skill, relying on the co-ordination of a powerful and accurate thrower, an aggressive and talented header of the ball and the astute deployment and back-up of colleagues, and so needs to be worked on in training, using defenders trying to clear, to come off in matches. The most effective throws are fast, low and flat, giving the receiver the best chance of directing his flick; if the ball is looped and falling, it makes it difficult for him to time his run and get power on his header, while giving time for defenders to compete.

The technique is as much about rhythm as sheer power. Physical strength is nevertheless a great help, as England left-back Kenny Sansom conveys here as he lets go during the European Championship finals match against Italy in Turin in June 1980. Note how his hands are turned outwards as his arms come down before following through and up into an 'angel' position behind him—'spinning like windmills' as Sansom describes it. Though it's important to arch your back as you approach the line to get the leverage and 'whip' required, the power comes from the arms and shoulders. A minority of long-throw specialists keep a split stance with one foot well in front of the other, but Sansom uses the technique that drags the trailing leg forward to join the guiding leg before the ball is released, finishing up on the toes on both feet placed together on or near the touchline. Developing the knack for the long throw is a question of patient practice. It's pointless sacrificing control and accuracy for distance. A long-throw expert is an asset to any team, and a ten-minute competition, as shown below, will soon discover any hidden talent.

Corners

Corner-kicks offer fairly regular chances for the attacking side to combine the efforts of at least two players in creating relatively simple strikes on goal, most often with headers. It is rare for a team not to gain a handful of corners during a match, and the average is nearer ten. They provide another opportunity to use planned and well-rehearsed ploys, and must therefore play a big part in the set-piece preparation and training of any side.

Like any form of tactical planning for attacking at a set piece, the corner is essentially a matter of playing to strengths, of making the most profitable use of the talent available in a team. If your side boasts a powerful and accurate kicker of the ball and two or three tall players who are good in the air, it makes sense to base that planning on the longer crosses to the

far-post areas. If you have a player adept at timing his runs and getting in telling flicks at the near-post, it will pay off to practise different crosses to him in training. If it works, stay with it; variety on a tried and tested theme is far better than variety for its own sake.

At the same time, there is no point in putting over a series of high inswingers if the keeper is consistently plucking the ball out of the air, or trying near-post moves if the ball is constantly headed out by an aggressive, well-placed defender. Corners must be tailored to the limitations of your side.

This is something that is particularly relevant to young players. Most boys under 15 or so find it difficult to reach the areas near goal with their crosses, and at a corner, where the distance is almost maximum and there is more pressure, it can really be a problem. Even if the ball does get over, there are rarely enough team-mates who are confident headers of the ball. The answer—and it's a viable

alternative, not a cop-out—is the short corner. There is no point in struggling manfully to emulate the professionals and then just lose possession when a constructive option is available. You should continue to work on your distance from crosses, of course, but also devise a number of ways for exploiting the short corner. This is dealt with in more detail on page 183.

For the senior ranks of the game, and particularly in Britain, the corner still means the longer ball for the most part, though the shorter versions are being used more frequently. Basically, the conventional corners break down into three broad types, based on the primary area at which the kick is aimed: the mid-goal area, the far post and the near post. While these areas overlap—and the distance from goal at each one can vary from two to 20 yards—they serve both as a framework for practising corners and an essential guide to the appropriate positioning of attacking players when they are taken.

▼ *Kevin Keegan hits a high corner during his three-season spell with SV Hamburg, when he helped the German club to their first Bundesliga title in 19 years and the European Cup final. Though Keegan is a fine finisher and a real handful on near-post crosses, Hamburg obviously decide to go for the long ball to the big attackers at some corners. Note his balance and concentration as he gets well under the ball; it is already well off the ground. It's important to practise long corners on a pitch with the ball placed in the quarter-circle.*

It is important that the positioning at corners is planned. Players should always be willing and able to react to changing situations, of course, to make intelligent runs where it matters, but they must have an organised base from which to operate. Spreading at random around the danger zone will not be enough; nine times out of ten it will cause confusion when players go for the ball and the well organised defence will win the day. All players should have allocated roles, adjustable for whether the corner is from left to right, for which of them takes the kick, the conditions and so on. Again, it is worth emphasising that this is merely a framework, not a fixed 'formation'. Corners is a question of hitting areas rather than players—and men should make sure they get there.

First, there should be at least one man beyond and well out from the far post, perhaps as far as outside the penalty area. He is looking to time his angled run to come in, possibly on the blind side of the defence, to get good height on the ball

played well away from the keeper. As many as three players may station themselves in this general area, usually the tall strikers and big defenders, who have moved up for the set piece. Having three players means it is very difficult for the defenders, who have the problem of trying to see ball and opponents at the same time, to concentrate on their task. This is made more taxing when one or more of the attackers makes a dummy run to the near post area.

Second, there should be a player closer to the far post just outside the edge of the six-yard box. He is ready to exploit a short run in but can also move back to go for the higher ball that beats the defence and nod it across or down to a player in a better scoring position.

Third, a player should be in the mid-goal area. Often he is close to or even on the line, and tall players can make life awkward for both the keeper and the defender on the far post.

Fourth, there must be at least one man

▼The simple corner is often enough to succeed if everyone does his job well—and the defence hesitate. In the European Championship match against Bulgaria at Sofia in June 1979, England's second goal came with perhaps the most basic of approaches—an inswinger to the mid-goal area. While the home side showed excessive concern with Kevin Keegan's movement at the near post and keeper Filipov displayed a distinct lack of commitment with his punching, centre-half Dave Watson timed his short run superbly to oust Bob Latchford and power the ball in. With the attributes of Keegan and Watson and the accuracy of Brooking and Steve Coppell, England had to look little further than practising two ploys at corners: this one and the near-post flick (see over).

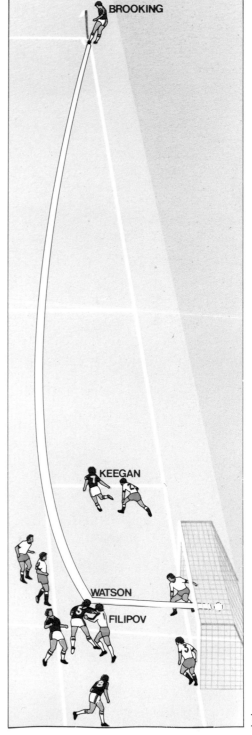

▼As a basic guide, a corner taken with the right foot from the left side (A, B and right) and a corner taken with the left foot from the right side (see overleaf) will tend to swerve towards the goal—the inswinger. A corner taken with the right foot from the right side (C and D) or taken with the left foot from the left side will tend to swerve away from goal—the outswinger. Thus just one player can produce both types of cross into the two main target areas, and a side with one accurate right-footed player and one accurate left-footed player can always use the same ploy or some variation of it. Playing inswingers with the outside of the foot is an extremely difficult and unpredictable skill and should not be tried. As with all crosses, the corner is largely a question of hitting areas rather than specific players and the attackers should position themselves, as a result of moves worked out in practice, in the best positions to make contact in those areas. The two prime target areas are the near post and the far post. The inswinger is the more common and effective ball to the near post, looking for the flick-on to players behind, but the one that curls high inside the post (A) is a desperately awkward ball for the man guarding the post and the keeper. The outswinging cross to the near post (C) can be met by a player on an angled run for a direct strike on goal. The long inswinger (B) can be difficult for defenders because it can bend late in flight, but the more common far-post corner is the one that drifts away from the keeper and into the paths of tall attackers (D), players either coming from deep positions near the edge of the area or, nearer the line, a man climbing to nod the ball back across for a team-mate to head or volley home. With all these crosses it's important to get pace on the ball; corners that float over or hang in the air are more likely to be taken by the keeper or headed clear by defenders because they give them more time to compete.

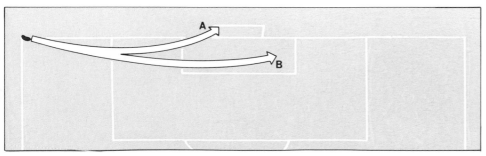

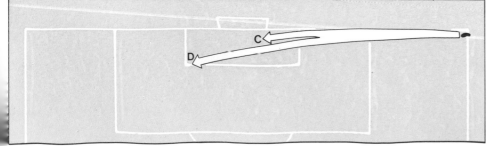

covering the front side of the goal, on or about the edge of the six-yard box. He is now often the key attacking player at corners. Studies have shown that corners taken to the near post area are more likely to produce goals than those hit to the far post. The difference is not huge but it is significant.

The great advantages of the ball played there are that the receiver is more likely than players behind to make contact and that, if played well, it can produce a wide range of options. Thus if he is not too far from goal the receiver might try a direct strike; he could flick it on over the defence to a player coming in at the far post; he can move 'off the post' towards the ball, pull-

ing defenders away a little and getting the merest touches over the 'pack' to send the ball on to a team-mate coming in at the near post or in mid-goal; he could move off the six-yard area towards the kicker for a shorter corner, intending either to receive the ball for a one-two or turn or, again, simply drawing defenders out of position.

Defenders find it difficult to seal the near-post area; for one thing the marker has to decide whether to stay goalside of his man or get on the 'wrong side', hoping he can get to the ball first. Clever positioning and movement here by one or two players, allied to an accurate kick, can cause all sorts of problems for the best of

defences and their keeper. Corner-takers should bear in mind that defences can become obsessed with covering the near-post area, and a conventional far-post cross after two or three near-post ploys in a match can easily catch them short of marking further back.

All these positions are only guidelines. Attackers must adjust their roles and their runs to suit the pace, height and trajectory of the cross. They must always be looking for the blind-side run behind defenders who are ball-watching, and for the space in front of defenders who, by contrast, are too concerned with their nearest opponent. They are often guilty of waiting for the ball, holding back to see what their

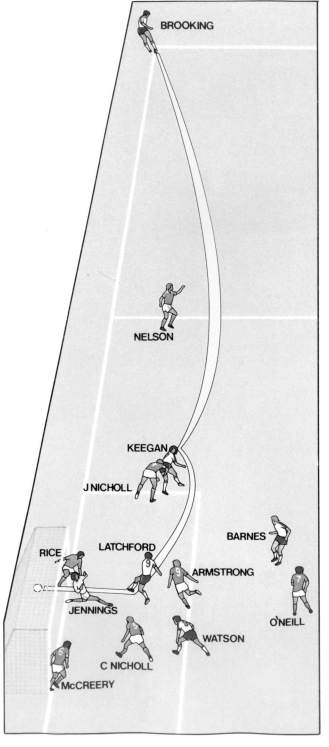

◄Statistical studies show that the corner played to the near post is more likely to produce a goal than the one to the far post, and that inswingers are more likely to produce goals than outswingers. The famous Trevor Brooking–Kevin Keegan partnership combined to help prove the point with England's first goal in the 4-0 European Championship win over Northern Ireland at Wembley in February 1979. This goal, which is shown from another angle on page 114, relied on the understanding built up in just a few hours of play and practice. Keegan made a sharp run off the near post to meet the hard low centre and flick it beyond his marker, Jimmy Nicholl, who had followed him out. The ball fell neatly to the feet of Bob Latchford, who had moved in smartly to the space at the near post. For teams with an accurate kicker of the ball, and a person good on the near-post, this tactic can provide plenty of variety on a basic theme.

▶ The inswinger to the near post works again, this time for Horst Hrubesch (9) to score the winner in the 1980 European Championship final in Rome. The cross was longer here (see diagram on page 149) and the big West German striker moved in on a classic angled run to come in behind the cluster of Belgian defenders to flash the ball past Pfaff into the net.

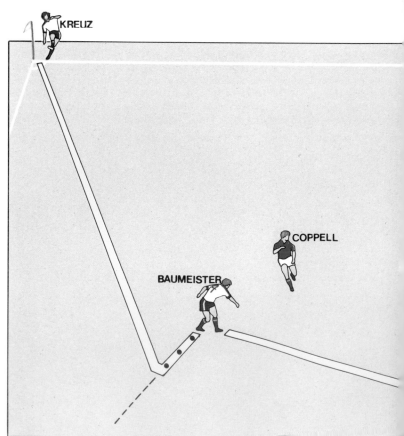

opponent is doing. Late, strong runs against hesitant defenders who should have attacked the ball can bring rich rewards at corners.

Players who are not allocated in the positions mentioned should fill the remaining space in the most sensible and constructive way possible. One midfielder, for example, can be just outside the area level with the centre of the goal, ready to drive home the poor punch from the keeper or weak defensive header; the winger on the other side can look for the long cross that beats all the big men and chip it back in or shoot; the full-back can move up to make himself available for the short corner.

The short corner provides a productive alternative to the longer balls for both professionals and youngsters. Taking advantage of the ten-yard rule at corners, you can create a two-against one situation to play a wall pass and set the taker free or, if a second defender comes to close the player down, and a full-back moves up in support, then with three-against-two. Whatever the method, the ploy makes a wider angle for the cross and from a position nearer goal. The man on the ball can also take it on towards goal with a dribble, he can shoot, or he can lay-it off square to a team-mate to shoot, or he can chip to the far post or play it towards the bye-line for the original kicker. The options are in theory many and varied: an increasingly common one, for example, is the hard, low shot-cum-cross into the goalmouth.

Thus while the short corner breaks the golden rule of getting the ball into the danger area quickly—indeed it always runs the risk of losing possession even before a threat on goal can be made—the advantages are attractive, particularly to a side struggling with more direct methods.

While it is important to continue to improve power kicking—for long passes far more than corners—dedicated practice using a range of well planned approaches and involving the whole team will ensure that one of the best chances to threaten the opponents' goal is not lost.

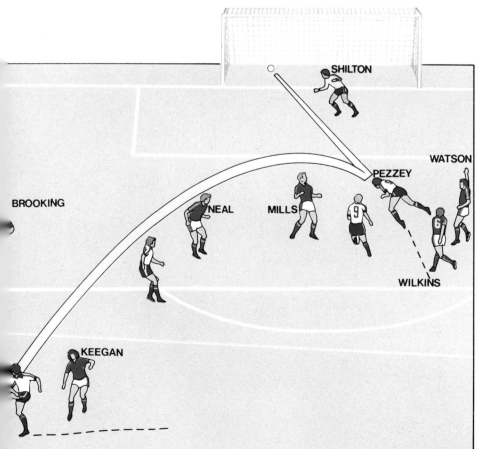

◄On two occasions in the friendly against England at Vienna in June 1979, Austria's centre-back Bruno Pezzey made a late run at a set piece to score with a long-range header. In the 70th minute, Pezzey would convert Robert Sara's free-kick to make the final result 4-3. But he also gave the hosts the lead, from a move that stemmed from a corner. Austria, sensibly playing away from England's traditional strength in the air at the back, elected to go for the short ball and Willy Kreuz played it deep to Ernst Baumeister. Perhaps the planned tactic was a ball played from there into the middle, or even a break to the bye-line for the ball played back, but with Steve Coppell covering back well and closing him down, Baumeister turned the ball inside to Kurt Jara, moving across in support. With a delightful touch Jara clipped an early ball at a tremendous angle to his run and it really caught the England players out. As Dave Watson stood appealing for offside against the retreating Kreuz—fatal with the early ball—Pezzey stole in front of him to send his powering header past Peter Shilton. Defenders tend to relax when the ball is played back well away from goal at corners, because they feel the immediate danger is past. But the attacking side have more options from the short corner, and they still have plenty of players up for the set piece, including the tall defenders. At the other end of the scale, short corners provide a simple and effective solution to the problems of youngsters not able to get sufficient power for the longer balls.

Free-kicks

Between a third and a half of goals are scored from set pieces. A small proportion come from corners and a tiny percentage from throws but the rest, at least 30% of the goals in football, stem from free-kicks. With defenders becoming better equipped all the time in terms of individual technique and tactical appreciation, and defences becoming increasingly well organised in terms of teamwork and discipline, the figure is on the rise. As scoring through open play gets more difficult, top teams spend more time working on their free-kicks in dangerous positions.

In doing so they are trying to capitalise on a number of distinct advantages that the attacking side enjoys in such situations, the factors which help to account for the high number of goals scored from

them. For one thing of course the ball is stationary, thus raising considerably the chances of a very accurate first touch, whether with a shot or a pass.

Second, the opposition must be at least ten yards from the ball, removing pressure from the kicker and providing space in which he can work. Third, moves planned and rehearsed to a high standard in training can be implemented in matches. Fourth, players can station themselves in the position which makes maximum use of their talents.

When opponents construct the defensive wall at free-kicks within scoring range, they automatically offer the attacking side yet another advantage—that of numerical superiority. If five men are in the wall, for example, it means that five defenders (excluding the keeper) are in theory marking and covering nine attackers (excluding the kicker). This can and should be used by the side on the ball to get players moving into dangerous

space and stretching the defenders not in the wall, even if the intended move is a sideways touch for a shot past the wall.

Finally, in the case of the direct free-kick there are options. There is no rule to say direct free-kicks must be taken with a shot on goal, and thus the defending side can be kept guessing. With an indirect free-kick, of course, they have the scant consolation of knowing that there must actually be two touches by different players to score. It is not surprising, then, with all these inherent advantages, that the free-kick is such a rich source of goals.

The higher the standard of the teams, the more significant these advantages become. The percentage of goals scored from free-kicks is far greater at professional than at amateur levels. Top players have more natural ability and this, combined with time to work on their moves, will result in more sophisticated and precise ploys. The more vital the match, too, the greater the likelihood that a goal will

come from a free-kick; space will be tight, restricting the chances of scoring from open play, and there will be more fouls—and therefore more free-kicks.

While the proportion of goals from free-kicks is lower at more modest levels of the game, any side will enhance their chances of success by following certain guidelines. They apply to a large extent to all set pieces, but are particularly relevant to free-kicks.

The first is quite simply to think before you act. Plenty of free-kicks are squandered because players try a move before team-mates are ready. Even with an easy two-man ploy, other players should be in the best positions and making the best runs to help it work. Time is on your side, so the rule is to look up, make sure everybody is clear about the tactic being used, and then take the kick when the moment is right. Remember it is the defending team, not yours, who have the problem.

Second, play to the strengths in your side. If you have a player with a fierce and accurate shot, play the ball to him in space for a crack at goal; if you have someone adept at making well-timed runs in behind the wall for a neat header, and another man able to place the chip for him, it would be a waste not to use that ploy. Success at set pieces depends on people doing their job well—and they will do best the job for which they are most suitably equipped.

Third, and linked to the last point, is to keep it simple. There is a great temptation to over-complicate at free-kicks, to play 'beyond your means' in terms of both skill and organisation. Moves might look great on paper, but the more players there are involved—and therefore the bigger the number of passes and touches—the greater the chance of it breaking down. This becomes more pertinent the further down the scale you play, since in elaborate moves everything has to be exact and co-ordinated to be effective. Generally,

the fewer the number of touches in front of the ball the better; the pass or shot that goes over or round the wall immediately takes the players in the wall out of the game. While you need alternatives—a defence will not always shape up the way you predicted—using variety and invention for their own sakes is pointless. As with corners, variety on a basic theme, exploiting the strengths of your team, will be far more profitable.

Fourth, the key to this whole tactical area is practice. The free-kick near goal presents a unique opportunity to come up with ideas best suited to your side and then rehearse and improve them until they are working again and again in training. Usually there is one player who is the controlling figure at such situations, and it certainly makes sense to have one man who decides and instigates the right ploy for the position. The last thing you want is a cluster of indecisive players hovering over the ball in matches.

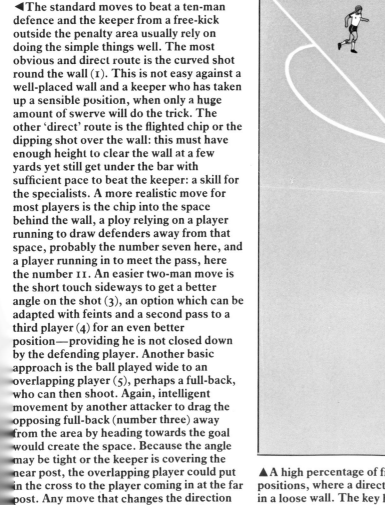

◀ The standard moves to beat a ten-man defence and the keeper from a free-kick outside the penalty area usually rely on doing the simple things well. The most obvious and direct route is the curved shot round the wall (1). This is not easy against a well-placed wall and a keeper who has taken up a sensible position, when only a huge amount of swerve will do the trick. The other 'direct' route is the flighted chip or the dipping shot over the wall: this must have enough height to clear the wall at a few yards yet still get under the bar with sufficient pace to beat the keeper: a skill for the specialists. A more realistic move for most players is the chip into the space behind the wall, a ploy relying on a player running to draw defenders away from that space, probably the number seven here, and a player running in to meet the pass, here the number 11. An easier two-man move is the short touch sideways to get a better angle on the shot (3), an option which can be adapted with feints and a second pass to a third player (4) for an even better position—providing he is not closed down by the defending player. Another basic approach is the ball played wide to an overlapping player (5), perhaps a full-back, who can then shoot. Again, intelligent movement by another attacker to drag the opposing full-back (number three) away from the area by heading towards the goal would create the space. Because the angle may be tight or the keeper is covering the near post, the overlapping player could put in the cross to the player coming in at the far post. Any move that changes the direction of the attack twice can cause confusion in the defence and this three-man tactic is a neat and economical way of by-passing the wall using fairly basic skills. In theory the permutations in these situations are endless, but the more players involved (and therefore the more passes and touches) the greater the chances of the move breaking down—and the opportunity being wasted.

KEEGAN

BROOKING

▲ A high percentage of free-kicks gained in the attacking third of the pitch are in wide positions, where a direct shot is not a realistic possibility and there may be only one or two in a loose wall. The key here is to be careful not to forget these situations when practising free-kicks in attack during training sessions, and work on getting the ball in towards the most dangerous spaces. Studies show that the chances of scoring from such positions are up to 90% higher if the ball is played to the near post rather than the far post. A classic example of the ploy was with the first goal of England's journey in the 1980 European Championship, during the 4-3 win over Denmark in Copenhagen in September 1978. The score came from another fine combination between Trevor Brooking and Kevin Keegan. With the Danes looking for the far-post cross but still marking Keegan tight, Brooking clipped in a slight outswinger and Keegan started a run, stopped and then stole a yard on his two opponents to get his head there first and turn it into Jensen's net.

185

◄Any ploy that distracts the defence or confuses the goalkeeper and helps to disguise the intention of the attacking side increases the chances of a score from vital free-kicks near goal. The standard move is two men making angled runs towards the ball, both shaping to take the kick, and is most effective when the ball is placed level with the centre part of the goal. It almost came off for West Germany in their last World Cup match in 1978, against neighbours Austria at Cordoba. The direct free-kick was from the most difficult position for the Austrians to defend against—almost in the middle of the lip of the 'D' outside the penalty area—and with a six-man wall there keeper Friedl Koncilia had problems with his positioning. Rainer Bonhof was the German general at free-kicks, and with his staggering ability to bend the ball (the remarkable goal he scored against England from a similar position four months before is shown on page 94), Koncilia and his defenders no doubt expected a swerving right-foot shot as he approached the ball (1). As he got close, however, he accelerated past the ball whilst Hansi Müller, who had come on as a substitute for Erich Beer only minutes earlier, emerged behind him on a late diagonal run from well wide of the point level with the end of the wall to strike a good left-foot shot (2). While Bonhof was picked up by Heinrich Strasser at the end of the wall (3), Müller's curling drive, reaching hip height and heading just inside the post, was pushed away for a corner with a spectacular dive from Koncilia. The keeper had done well not to go across for Bonhof's shot round the other side of the wall and had riskily kept his options open to get across to a ball he saw late. It was almost the first time in six games during the tournament that Bonhof had not taken a German free-kick awarded in the attacking third of the field, but he had suffered a notable lack of success in Argentina (with his passes from free-kicks as well as his shots) and it appears that late in the day the German camp risked ruffling his feathers by suggesting an alternative—one that very nearly came off. Though there is an obvious need for teams to be organised and disciplined at set pieces—and that means having one man who determines the best move in any given situation—any rigid framework would deny the very improvisation that the advantages of free-kicks in these positions permits.

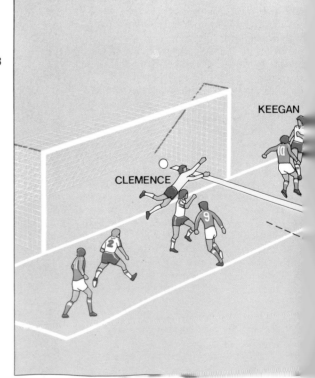

Training for free-kicks is as much about discipline and organisation as it is technique and improvisation. Each player in the side should know what is happening at every move, and how they can be most constructive, even if they are not directly involved. There should always be an 'opposition' to beat in practice (after perhaps a few dry runs to get the idea on more complicated ploys), using defenders who will stay back at free-kicks. It is no point in having a wonderful move that works only against a shadow defence.

As well as practising the actual moves, players involved should spend time sharpening the skills that help to beat the defensive wall and make them possible —notably the chipped pass or shot and the swerving shot, as well as basic power shooting from anywhere between 15 and 20 yards. Colleagues who will regularly work ploys in matches should find extra time to enhance their understanding and co-ordination in training: for example, the 'chippie' and the player he is looking to find with his pass at the far post or with the ball played into space just behind the wall. 'Practice makes perfect' should apply to free-kicks perhaps more than any other area of tactical play, simply because there will only be perhaps one or two chances a match in which to capitalise on the advantages the situation affords—and it is a crime to waste them through lack of effort or preparation.

Anything within reason and the rules that helps to deceive or distract the opposition—who have been practising their defence against free-kicks, of course —is useful providing it does not reduce the efficiency of the 'active' players in the operation, especially the initial kicker. The most basic ploy, one which is almost universal now, is two players running in at different angles and shaping to take the kick, as described opposite. But the more movement the better, both in front and behind the wall.

It is the attacking side who have the initiative. They move first and the defence must respond to them, so they must keep the pressure on the opposition with decoy runs and the constant search for space. With a little extra attention, this important aspect can be worked on and co-ordinated in training.

For the swerving shot, it always helps to reduce still further the view of the goal-keeper. This usually means putting one player (perhaps two) on the end of the wall, blocking the keeper's view of the ball—and diving out of the way as the shot comes at him to go round the wall.

▼ While the Brazilian and Peruvian players in the 1978 World Cup finals continued the pattern they had set in the 1970 and 1974 tournaments by looking for yet more ways of beating the wall by joining it, the Dutch still tended to hope that skill would be enough on its own. Here, in the final against Argentina in Buenos Aires, Rob Rensenbrink tries an ambitious curling shot against a five-man wall, taken from a position level with the near post. Though keeper Ubaldo Fillol doesn't have a good view of the ball as it is kicked, he soon picks up its path as it passes the wall. One or two players on one or both ends of the wall can be very useful in such situations; he peels off the wall as the ball is kicked, hopefully through the space he occupied. It can cause that crucial split-second delay in the reactions of the keeper, and the attacking side has plenty of spare men available for the job when the opposition build their wall. Obviously it relies on having a player capable of bending the shot accurately.

◄ **'Keep it simple, do it well'** is one of the basic maxims of good football, and while it's usually applied to open play it can also extend to set pieces—and certainly to the free-kick that gained the Republic of Ireland a draw from the European Championship qualifying match against England at Dublin in October 1978. The visitors had nine men back for the kick wide outside the area, including two forwards (Coppell and Keegan) in the six-yard box. With Neal, Hughes and Thompson there too, they were all set for Liam Brady's chip to the big Irish strikers and defenders, whether to the near post or the far post. But Brady had other ideas and played a firm sidefoot pass to Gerry Daly in space on the edge of the area. Hughes and Thompson rushed out to try and close him down, but Daly hit the ball sweetly with his right foot and his low shot beat Clemence just inside the post. While there is an obvious question mark about the England marking, all credit must go to Brady for seeing the chance and to Daly for converting it. No matter how well a move is rehearsed for a given position near goal, you should always be aware of what's happening; don't spurn the easy alternative if the chances of reward are far higher than from a complicated three-man move you've been practising all week.

GLOSSARY

ANGLE OF RUN Direction of a player's run in relation to the path of the ball and/or the goal.

ATTACKING THIRD Approximate area of the pitch in which a team can normally expect to launch a direct threat on goal.

BACK FOUR Conventional defensive line comprising right-back, two centre-backs and left-back.

BACK OF THE DEFENCE Space between the goalkeeper and the nearest defender.

BALL Universally used as an alternative term for pass: through ball, early ball, 'good ball', etc.

BALL PLAYER Skilful player, most often a midfielder, noted for his ball control, fine touch and creative play-making.

BALL WATCHING Tendency for both individuals and groups of players, especially defenders, to concentrate only on what is happening on and around the ball, and to be unaware of movement of opponents elsewhere, particularly on their blind side.

BLIND SIDE Side of a player or group of players away from the ball. The blind-side run is when a player moves undetected into space behind opponents, a ploy to which ball-watching defenders are extremely vulnerable.

BLOCK TACKLE Totally committed tackle where a defender meets an opponent in a standing or crouching position and puts his whole weight behind the challenge in an attempt to win the ball.

BODY SWERVE Movement by the man running with the ball which aims to wrong-foot his opponent.

'BOX' Penalty area. The 'six-yard box' is another term for the goal area.

BYE-LINE Goal-line.

CALLING Vital aspect of team play where colleagues with a better view of the play than the man on the ball can help that team-mate, often after providing the pass.

CENTRE Older and unfashionable term for cross, both as noun and verb.

CHECKING Trying to gain a yard or two on your marker by going towards the ball, stopping, and moving off sharply in the other direction—or vice versa. Also called checking out and checking back.

CLOSING DOWN Advancing on an opponent in possession to restrict space in front of him while covering his path to goal.

COME OFF YOUR MAN To move away from your marker (usually away from your opponents' goal) in order to create space in which to receive the ball.

CONTROLLING SURFACE Part of the body used to receive a pass.

COVER When a player occupies the space behind a team-mate who is challenging the man on the ball, he is covering that player. In team terms, it means having enough players 'behind the ball' (goalside of the ball) to defend adequately.

CROSSOVER When a player running without the ball crosses the path of the player in possession, and sometimes called the 'scissors'. The ball can be taken by the supporting player (the switch or 'takeover'), or his run can be used to create space by taking a defender away from the ball.

DECOY RUN Movement where a player runs into a position to pull defenders away from certain parts of the pitch in order that a more effective pass can be made to a team-mate filling the resulting space.

DEFENSIVE THIRD Approximate area of the pitch in which a team's priority is to prevent the attacking side striking on goal.

DEPTH In defence, the provision of cover; in attack, support behind and in front of the man on the ball.

DIAGONAL RUN Run made with or without the ball at an angle across the pitch.

DRIBBLING Somewhat old-fashioned but concise and accurate term for running with the ball under close control, and usually involving an attempt to beat one or more opponent.

DUMMY Skill used to disguise intention, applicable in several areas of the game, notably when committing an opponent to a tackle before slipping the ball past him; and shaping to take a pass and letting the ball run through to a team-mate behind.

EARLY BALL Pass played as the first possible opportunity, usually into space for a team-mate to run on to. The classic example is the ball played in behind the defence before the opposition have a chance to cover.

FAR-POST BALL Pass played to the area around and out from the post farthest from the passing player, and normally a high cross. A far-post run is a run to this area from a deeper position.

FEINT Almost synonymous with the dummy, though used mainly to describe wrong-footing movements when running with the ball.

FILL IN To cover the position and role of a defending colleague when he has been forced to move away from it. It most often applies to midfielders dropping back to help out the back-four players.

FINAL PASS/BALL Pass played at the end of a

move in the opponents' danger area, the ball which should set up the direct strike on goal.

FINISHING Ability to convert the final pass or, more broadly, the art of 'snapping up' any chances or half-chances near goal.

FIRST-TIME PASS/BALL Using only one touch to receive and pass the ball; first-time play is a move made up of one-touch passes.

FLANK Area near the touchline, within 12 or 15 yards of it; the 'wing' was the older term for it though the word flank tends to be used also for wide defensive areas.

FREE MAN Player in space and unmarked.

FRONT PLAYERS Two or more usually three members of a team who rank as out-and-out forwards, whether their roles are as strikers, target men or wide players.

GOALSIDE Position of a marker when he is nearer his goal than his immediate opponent. 'Staying goalside of your man' is a fundamental rule of defensive play.

HALF-VOLLEY Pass or shot where contact is made with the ball immediately after it hits the ground.

HANDING (PASSING) ON Technique used by a defence working a zonal system of marking. As an opponent moves out of one defender's area or zone, he is 'handed on' or 'passed on' to the defender responsible for the next zone.

INSTEP Upper surface of the foot, and the basic area of contact for most forms of shooting.

JOCKEYING Holding up or deflecting the advance of an opponent with the ball near the danger area, usually by trying to force him towards or along the touchline.

LATE TACKLE Challenge which, whether intentional or accidental, makes unfair contact with the player after he has played the ball.

LAY-OFF Short pass played with any part of the body or foot, usually first time.

LOSING YOUR MAN/MARKER When a player gains space away from or behind the opponent who is marking him in order to receive a pass; often achieved by checking.

MAN-FOR-MAN-MARKING Defensive system where each player is responsible for marking a designated opponent in the important defensive areas of the pitch.

MARK To take up a position in relation to your opponent that enables you to challenge for the ball and, ideally, to prevent your opponent receiving it.

NARROWING THE ANGLE Moving nearer to an opponent in an attacking position in order to reduce his passing or shooting angles. The expression is used almost exclusively for when goalkeepers come 'off their line' to reduce the area an opponent has to aim at with his shot.

NEAR-POST BALL Pass played to the area around and out from the post nearer the passing player. A near-post run is a run to this area from a deeper position.

NICKING THE BALL Dispossessing an opponent by touching the ball away from him.

NUTMEG A ball played between the feet or legs of an opponent and 'collected' on the other side of him. In the USA this is known as the 'small bridge': the 'large bridge' is when a player pushes the ball to one side of an opponent and then runs past on the other side to collect.

OFFSIDE TRAP When a defensive unit, usually acting on a call or signal from the 'bossing' player, moves forward in such a way to catch at least one opponent in an offside position.

ON THE BALL When an individual player is in possession he is 'on the ball'. 'Off the ball' refers to any movement away from the immediate area around that player.

ONE-TOUCH PLAY See first-time pass.

ONE-TWO Any passing move involving a return ball, and usually used as alternative term to wall pass.

OPTIONS Common term for the alternatives open to a player on the ball.

OVERLAP A supporting run made from behind a team-mate and on the outside of him to a position well in front, whether to receive the ball or simply draw the attentions of defenders. The run is most often made near the touchline by full-backs.

PARK Colloquial British term for the pitch.

PENETRATION Term sometimes used to assess a team's ability to break through the opposition defence into dangerous positions.

PUSH AND RUN Simplified description of the style of play resting on quick passing and continuous, mobile, all-round support, where a player plays a short ball to a team-mate and immediately makes his run into space, often for the return pass. As a good football 'habit', it is sometimes called 'give and go'.

RECOVERY Movement of a defender when his side loses possession from a position on the wrong side of the ball to a position goalside of the ball.

RECOVERY TACKLE Tackle made from a position on the wrong side of the man on the ball.

REVERSE PASS When a player carries the ball in one direction, shaping to play the ball or continue his run in that direction, but suddenly plays it back the other way to a team-mate in support.

ROUND THE BACK A player has got 'round the back' or 'behind the defence' when he has passed the last covering player and is

in a position to run at goal or, nearer the bye-line, to cross the ball.

RUNNING OFF THE BALL Any tactical run to support a team-mate on the ball, whether to draw defenders or to create space to receive a possible pass.

SELLING YOURSELF Committing yourself to challenging for a ball and being beaten by your opponent.

SET PIECE The situation at the restarts after an infringement or when the ball goes out of play: goal-kicks, throws-in, corners, indirect free-kicks and direct free-kicks, including penalties.

SET PLAYS Moves worked out in training to exploit set pieces, mostly from corners, free-kicks near the opponents' goal and long throws.

SHADOW MARKING Where one player is assigned to mark a dangerous opponent closely for the whole match, trying to 'mark him out of the game'.

SHADOW PLAY Training technique where the players create movements without opposition.

SHIELDING Maintaining control and possession of the ball while looking for support by keeping your body between the ball and the challenging opponent, usually when facing your own goal. Also called 'screening the ball'.

SHOWING YOURSELF Making it obvious to the man on the ball you are available for the pass; usually applied to front players coming off their markers to collect the short ball from midfield.

SLIDING TACKLE Tackle made by sliding your supporting leg along the ground, and most often made near the touchline.

SPACE Goalside area between any player and his nearest opponent.

SQUARE BALL Any pass made across the pitch, approximately parallel to the goal-lines. A 'crossfield ball' is a long square pass played from one flank to another.

SQUARE DEFENCE A defence spread in a line across the pitch. Such a defence is lacking depth and is vulnerable to the ball played between two of its members into space behind them, allowing an opponent a clear run on goal; the defence is then said to be 'caught square'.

STRETCHED DEFENCE When the defence is spread out and there is no cover, often when the opposition suddenly switch the point of attack.

SUPPORT PLAY A player is 'in support' when he makes himself available in space to receive a pass from the man on the ball. Support play covers any run, movement or ploy that enables him to achieve it.

SWEEPER Defender, usually an extra man, who plays behind the rest of the defence and covers them.

SWITCHING THE PLAY Changing the point of the attack, notably with a crossfield ball.

TAKING A PLAYER ON Trying to beat a defender by dribbling past him.

TAKING A MAN AWAY When a player runs off the ball and takes an opponent with him, trying to create space for the team-mate on the ball to exploit. Also called 'pulling', 'drawing' or 'dragging' defenders away, especially when applied to moving into wider positions in the attacking third.

TARGET MAN Misleading expression that denotes merely a part of any front player's role—to present himself as a target for midfielders' passes and then hold the ball and/or lay them off, in turn going to look for a new position.

THIRDS OF THE PITCH Approximate divisions of the pitch useful as a coaching 'tool': the defending or defensive third, the middle third and the attacking third.

THROUGH BALL A pass played between two defenders into the space behind them for a team-mate to run on to. Most often played from midfield behind the defence.

TIGHT A player is tight on an opponent when he is marking him very closely.

TURNING Receiving the ball when facing your own goal and controlling the ball as you move to face your opponents' goal. Turning a man, or turning against a defender, is when a player being closely marked receives the ball and moves with it into space behind his opponent, thus having to beat his man on the turn.

VISION Being aware of the movement off the ball before you receive a pass—and being able to see and exploit subtle passes and patterns of play.

VOLLEY Any pass or shot with the foot where contact with the ball is made above the ground.

WALL Line of players forming a human barrier against a free-kick near goal.

WALL PASS Exchange of passes between two players and used to beat an opponent.

WEIGHT Pace of a pass in relation to the position and movement of the intended receiver.

WIDE PLAYER Front runner or attacking midfielder who tends to play near the touchline, but not necessarily a winger.

WINGER Attacking player whose main role is to play out wide and get to the bye-line and supply crosses to team-mates in the central areas.

WORK-RATE Overused and abused professional term coined in the 1960s to describe a player's overall physical contribution to the team effort, particularly his running off the ball and covering.

WRONG SIDE A defender is the wrong side of his opponent if he allows that opponent to get between himself and the goal.

ZONAL DEFENCE Defensive system in which each member has an approximate area or zone, and is responsible for picking up any opponent who enters that zone.